GW01390046

To Hear A Nightingale

by
John H Cooke

9 780956 415684

ISDN 978-0-9564156-8-4

Printed by Vale Press Ltd
6 Willersey Business Park, Willersey, Nr Broadway, Worcestershire WR11 7RR.
Tel: 01386 858900   sales@valegroup.co.uk

*This book is dedicated to the memory
of my parents and sisters*

ACKNOWLEDGEMENTS

When finally putting pen to paper, to record my memories of growing up in the 1930s and 40s, having received encouragement from both family and friends, I became aware that to achieve this I would need a lot of help from these villagers, both past and present, if it was ever to get off the ground.

The response I have received has been huge in information and photographs and for that I would like to thank the following: Ann Brain, Betty Bryan, my cousin, Peter Cooke and his wife Joan, niece Gill Young, Chris Payne, John Wilber, Jack Hands, my neighbour from 1933 to the time I left Ilmington in my early twenties and by pure coincidence, on my return to the village some three and a half years ago, became my neighbour again.

To Sheila, my oldest daughter, for her dedicated work on the family tree, and my three other daughters, Myra, Julia and Thelma for their constant encouragement. To Stephen Wright whose skill with his camera and photographs are remarkable; finally to Gwen Sabin whose patience and nimble fingers have spent many hours on her computer and has made this project possible.

To all these generous people I extend my sincere gratitude.

CONTENTS

FRONT STREET & MY FAMILY
& NEIGHBOURS

I was born on the 18th July, 1928, the youngest of five children and the only boy. Our parents were John (Jack) Henry Cooke and Myra Frances - who was always known by her second name - and we lived in No. 1 Front Street in the North Cotswold Village of Ilmington. There were six cottages all built with Cotswold Stone with slate roofs, each cottage had two up and two down. My four sisters shared one bedroom and I had a cot in my parent's room. Rather a tight squeeze you might say. My sisters in order of age were Rita, Vera, Elma and Myra and then, of course, me, who had the same name as my father.

The row of six cottages on Front Street - ours was Number One

Each cottage had a long narrow garden. At the bottom of each one there was a pig sty and three, yes three, toilets - two households sharing one. Also there was a large shed with a copper. This building was known as the brew house. All these outbuildings were built of brick. This wash-house was shared by numbers 3 and 4, while we at number 1 shared with No. 2 the washhouse on the end of our cottage while numbers 5 and 6 shared the one built on the end of No. 6. Outside our cottage was a large mangle. I can see my mum now folding the washing, smaller and smaller as she passed it through after each fold. When she had finished, it was practically dry and then finished off by hanging it on the clothes line which stretched down the garden.

In the garden there was this old apple tree and I remember Dad picking the apples which were Blenheim Orange. My mother then wrapped them in tissue paper and kept them in a drawer until around Christmas time. The tree never bore a lot of apples and this is why they were treated like gold-dust. A number of the old

Cottages viewed from the other end showing the wash-house

orchards years ago probably had two or three of these trees and they are not very prolific producers and, therefore, I would think this is why they were never grown commercially. I did buy one of these trees around 1990 and had it for 15 years but it never bore an apple! The taste was unbelievable and easily comparable to a Cox's Orange Pippin.

My first photo - aged about ten months

I remember my father had a motorbike which he kept in the shed at the bottom of the garden but I never saw him ride it. This motorbike was a Douglas Twin. Obviously, my three older sisters did because mother said that when my third sister Elma, used to hear him coming, she got very excited because he would stop and put her on it and take her down the garden. After that, when my youngest sister and I came along he probably couldn't afford to run it.

The Cooke Clan - the photographer came at lunchtime, hence the pinafores

In number 2 were Sonny and Lucy Bryan and their son John who was three weeks younger than me. They were really nice, kind neighbours. Like the time we all had flu, and my father not getting home from work till late, my mother had no one to fetch the

Outside Mabels House Farm, Back Street, aged two years, ten months

medicine from the doctors' surgery in Shipston. The medicine was always placed in a large box outside the surgery so that people could collect even out of surgery hours. Sonny, without hesitation, said he would go on his bicycle and fetch our medicine even though it was a terrible, dreadful, windy wet night. Mother told me this story some time later along with the sad news that Sonny fell ill with pneumonia and died, just 27 years old, a year or two later.

Mrs Bryan and John then moved into the Manor where she, as far as I can remember, lived and worked for the rest of her life. Our new neighbours were Mr & Mrs Jack Gaydon and their son, Jackie, who was some four months younger than me. Mrs Gaydon, whose first name was Nellie but always known as Polly, had two sons from her first marriage - Frank the eldest who was a Master Baker, and Sidney, who I believe, was a chef. Both of them lived and worked in Weston-super-Mare. They had, like Mrs Gaydon, a strong West Country accent. They used to visit once or twice a year. Mrs Gaydon obviously originated from there as she, with Jackie and later Dorothy, who was born around the time we moved to the new council houses in 1933, had frequent holidays there in the summer.

In Number 3 was Aunt Mary (Sabin) who, as I remember, was a tall, slim lady with snow-white hair tied back in a bun. She always wore long clothes and a pinafore and I am sure that outside her back door there was a water pump where, I presume, we got the water from which was shared by all six cottages. She often came along and complained to my mother that we children had stolen her gooseberries.

Next door, at No. 4 was Mrs Summers and her son Dick. Mrs Summers was a tiny lady – not above five foot and Dick, her son, wasn't very tall either. Dick was employed by Mr Jack Foster as a carter and in his spare time he used to mend people's cycles, punctures, put spokes in etc. He was a very handy chap to have around.

Number 5 were the Miss Browns, two spinster sisters. I don't remember a lot about these ladies or what they did for income etc.

Originally, Number 6 was occupied by a Mr & Mrs Tom Smith and they had four children there, two boys, Bill and Bernard and two girls, Ethel and Gwen but had later moved to one of the cottages in the row that is between Whitehouse Alley and the shop of Biles. Their place was taken at No. 6 by my father's youngest sister and her husband, Auntie Flo and Uncle Frank, always known as Wink. Next-door to us, but on the other side of the roadway, was Mr Fred Dumbleton and his wife and his brother who was called Taggart. Mr Dumbleton was a lay preacher at the Methodist Church and during the summer they used to entertain the Salvation Army. The Band came up and gave services on the bottom green. Taggart used to come and lean over the gate and sing a song to us which was called Barney Goo Goo, Barney Goo, Barney Goo, the man with the goo goo eyes! Sadly, Taggart died and the smell of Chrysanthemums always reminds me of Taggart.

Each November, Mr Gaydon always built a big bonfire in the garden and placed a guy on the top and, of course, it was quite a big celebration in those days. The children all had fireworks and we all had sparklers.

The Catholic School before it became the Catholic Church.
The house on the right then became the priest house

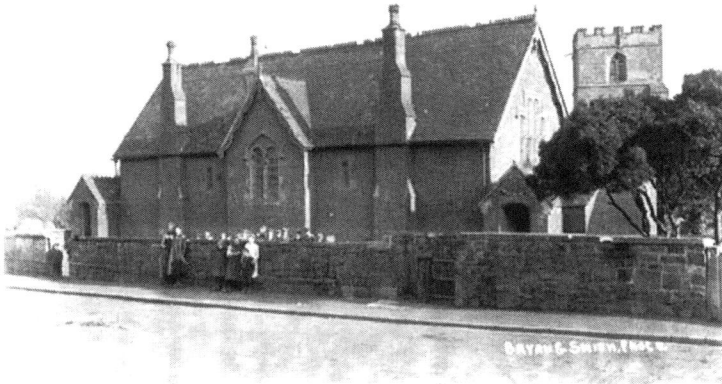

The Church of England School in Back Street

This one particular year, the fire was going and my father came home from work with his bicycle and carrying on his back was a bag and in that bag was a little pig that we named Guy. My mother used to feed him and as the pig got older it got to know the sound of the bucket she was mixing the feed in and it used to start creating. He was fed on vegetable waste and mother used to boil pig potatoes (the small potatoes which were too small to use in the kitchen) that were kept in a separate bag. Mother used to boil them up and mix them with the meal for his feed which was always in the afternoon. As he got bigger, every time he could hear my mother mixing it, he used to stand up and put his front feet on the door of the pig sty and look over and start shouting. Obviously, a few months later, around March time, poor Guy was unfortunately killed but this was all done whilst we were at school so that we wouldn't see anything of it. The pig was taken to my Gran's home in Middle Meadow where it hung in her dairy for a couple of days before being cut up into joints. The hams and the bacon were put in a salting trough (a shallow trough about five foot long and three foot wide) and they were preserved with salt, brown sugar and saltpetre. This was rubbed into them every day for perhaps 10 days or so and then the hams and bacon were hung up in muslin to keep the flies out. They were hung on the kitchen walls.

Whenever I hear the name linseed it reminds me of when I was about four, I had swollen glands on the right hand side of my neck and the Doctor came and advised mother to poultice it twice a day with linseed. It was painful and hot and I was a bit reluctant to have it done but I was told if I didn't have it done, the gland would be cut out which I think was said to frighten me. Eventually it went.

One of The first memories I had was of the Catholic School which was where the former Catholic Church is now. A Lot of children from the village attended this school and one of the teachers was Myra Biles. I think she taught arts and crafts. I was only around two and a half, when I used to go there and I spent the biggest part of my time, sitting on Myra's lap. I don't know why I used to go but guess it was probably because it gave my mum relief from looking after me and more time on house chores.

The Catholic Church used to be at Foxcote House but eventually they decided to move the Church down to where the Catholic School was. Apparently the pupils got less and less and they decided to close it and all the pupils transferred to the C.E. School instead which was at the top of Back Street. This school had been built in the early 1900s. It was built on the left of the path leading down and in line with the Church, while the school house was built on the right of the path. That building exists today.

When I started school at the age of five, I was in the infant's class which was separated from the other classroom by an internal wall and a door. Our teacher was a Miss Steele who came from the hamlet of Willington which is situated about a mile and a half the other side of Shipston. She cycled from there each day a round trip of around 11 or 12 miles.

1935 infants class - me and my close friend, Geoffrey Freeman, standing in front of our teacher - Miss Steele

MOVING HOME

Behind the first three cottages at the bottom of Front Street was a grass field, farmed by the tenant, Jack Sabin whose farm in Back Street was owned by the Council. With the need for more housing to accommodate the growing population, the Council took the bottom half of this field in 1932 to build 10 three bedroomed houses, not with Cotswold Stone but of brick. I suspect this was to keep the cost down. They were built in three blocks, four in the first, two in the second and the last four in another.

They were completed in 1933 and my parents were allocated No. 2 with Mr Gaydon at No. 1, so he still remained our neighbour. So in the late summer, and with the loan of Uncle Harry's horse, Robin, and trolley and father's brother, Uncle Bill, we moved the 400 yards or so from No 1 Front Street to our new address, No. 2 New Council Houses. My parents,- mother especially were in seventh heaven.

I have mentioned Mr and Mrs Gaydon in Number One - he was the village mole catcher which was done mostly in the spring and summer when moles are more active nearer the surface. Like their food, which of course are worms which in winter are deeper underground. Gardening was also in his occupation and he worked in the garden of Sansome House in Back Street. In winter he did a lot of draining and ditching. You would often see him with the tools of the trade on his shoulder which were a graft, a type of digging tool, the blade being any length from 13 to 18 inches, slightly cupped and tapered from about 6 inches at the top down to 4 inches at the bottom and a scoop - this was a cup blade some 8-9 inches in length, curved into a swan neck on a long handle for scooping out loose crumps and bottoming out the narrow trenches for the purpose of laying clay pipes each about a foot in length and laid butting up to one another.

Next to us in Number Three were Mr and Mrs Hands and their young son, Jack. Mr Hands, whose first name was Thomas worked for Mr Rainbow, a farmer in the village of Darlingscote, some two miles from Ilmington and about half way to the market town of Shipston-on-Stour. Mrs Hands became one of the post ladies when George, who had ben born some three years after Jack, started school, the other one being her sister, Mrs Beatrice Boswell who delivered the post to the top half of the village while Mrs Hands delivered the bottom half. She also included the village of Admington. She would finish the village along the Mickleton Road, up to Larkstoke and then on to Admington and then round to join the Stratford Road to her last delivery at York Farm owned by Mr Purser. She did this for many, many years, by bicycle in all weathers, winter and summer and always in a cheerful manner.

Living in Number 4 were Mr and Mrs Hughes and their family of three boys, Laurence, Howard and Eric, the youngest. Their fourth child and their only girl was Kathleen. Mr Hughes, whose first name was Amp, worked as a groom for many years and did a lot of breaking in and training young horses. He walked with quite a limp, the result of a riding accident when a young horse shied and threw him. His foot, being caught in the stirrup, he was then dragged some distance by the frightful animal. Luckily for him it was in a field thus avoiding what could have been a lot worse. He did return after quite a time, recovering as a groom but gave up breaking horses.

At Number 5 were Mr & Mrs Moore and their family of four girls. Mr Moore served and survived the First World War, despite being gassed. He was always known as "Spetter". They had moved down here from up north where Mr Moore had worked in some type of industry that was affecting his health. With relatives living in nearby Mickleton, he moved to Ilmington.

Mr and Mrs Peachey lived at Number 6 with four boys and a girl and over the following years, they had two more boys and girls – nine children in all. Mr Peachey whose first name was Bernard, was a hay tier because this was years before hay bales. The hay was stacked in ricks and then thatched to keep the weather out. Farmers would sell any surplus ricks to hay and straw merchants who would then pay Mr Peachey to cut and tie the hay in trusses, so it could be transported to wherever it was required, often by horse and waggon and sometimes to railway stations to be taken by goods train.

No 7 was the home of Miss Bryan, a retired postmistress who had run the old post office up the top of the village for some years.

In No 8 lived Mr and Mrs Norman Hall and their son Ralph. Mrs Hall was May Boswell before she married Mr Hall and she was the daughter of Mr and Mrs Boswell who ran the Red Lion Public House. She was a longstanding member of the Church Choir.

No 9, was the home of Mr and Mrs Wilson – they were my uncle and aunty. They had moved from Foxcote with their daughter Theresa. Uncle Evelyn was a bricklayer and worked for a builders firm in Shipston. He was also the local barber and cut most of the neighbours' hair, usually on a Sunday morning.

One of my best friends was Geoffrey Freeman who lived with his Mother, Father and Sister at No 10 New Council Houses. Geoffrey's parents were Joseph and Alice Freeman and his sister Kathleen.

Although modern at that time but basic by later year's standards, it must have been like a palace to what mother had had in Front Street. The layout of the ground floor, starting at the front door which opened onto a small hall which was 3-4 feet square, directly in front were the stairs, the door on the left opened on to the living room. As you entered the living room, on the left was the only window with wooden frames with two metal opening ones and an opening skylight at the top of the fixed centre one. Directly in front, in the alcove, a built-in cupboard with two doors and over the top, three shelves. Adjoining this was the fireplace, being a black open range with oven on one side, the fire grate in the centre. This had an iron grill shelf at the bottom and one at the top which could be moved up or down into an upright position so that it would give you a greater depth of fire. Over the top, a hinged bar with notches for the purpose of hanging kettles or pots. Over the oven was a large hob and another smaller one on the right-hand side. Above the fireplace was the mantelpiece on which, at each end, were two tall tins which originally were for tea, both had pictures of Indian women picking the tea leaves. In one of them, mother always kept all her receipts and the other one was full of bits of string, boot laces etc. There was also an old jug which used to hold all the spills – spills being made either of paper or bits of wood for lighting the candles or lamps to save striking matches. At the bottom, a fender with brass knobs at each corner, lying at the bottom and resting on the end bars were the fire tongs, poker and a flat iron bar in the shape of a letter L for the purpose of raking out the ashes from under the oven and pushing hot coals to adjust the oven temperature. To the right of the fireplace, another smaller alcove which mother used to keep her sewing machine in. On the opposite wall was a cupboard under the stairs where all our coats and shoes were kept. To the left of that was the door into the kitchen.

The kitchen - on the right hand side was a door to a walk-in larder. On the side wall there were three shelves the full length and at the end there was a Welsh slate cold slab. The little window at the top was covered in mesh to keep the flies out. Opposite the door into the kitchen was the backdoor. To the left of the back door, was a brown Belfast sink, built on brick pillars, with a window above. Opposite the sink was a pine table which mother used for preparing all the meals. On the right, facing the table was a door which led to the bathroom. In front of the door, straight opposite, was the copper and to the right of the copper, adjoining it was the bath and with one tap for cold water which would have been a godsend to my parents. All the walls were just brick. There was no plaster in the kitchen, bathroom or the larder but were painted in Council colours, being the bottom half brown and the top half green and the ceilings were a type of whitewash called distemper – obviously white. It was a powder mixed with water.

The front room was plastered and the walls were decorated in a very pale blue, also distemper and the ceiling was white, the same as the kitchen ceiling.

Upstairs – the stairs consisted of 14 treads, the last two being on a bend which went on to a landing. On the left was the master bedroom at the front of the house which had a built-in wardrobe. On the opposite wall, there was a little fireplace. This was my parent's room and this I shared with them as I had four sisters still at home.

Opposite the main bedroom, was another door to the small bedroom and at the end of the landing was the second bedroom which my two elder sisters had – my two younger sisters had the small room. All the rooms were distempered like those downstairs.

Being at No 2 of a block of four, the right of way to access the back was down the side of No. 1. For No. 3, their rear access was around the side of No. 4. Out the back, we went down two steps and diagonally to the left there was a brick building which stretched from No 2 to No 1 with a flat concrete roof: it had two compartments – the first was the coal shed and the second was an outside toilet which consisted of a bucket.

Directly outside the toilet door was a six foot wooden partition fence between Nos 1 and 2. Up against the house wall and against this partition fence there was a large corrugated soft water tank for catching surplus rain water off the roof: always covered over with a sack to keep debris out. Mother used it a lot for rinsing clothes and washing our hair.

The path from the back gate and the back gardens went right down to the Armscote Road – nearly 100 yards long and around 20-30 feet wide. At the top of this garden there was two wooden sheds. Although it was our back garden, No. 1 had a garden shed back to back with ours where father kept all the tools, bicycles, etc.

The garden was still field and father paid Austin (Manty) Sabin the sum of thirty shillings (£1.50 today) to dig it. Down the right-hand side, father planted blackcurrant bushes and gooseberries. Right at the bottom down the path we had a big clump of rhubarb and later on he brought home three magnum plum trees and planted them at the bottom. Being that it was such a long way round from the front of the house to Front Street and the Armscote Road father, like everyone else, made an opening in the hedge at the bottom for a short-cut. The Back garden had a gentle slope to the boundary edge on the Armscote Road which had a ditch either side. There were no dividing fences between the gardens, each garden being from furrow to furrow which in all probability had been ploughed out by a pair of horses decades before for drainage purposes, being as the subsoil was heavy yellow clay. The front gardens were divided by chain-link fences. Ours was divided from Number 1 and the path from the front doors divided us from Number 3 and so on along the row. The boundary fence was also chain linked and outside this was the road which was made of stone. It ended beyond No 10 in a circle for the purpose that delivery carts and waggons were able to turn to come out.

At this time, Electric Companies were starting to bring electricity to the area. We had no electricity and all our lighting was by oil lamps or by candlelight. Workmen put up a great big power station on the Fosseway near Darlingscote and they were erecting all these large pylons. My Uncle Roby worked for this company erecting the pylons. He lived in the first cottage next to Whitehouse Alley with his wife, Aunt Lil – and they had three daughters, Evelyn, Sylvia and Daphne. Evelyn the eldest would be about eleven years of age, Sylvia about seven and Daphne round about five. One particular day, he cut his hand and just wrapped a handkerchief around it. Apparently it went sceptic, so he went to the doctor who told him that it was poisonous. He went into hospital where they lanced this thing. Unfortunately, all the poison had gone up his arm and they decided it had gangrene and they had to amputate his arm. Even worse it had gone past that into his body, hence he died of blood poisoning – that was in 1934. Tragically, Aunt Lil his wife, who suffered badly from arthritis died one year later, in 1935 and left all the girls orphans. To start with the girls were looked after by relatives but later on they had to go into an orphanage in Birmingham. They used to come over in school holiday times in the summer and stay with different Aunts. They all grew up and left school. Evelyn did come back and married a local boy – Derek Hemmings and they lived in Shipston. Sylvia, who had a cleft palate, worked in Birmingham but we lost touch so I don't know what happened to her or Daphne.

About the time of King George VI Coronation in 1937, Mr and Mrs Gaydon who lived in No. 1, moved to a bungalow down Whitehouse Alley which is off the Lower Green. Our new neighbour was Mrs Coaton who was Mrs Hands' mother from No 3. Also Mr and Mrs Freeman at No 10, the parents of my very close friend Geoffrey, moved to Junction Cottage which is situated on the road to Compton Scorpion.

This property was built on the side of the old tramway which in all probability served as a station as the road would surely not require someone in residence to open and close the gates for a horse drawn tram to and from Stratford twice a day. There was quite a lot of ground with this property, a good half a mile of the old tramway. They kept chickens and reared turkeys and late on had a couple of goats, a pigsty and a cob which Geoffrey and I would often ride and the family would go for a drive on a Sunday afternoon in the summer, weather permitting. Their place at No. 10 was taken by Bill and Mabel Cooke, my second cousin. They had moved from the house along the Mickleton Road on the junction leading up to Larkstoke.

This cottage was built of brick and was known as The Brickle. Bill worked for Wilsons who had the farm at Larkstoke.

In the days before immunization, our family, like all others, caught and suffered all the illnesses that went around the village through school contact on a regularly yearly basis. Illnesses such as, measles, mumps, whooping cough, pink eye, impetigo and chicken-pox. Doctors were kept busy visiting houses where sick children were and then had the problem of fetching the appropriate medicines and ointments for different ailments.

Our doctor, was a Dr Walker who was one of three doctors whose surgery was in Shipston, the others being Dr Harris and Dr Stein. I remember on one occasion we were recovering from one of these ailments in late spring, sometime in May. Dr Walker called in to check on our progress and said to mother, "Put their coats on, what they need is a good dose of fresh air". So out we went into this open top car and off we went down the Stratford Road, round through Admington, onto the Mickleton Road and back home. What a treat – better than all the medicines and our very first ride in a car. What a wonderful kind doctor he was. Everyone was so sad when he moved on. Our new doctor was a Dr McMullen, a big man with huge bushy eyebrows and a Rugby Union man, who had played at University and Club level until he qualified as a doctor. He had numerous photographs of Rugby teams hanging in his surgery.

When my oldest sister, Rita, left school she went to work for Mr and Mrs Sherrat who owned Berryfields Farm. Her main job was looking after their three daughters. She used to bring the eldest, Audrey, to school in the morning and fetch her home in the afternoon. To get to Berryfields by road was quite a jaunt. You had to go down Armscote Road to the crossroads, turn left into Gypsy Halt and from there it was a good mile and a half, down a cart-track and across a couple of fields. The shortcut which was down a track known as Bald Addledon which was just across the road from the bottom of our garden. This track gave access to all the fields down the track and at the bottom was a field full of scrub and bushes which, incidentally, was a favourite place, so quiet and peaceful, for nightingales. On lovely May evenings their song filled the air with a sound that took your breath away and made you stand in awe and wonderment of how a bird so plain and inconspicuous could create such a beautiful sound – a sound alas you seldom here now. To get back to the shortcut to Berryfields, across the scrubfield and across another grass field and you were there – a distance of about a mile. I remember going down there with my two younger sisters during the summer holidays and having tea on the lawn and playing hide and seek among the farm buildings. They were really a very nice family.

It was on days like this that we became friendly with a man by the name of Ben Tandy who worked for Mr Sheratt. Ben was a nice quiet man, always smiling. He came from Bretforton where his mother and brother Jim lived. Ben lived in at the Sheratts and was quite good with machinery. He rode a motorbike and would travel home when he had a day off. Mr Sheratt was the first farmer that I can remember having a tractor and of course Ben became the tractor driver and for years after, that was what Ben did. He became a really good friend of my family and used to call in on a regular basis for a cup of tea and a slice of mum's cake. Neither he nor his brother Jim ever married. Ben had a wire-haired terrier which he call Nip. She had a black head and tail and the rest of her body was completely white. She would go round the farm with him while he carried out his work. She was about 18 months old when we used to go down there. Ben, having had her since she was an 8 week old pup. One early summer evening, after we had finished our tea, father was about to go out to the garden and my sisters were washing up. There was a knock on the backdoor, one of my sisters opened it and there stood Ben, smiling as usual. On hearing his voice, mother called, "Come in Ben, I'll put the kettle on, have a seat." He always sat by the table. Father, having delayed his exit, enquired "How's work Ben" and Ben finished his mouthful of cake, put down his cup and replied "Really busy with the tractor, now spending hours out in the fields and helping out on neighbouring farms and I am unable to take Nip with me and hate having to leave her shut up all day and that is the reason for my visit. Would you and your family have her and look after her. It would be a huge weight off my mind and I know she would have a good home and I wouldn't want her to go anywhere else." Father paused for a few seconds, which seemed to me to be minutes, while I waited with baited breath. Finally he said, "Yes, Ben, we'll take her." Ben replied, his smile lighting up his face and said "Thank you, that is a weight off my mind" After a few days Nip became one of the family. I couldn't wait to get home from school to take her out for walks. However, there were a number of occasions I came home and found no Nip. Despite mother's efforts to keep the backdoor shut, she escaped and made her way back to Berryfields, resulting in me having to go down there to fetch her. Eventually, after a few weeks, she settled down and was free to go in and out as she chose. However, she always knew when Ben came to visit, for she would hear the sound of his motorbike and would go to the backdoor and wait with wagging tail for Ben always stopped at the bottom of the garden and walked up to the backdoor. When he left, he always gave her a pat and said "I'll see you again soon" for he must have missed her such a lot. This was the start of a long and happy time for no matter who went out, Nip wanted to accompany them and was really disappointed when told she couldn't go.

When Rita left Berryfields a year or so later she went to work as a housemaid for Major and Lady Rosemary Gresham at Sansome House in Back Street. Lady Gresham was a beautiful young woman who used to advertise Ponds Vanishing Cream in the glossy magazines. Major Gresham was a keen horseman and had a stable of some really good hunters and point-to-pointers. In fact he had one mare called Glengarrig that was unbeaten for two or three seasons. His head groom was Mr Ledger, a man with a real cockney accent who lived in a cottage next to the stables.

Major Gresham's mother, whose title was the Countess of Erol, lived with them – a very elegant lady who was always immaculately dressed.

By this time, Vera, my second sister, had left school and was in domestic service in Stratford. Rita, having left Major Gresham, was now in service at The Folly in the village of Halford for a Miss Penson where the cook-housekeeper was a lady by the name of Annie Cox who, like Miss Penson, thought a great deal of Rita. Miss Penson was a generous and kind lady, who, each Easter, for a number of years, gave my two remaining sisters and myself, an Easter egg in its own box with the egg decorated with edible spring flowers such as violets, primroses and cowslips, the like of which my parents could never have afforded and each Christmas lovely presents also. Annie, who had worked for many years for Miss Penson, lived in at The Folly as did Rita for the time that she worked there. When Miss Penson died, a few years later, she left Annie a cottage in the village which she had purchased a while before and a sum of money for her to furnish it. Annie, who remained a spinster all her life, lived there till her death in the 1960s. She kept in touch with my mother right up till that time. Also when Rita married in the mid 40s, she lived in a cottage in the next street to Annie and so they visited one another every week until Rita moved in the early 50s.

COUNTRY PURSUITS

When I was about seven my father took a job timber falling which, being away from the area, meant he was away from home all the week and only came home at weekends. He and his brother, Uncle Bill, would set off late on Sunday with tools strapped to their bicycles, ie axes and a crosscut saw which was about six feet long with huge teeth and very sharp, operated by two men who, on each stroke pulled the saw towards them. Operating this together made it look so easy and effortless and I'm sure it wasn't.

Uncle Bill lived in a house at the top of Grump Street. We children looked forward to them returning on Saturdays for father would bring us a bag of bluebird toffees which was a real treat and mother would give us one or two each day. This routine went on for months until it became too far to travel so they returned home and went to work for a local builder by the name of Mr Clifford.

I remember when the fox cub hunting season started in September, mother would get us up early to go to the meet around Larkstoke to see the hounds and huntsmen in their scarlet coats. There were two hunts that used to hunt around here, the North Cotswolds whose kennels were at Broadway and the Warwickshire whose base was at Kineton.

This was also the time of year, mother like a lot of women, would go blackberrying. When she had seen us off to school, she would go down the fields at the bottom of our garden, dressed in an old mackintosh she kept for the job, with a belt round her waist. Onto this she would have a small round basket made from soft rope and string that held a couple of pounds of fruit hanging at the front. Two or three buckets and a walking stick not used for walking but to pull down the berries she could not reach. She would leave sandwiches for our dinner and always a note to let my sisters know where to meet her when we came home from school at four o'clock for they had to carry the fruit of her labours home.

Her hands would be deeply stained with blackberry juice and full of thorns which would be removed each evening for this was not just a one off job, it would last as long as there were blackberries to pick. She must have walked miles during a season.

Then there was the job of taking them up to the carriers who lived at the bottom of Foxcote Hill. This was done with the aid of our old pram, this being a hard task in itself for there were two quite steep hills to negotiate on a journey of well over half a mile. There the fruit would be weighed and tipped into wicker baskets ready to be taken to where they would be used. This could be a jam factory, canning factory or a dye manufacturers. She would be paid 6d ($2^1/_2$p today) a pound. Mother used the proceeds to buy our winter boots and shoes, mostly boots for girls as women wore boots in those days for everyday use.

WOMAN'S WORK

In the days when very few married women had a full time job, their time was spent running the family home, a full-time job in itself for, in the days before we had electricity, the heating and cooking was all done by coal fire. So I think it only right to give a description of a typical week in the life of a wife and mother. Starting with Monday, she would get up at six o'clock or before. The first job was raking out the ashes from the black cooking range in the living room, laying and lighting the fire with kindling wood and small bits of coal brought in the night before. Then, filling the kettle and placing it over the fire suspended from a hinged bar to make the first pot of tea. Next remove the pan at the front and take up the ashes and then out into the bathroom to light the copper, already filled with water for the weekly wash. By this time, if the fire was going well and the kettle boiling, time for a welcome cup of tea. This would be drunk while laying the table for breakfast. Around a quarter to seven she would take a cup of tea up to my father, followed by checking that the fire under the copper was burning well which would then be topped up with a shovel full of slack. This was small bits of coal and dust which mixed with the dregs of the teapot which was always used to dampen and bind the coal bits together. This was always done whenever the teapot was emptied. Father had made a partition with bricks on the side of the coal-shed for the slack coal to be stored. Father would get up at seven. As soon as mother heard him coming downstairs, she would prepare his toast. He always had toast for breakfast which, of course, had to be done in front of the fire with a toasting fork. Our fork was a three pronged one of steel about a foot long which could be extended to double that size, if the fire was too hot so as to prevent burning one's hand. At about 7.30, with father off to work, she would then come upstairs and make sure we were awake and getting up. She would then prepare our breakfast, which in the winter would be porridge which she would make while we washed and did our hair. Having finished breakfast, one of my sisters, usually the oldest at home, would go up to Dowler's farm in Middle Street with a can to fetch the milk. That done, it would be time for school. Mother would then have five minutes for another cup of tea and a bit of breakfast. It was then time to start the washing. My father had made two platforms that fitted over the bath on to which two zinc baths were placed, one for washing, and the other for rinsing. This was before the days of detergent. It was then Sunlight and Carbolic soap - these would be rubbed onto the clothes and with the hands, rubbed and scrubbed to remove the dirt, rung out and rinsed two or three times before ringing out again ready for hanging out to dry. With the sheets and pillowcases, these were usually boiled in the copper, rung out, several rinses and placed in a bath containing a blue bag. This was used for whitening, then rung out again and then put in a wicker clothes basket and then down the garden to be hung out on the clothes line. This stretched almost to the bottom of the garden, supported by four posts positioned by the side of the grass path. The line was of strands of wire twisted together to a thickness of a pencil which was strong and flexible and virtually break proof as no one wanted all their hard work undone by the line breaking and dragging the washing on the garden, thus having to go through the procedure again. The washing was held on the line by handmade wooden pegs. These were made by the gypsies from Willow, Hazel and Ash whichever was available where they made their camp. Pegs would be about five inches long, stripped of their bark, split three quarters of the way up, the split then tapered on the inside to allow it to be pushed down onto the clothes and line. About an inch from the top was a narrow strip of tin held on by a small tack, thus preventing the peg from splitting right up to the top, very effective they were.

This done, it would be time for the next job, upstairs with the slop bucket, which was about a third full of soapy water for the purpose of emptying and rinsing the chamber pots and making the beds. After this would be a well earned morning break which could be a cup of cocoa or a small glass of stout. Mother would then use the washing water to scrub the front and back doorsteps and finish them with a pumice stone. This would be done in circular movements. It would now be time to think about lunch or what we used to call dinner for we would come home from school for dinner – no school dinners in those days. We would leave school at 12 o'clock, have dinner – usually sandwiches – for mother would always cook for the evening, which on Mondays would be cold meat from the Sunday and bubble and squeak with pickle or chutney followed by a pudding of some sort. We had to be back at school for 1.30. Mother would usually wash the kitchen floor with the remaining water in the copper. Late afternoon would be time to check the washing. Any that was dry would be folded and placed in the clothes basket. Often in winter it would be stiff as a board with frost.

Tuesday was normally ironing day. This was done with flat irons. These were made with really heavy metal, which were stood on their heel in front of the fire to heat up. They would be lifted off with a kettle holder to save burning your fingers for they would get very hot. To test them for heat you spat on them. If it shot off that was the sign they were ready. Mother used to iron on the table that stood in the middle of the living room. She placed a blanket, doubled on the end of the table then covered by an old sheet kept for the purpose. On the table would be a stand for the iron and a basin for water to sprinkle on the items if they were too dry.

Often when the washing was brought in from the line, very dry, it would be sprinkled with water, rolled up and placed in the basket ready to iron.

Wednesdays - mother would usually spend the morning cleaning and dusting the bedrooms, down the stairs and the small hallway. Our dinner would probably be rabbit in some form or other. It could be stew, rabbit pie or a favourite of mine – roast with onions, herbs and bits of bacon. Mother could skin and joint a rabbit in about 15 minutes. I suppose it was from plenty of practice. In her time she must have done hundreds. There was nothing like coming home on a winter evening to the sight of a roaring fire and the smell of rabbit roasting in the oven. Saucepans simmering on the hobs with vegetables to be followed by steamed or boiled puddings. It could be any one of jam, treacle, sultanas or spotted dick. Often it would be suet crust pastry in a basin with bottled fruit done in the summer, such as gooseberries, plums or damsons all with custard, made with whole milk. Mother was a really good cook who could make a meal out of practically nothing. In those days there was very little waste. What could be was preserved while most vegetables were seasonable.

Thursdays – the day for putting the aired washing away in the appropriate drawers. We had a trunk for the bed linen in mother's bedroom also a blanket box which was kept in the wardrobe which was built in over the stairs. Mother would visit her mother in Middle Street for an hour or so in the afternoon before returning for when we came home from school and to prepare and cook tea.

Friday was a day for the living room to be given its weekly thorough clean, starting with the fireplace, the space under the oven would be raked out through a removable plate at the front and the ashes would be taken out. The grate would be black leaded and polished so that it shone like silk. The floor was swept and the linoleum was also polished plus all the ornaments would be put on the pine table, the sideboard and the drop-leaf table polished, also the shelves and the cupboard would be dusted and polished with Mansion furniture polish. The ornaments would then be dusted and replaced to their allotted space. The oil lamp would have the wicks trimmed, the globe and funnel would be carefully washed and thoroughly dried and the oil reservoir would be topped up with paraffin Also the daily task of bringing in the wood and coal, having first chopped the kindling which could be wood from a faggot, pine blocks or any rotten branches that had fallen out of the trees. This task became mine from the age of ten.

Saturday was the day for cake making as well as pastry for pies and tarts. My sisters often did this and they, like mother, were really good cooks. Elma was a very good pastry cook and always made it during her time she lived at home. Saturday night was our bath night and also when we had our weekly dose of syrup of figs.

Sunday was the only day when everyone didn't have to get up early, so mother would call us to get up around a quarter to nine. We children would all have clean underclothes which mother had laid out the night before and Sunday clothes. After breakfast it would be time for Sunday School. This we held in the school each week at ten o'clock. Our teachers were Mrs Warren who lived in a cottage by the school and Gwen Smith. At around ten minutes to eleven, we would line up outside and then walk the hundred yards or so down to Church for the morning service for which we had been given a penny for the collection. After this, and before the sermon started, we would be led out and dismissed to return home. Often, we took a long diversion which entailed retracing our steps back up to the school, then turning left and along to the bottom of Campden Hill where Mr and Mrs Roy Garrett, who kept a small shop selling mostly sweets. Outside Mr Garrett had a petrol pump which was operated by a handle which, when turned anti-clockwise, would push the plunger down and then bring it up when turned in a clockwise direction, delivering one gallon each time. This was registered on a dial with a pointer and numbers from one to zero. They also sold paraffin for the purpose of lighting. Mr Garrett also ran a taxi service. To return to visiting the shop as I mentioned, we each had a penny for the church collection and at times, one or two of us would have been given two half-pennies. This became a temptation too great to resist, resulting in the trip to purchase after having only put in a half penny into the collection. We had the other halfpennies to spend on sweets which usually went on halfpenny bars of toffee which could be ordinary brown or a favourite of mine – liquorice toffee. Looking back, it wasn't a very nice thing to do but sweets were more or less a luxury in those times for there was little or no money for such treats.

On returning home it would be approaching dinner time which would always be a roast of either beef, lamb or pork, the latter being eaten only in winter from October to March. As the old saying goes (like rabbit) only when the month contains an "R" in the spelling for in the spring and summer it was said and believed that pigs would sweat and therefore lose tenderness and taste, a tradition, I must admit, I still follow today. We always had a pudding of some sort – it could be pie, crumble or steamed or even rice. After the washing up was all done, depending on the weather and what our parents had planned, in the spring we would go for walks down the country roads while our parents had time to themselves. What a time to be out in the countryside. Hedges and trees bursting into bud, and to hear the birds like the cuckoo, the sweet sound of the blackbirds and the wonderful song of the songthrush. The yellow hammer announcing his lunch with a little bit of bread and no cheese, while in the tops of the mighty oaks and elegant elms were the cluster of nests with their young being tended to by their noisy parents. The rooks and crows, who are some of the first to nest, preparing them in February where, according to the old saying, if they nested at the very top of the trees we were in for a good summer. If they nested below then the summer would not be so good with more rain and cloud. Then there were the spring flowers along the hedgerows whilst on the banks of the ditches were the intense blue of the violet with their sweet scent. The carpets of yellow primroses covering the ground in the spinneys and copse and in the large woods, the white flowers and deeply scented plants of woodruff, the yellow heads of aconite – all these could be found along with the deep yellow of the celandines. Then in May many of the woods would be carpeted with bluebells. The hedgerows would display the clusters of small white flowers of the hawthorns (or May Blossom as it was called), hence the saying' Cast not a Clout till May be out'. It was in these tall hedges that the magpies built their nest. Like most large birds they would be of twigs. These domed nests are very untidy in appearance and quite large.

SEASONS

Spring and summer would be the time for family walks which usually finished up visiting various relatives like Uncle Ernie and Aunty Roz Proctor and their son Wilfred and daughter Edwina. They had a farm called Oakham over Campden Hill in the village of Ebrington. After Sunday dinner we would set off up Foxcote Hill, along the Charingworth Road and then cut across country to their farm, a distance of around three miles. Those three miles were full of interest, with the various wildlife and, on clear days, views which could stretch for miles. Once there, Wilfred and Edwina would show us around the farmyard to see the calves. They had quite a large dairy herd of shorthorn cattle. Also chickens and ducks were all around while in the pigsty were pigs of various sizes, most of which would be sold for porkers and bacon, depending on size. Auntie made a lot of butter which would be taken to Stratford market every Friday along with eggs from both chickens and ducks. The time seemed to fly by with so much to see and do. Then, we would be called in for tea of bread and home-made farm butter and jam. Sometimes, jelly or blancmange and home-made cake which we were always ready for. What with the fresh air and exercise, we had healthy appetites. We all had tea with the exception of Uncle Ernie for he would be doing the afternoon milking, the cows having been brought in by Wilfred. That was his job and we would all help whenever we visited. At around half past six, we would say our goodbyes and thankyous and set off on the three mile walk back home for it was school the next day. We didn't need any rocking that night but we thoroughly enjoyed the visit which we probably made two or three times during the summer.

Another of our walks was what we called 'round the avenue' for which we would set off after tea up Foxcote Hill but instead of taking the Charingworth Road we would go straight on through the gates onto the Foxcote Estate. There were no roadside edges but huge beech trees both sides of the road. These went all the way along to the big house. The open fields either side of the road were backed by woodlands. On the right about half way to the big house and about two to three hundred yards from the road was a red brick building with three or four arched openings, like a cart hovel. I never quite knew what it was used for. The house which was very big stood back from the road on the left separated from the side of the road by an iron fence about four feet or so high with a gate at each end onto the driveway up to the front door. Between the drive and the fence was lawn. The road at the end of the fence turned right towards the Campden Road or straight on which dropped down into a dip where, at the bottom, on the left was a cottage for probably one of the

Uncle Hobble with his terrier and pet fox

estate workers or may be a gardener. Over the top of this dip was a wooden foot bridge which led from the house grounds to a summer house on the opposite side of the road. You can imagine the ladies of the house with visitors strolling across the bridge with their parasols on a hot summer afternoon to sit and talk in the peace and quiet and shade of this summer house. On the left and to the right of the big house you could catch a glimpse of the lake which usually had mallard ducks on it. Following the road from the dip you came to one of the estate farms. This one on the right was farmed by tenants, Mr and Mrs Dyer with their children, Sonny and Patricia. To continue our walk we would turn right at the summer house and follow the avenue towards the Campden Road., This stretch had many trees of different varieties on either side, where often you would see squirrels running along the branches and jumping from tree to tree and possibly a Jay – a colourful member of the Crow family. These birds would always be found near Oak trees for acorns are their main source of food especially so in winter. In the autumn they would bury hundreds in the ground to keep them through the winter months. Naturally they would forget where

My parents and youngest sister with our terrier, Nip, before the Sunday walk

some of them were. So if you are walking through the woods and come across a small oak sapling, chances are it was buried and forgotten by a Jay - one of nature's ways of reproduction.

On reaching the Campden Road and to the left about a hundred yards or so, was another estate farm – this one farmed by Mr Bell but we turned right back towards the village. A little way along this road on the left and slightly down a hill, a road led to the farm called Wood Meadow, where my grandfather and grandmother lived as tenant farmers and my mother and sisters and brothers grew up – a wonderful place to live in the summer but could be very hard in winter for mother would often tell us of snow drifts up to and over six feet deep. It must have been extremely difficult getting to and from the village for they had to walk to school in the village which mother said you often didn't know if you were walking on the road or on the hedge. They must have been exhausted when they reached home for Campden Hill is the highest in Warwickshire. On reaching the bottom of the steepest part of the hill, we would sometimes call on Ginny Newman who we, as children, called Aunt Gin. She lived in the second of two detached cottages, entering the village or the second from the last on the left hand side leaving it, or we would call on Auntie Frances, who lived in the third from the bottom of a row of cottages on the left. I can just remember Uncle Hobble, Auntie Frances' husband – he was my father's uncle, (Grandfather's brother) whose real name was William George Cooke but everyone called him Uncle Hobble. I remember him taking me out to the back garden and up these stone steps to the pigsty at the top of the garden, picking me up and showing me what I thought would be a pig. Instead it was a fox which he had raised from a cub since its mother had been killed and was the only survivor of the litter - obviously it was very tame and had no fear of humans or dogs for it spent a lot of its time with his terrier. Alas, Uncle Hobble died when I was four but I will never forget him showing me this fox which lived for quite a few years after Uncle Hobble. Auntie Frances fed and cared for it for the rest of its life because there was no way it could have survived in the wild on its own. Another visiting place on our walks was in Middle Street where my grandmother lived with Uncle Harry, my mother's brother, who will be given a more detailed description in a later chapter – Farms).

Another walk which we often did was up the village to the Red Lion, down Featherbed Lane to the ford and then right along the gated road towards Compton Scorpion until we reached the turning to the Shipston Road, where we would turn right on to Pig Lane. This was an old drover's way which the farmers, in years gone by, used to drive their stock to Longden Road (Darlingscote) or to Shipston Market. Pig Lane was a steady climb through three gated fields, out on to and over the Foxcote Road. On up the lane and through a small wood, across a field and then a huge open field called Nebsworth, with its row of big beautiful oak trees which could be seen for miles. This, of course, overlooked the village, a truly magnificent view and where in the 1800s a racehorse trainer, by the name of E P Wilson, galloped his horses. One of these, a horse called Voluptuary, won two Grand Nationals. His stables, in Middle Street, were where Mr Dowler had his farm. From Nebsworth and down a slight incline you came out onto the Campden Road, just a few yards from the Foxcote Avenue entrance. There were lots of walks you could take around the village and over my childhood days I would have done these countless times.

Autumn

The walks at this time of the year were the same as those in Spring and Summer with the exception of Ebrington which I don't remember visiting at this time. The rest we did and changing seasons brought different things to see, all the berries, like blackberries, elderberries, hips and haws ie Hawthorns. Not only were these colourful but vital for birds and wildlife if they were to survive the winter. Then there would be the wild fruit for instance, the Sloe which is the fruit of the blackthorn. It is a small round fruit, the colour of damsons but as hard as bullets which the old folks called bullies but nevertheless these would make sloe gin, a drink that would warm the cockles of your heart on a cold winter's day. The blackthorn is the first species to flower – you will see the wild flowers in the hedgerows in March which bears the saying "of the blackthorn winter" as the weather never seems to get warmer until it has finished flowering. The wild cherries which you could often find on the edge of woods, the wild plums and the crab-apples which grew in the hedgerows, I remember gathering these from Uncle Harry's fields for mother to make crab apple jelly. This could be eaten like jam on bread and butter or with roast pork; either way, it was delicious and a vital addition to mother's store cupboard. Then of course, there were the nuts. I remember us going up the Campden Hill, just round the first bend and on the right, a gateway that opened onto a track that led to Hill Barn. On the left of this track was a hedge which was just full of hazel bushes and what do you get from these bushes – hazel nuts – just clusters of them. We used to pick them usually in October just as they were starting to go brown. They would be taken home, placed in an air-tight weather-proof container and buried in the garden where they stayed with their position marked until a couple of weeks before Christmas, then dug up and taken out perfectly ripe, and yes, sweet as a nut. It would be difficult to achieve this today for there are so many squirrels which take them before they are ripe and store them like us for use in the winter.

Then there was a special walk we only did in the autumn. In late October, we children would set off after Sunday lunch – we would go up the village to the lower green, down Whitehouse Alley, through Mabels farmyard, over back street, through the rick yard, into the field called Little Meadow, across to the far left hand corner into Big Meadow which, in the summer, was full of flowers, I remember specially big white daisies which everyone called Moon Daisies. These seemed to thrive for it was the only field that I ever knew that had so many year after year. From here we had a steady climb through two more fields, over a stile into a field that fell away to the left at the top and immediately in front was a row of huge sweet chestnut trees. These were the purpose of our walk, for they would be shedding what we had come to gather – chestnuts. We always gathered so many that we gave a lot away. We would always have roast chestnuts done on the bars of the open range and for those lucky enough to be able to afford turkey for Christmas, which we never had, for the traditional chestnut stuffing. This walk, like so many we did, was quiet and peaceful with always something interesting to see.

Our walks in winter depended on the weather. If it was raining, or likely to, it would be a no-go and, of course, when it was suitable we would keep to the roads for the fields and tracks would be far too muddy. The only time we were allowed off-road was if we had snow; even then it would have to be a good covering for it meant we could go up Foxcote Hill and into Mr Foster's field that were ideal for tobogganing or sledging as we called it. This field was quite flat at the top, then in the middle was a long steady fall right down to the bottom where it levelled out before the

Sledging on Foxcote Hill, Winter '45/'46

boundary hedge. At the bottom, a distance of some 5-600 yards, on the right hand side of the slope, the field had quite a steep bank while on the left, not quite so steep but with the hazards of a large rabbit warren, which we tried to avoid naturally. Some unfortunate people, who not knowing these hazards, would finish up in the snow sometimes with broken sledges which ended their enjoyment until repairs had been carried out back at home.

These afternoons on Sundays and often for us, Saturdays as well but Sundays were the time for families. Children, young adults and parents would gather up there for a wonderful afternoon sport, where, if the snow was powdery the going would be really fast and speeds of up to 50mph and over could be reached especially on a large sledge with four or five people on it. In fact, when I worked in Blackwell for Mr Hicks, Jim, his son, used to sit up in his bedroom and watch us through his binoculars. He reckoned some of them came down at up to 70 mph. Whatever the speed, we all had a wonderful time. We boys used to like going down lying two or three piled on top of one another, face down. We couldn't wait to get back to repeat it over and over again. Despite it often being bitterly cold, it didn't seem to bother us for we would come home probably wet through with healthy appetites and ready for tea, hoping we could do it all again the next week-end. Another of our favourite winter past-times was sliding. Whenever we had prolonged hard frosty weather, we would go down the Shipston Road past the Blackwell turn, down the small hill and in the field on the left was quite a large and not too deep pond with a few willow trees. Ponds always had Willow trees closeby for they thrived in moist condition and were lopped every several years or so when their branches were large enough to be cut and used for fencing rails. We would test the thickness of the ice to see if it would bear us. If we thought it had sufficient strength, we would edge forwards towards the middle. If there was the slightest crack we would carefully retreat to the edge and once on safe ground, we would break the ice, often with the heal of our boots, in as many places as we could to allow the water below to rise up and cover the pond, so the frost could build up the thickness. We might have to do this several times before it was safe enough for us to use as a slide. We would take a run from the field and slide from one side to the other, one after the other, over and over again – great fun!

ELECTRIC JOY

Around 1937/38, the village welcomed the arrival of the electricity supply. Although having been introduced to the towns and cities before, it took a while to relay it to outlying villages. It would have been a blessing to the housewives, although still in the stages of development. In the decades before plastic was even thought of, the wires were covered with rubber and the outer covering was of braided cotton fixed to the walls with tin clips. The light switches and fittings were of Bakelite. There were no power points. The first appliance my mother had was an electric iron which she had to plug into the light holder, having first to climb onto a chair to reach it. The fitting was also of Bakelite and like a light bulb had a bayonet fitting – no health and safety in those days – and, of course, turned on and off at the light switch. It must have been a blessing after years of using flat irons

King George VI Coronation 1937

heated in front of the fire. As I have mentioned, there were no power sockets so mother still had to use her primus stove which she acquired a few years before to boil the kettle and other cooking jobs. Even so, she still had to use the range but the primus was far quicker than lighting the fire. The primus stove was a tremendous addition to the kitchen. It was made with a round brass container that held about two and a half pints of paraffin. This was attached to three steel rods which formed the legs that held it about one and a half inches from the bottom. These rods extended up to support the round grid at the top, the tank had a brass threaded filler cap plus a brass pump in the side. At the top of the tank and in the centre, a brass tube about four to five inches long which had a small threaded brass nipple with a very small hole in the centre. Under this was a small round shallow tray and above this was the burner and spreader. This was a metal cap which had numerous holes pierced all round the side. To light it, you first had to prime it. To do this you had to fill the tray under the burner with methylated spirits, light it, and when it had almost burnt out you pumped the paraffin up to produce a gas like flame around the spreader. The heat, of course, was governed by the amount of pumps you gave it. If by chance for some reason the pressure fluctuated you had a little tool called a pricker. This was a metal strip with a short piece of very thin, strong steel wire that you pushed into the small hole in the nipple to remove any obstruction. The coming of electricity was, no doubt, a blessing to the housewives who were lucky enough to have it for it removed the daily chore of maintaining the oil lamps that needed regular re-fueling and frequent wick trimming beside careful handling and washing of the glass chimney and globe. Not only this but the small carrying lamps used for taking upstairs which were much better than candles that most ordinary people used and the constant battle to keep them alight when on the move, especially opening and closing doors. To have instant light by the flick of a switch in all rooms was a feeling of sheer joy and relief from the daily routine of keeping oil lamps in good working order especially in winter when daylight is short and the nights are long. Around this time of the Coronation, Elma my third sister left school. The previous year she had suffered an appendicitis and been taken to hospital in Shipston with severe abdominal pain where she underwent an operation to have her appendix removed. She was in hospital for three weeks and then spent three weeks at home convalescing. It was during this time, she took up needlework in the form of embroidery and over the next few years, in her spare time, she made the most beautiful table-cloths, chair back covers as well as runners for dressing tables.

Around 1938, the Council saw the need for larger houses to accommodate larger families so they built four houses at the end of our row, each being of four bedrooms. These were built by a Shipston based firm of Wards. (Some years later our road was renamed Bennett Place after Sam Bennett, the well known character from the village.) These new houses were allocated as follows -

In No. 11 were The Langstons, No 12 would now be The Hughes Family, currently living at No 4. In No 13 would be Mr & Mrs William and their four children, two boys and two girls of whom, only two were still at school, the other too having left. In No 14 was Mr & Mrs Hall who had moved from a cottage up Campden Hill with their six children, four boys and two girls. With the Hughes family having moved to No 12 this left No 4 to allow us new neighbours. Moving in to No. 4 was a Mr and Mrs Edwards who had moved from Compton Scorpion with their three sons, Aubrey, Dennis and Geoffrey. Mr Edwards, known as Billy, had worked for a Mr Wilks as a butcher in the village of Honington. It was in this capacity, while mincing the meat for sausages, Aubrey, the oldest boy (who incidentally was about three weeks older than me, and about 5 or 6 at this time) watched how the meat was placed in the top of the machine where it was pushed down and then came out the side as mince which was then mixed with other ingredients to make into sausages. Aubrey, like all children would be, was fascinated by all this and whilst his father's back was turned, climbed up on to the stand and proceeded to push the meat down with his left hand too far, resulting him losing one finger and most of the other three. When the surgeons operated they removed the remaining fingers down to the knuckles so he finished up with his thumb and palm of his hand. Luckily Aubrey was right handed and over the following years he could do practically anything with this.

SHOPS & CRAFTS

Our Village, being some 3-4 miles from the small market town of Shipston-on-Stour and 7 miles from Stratford, people were more or less dependent on village shops and tradesman for the service they provided, not only food but people to make and repair various things that were needed by farmers and village people, so I think it only right to start with the staff of life – bread. We had no less than three bakers in the village. Starting at the top, there was Valenders whose bakery was at The Grey House down Valenders lane which was in the grounds of and owned by the Manor. I remember seeing the bread and cakes on display in the window overlooking the lane. Next, opposite the Manor Gates were Mr & Mrs Frost who did a lot of the baking with the help of Charlie Sabin who also delivered by horse and trap, twice a week – Wednesdays and Saturdays. I remember mother would sometimes buy small fancy cakes for a Sunday teatime treat. I can see Charlie now, coming down the back path with a basket over his arm containing the loaves and cakes to No. 1 and then to us. He would come in and place the bread and cakes, if we were having any, on the table, pick up the money mother had left ready and say "The usual for Wednesday" and mother would tell him yes but occasionally on a Wednesday she would order a small brown loaf to deliver on Saturday to have for tea on Sunday. Charlie also delivered to Darlingscott and outlying farms and cottages as far as Far Longdon which is past the Longdon Road for Darlingscott Station and then to the farm and cottages along the Compton Scorpion Road and then onto the cottages and house at Foxcote. I have often wondered how he managed these outlying places in bad weather like snow and ice. Down the bottom of Middle Street was the quite substantial business of Mr & Mrs Biles, for not only did they have the largest bakery but a really well stocked grocery shop and also a butcher's shop. To start with the bakery, they employed Mr Hathaway who did

The Biles Bakers posing with delivery trap

most of the baking and Mr Fred Paintin who helped with the baking and delivering. Next, Mr Tommy Grimley, who looked after the ponies and the sheep. The ponies were kept in the field called Biles Close which is opposite the bottom green, while the sheep were in two large fields down the bottom of the village next to the Stratford and Mickleton Roads. Tommy also delivered – his rounds were Admington and Upper Quinton as well as Larkstoke. His delivery days were Tuesday and Friday while Fred's were Armscote, Blackwell and Tredington, quite a large round and he also delivered twice a week on the same days. The grocery shop was in part of the house which stands back on the right hand side before what used to be Dowler's Farm. This was run by Mr and Mrs Biles and their oldest daughters, Flo and Myra. The butcher's shop which was next to it was run by their son, George and Algie Hale who was also the slaughterer, assisted in this task by Tommy Grimley. They used to carry this out behind the Howard Arms and we used to stand at the top of Hobdays Bank and watch them bring the lambs out of one of the pig stys, slaughter it, put it on a barrow and take it round the back of the butcher's shop to dress and hang it for a while before jointing it ready for sale. Other shops in the village were Mr & Mrs Garrett at the bottom of Campden Hill which I have mentioned in an earlier paragraph and later Mrs Hathaway who lived in a cottage lying off the bottom green. She sold sweets, candles, matches, along with knitting wool, needles, cotton and soap.

The Post Office which was run by Mr & Mrs Edwards, was the house next to Frost's bakery and on the corner of Featherbed Lane. Mr Edwards was also a reporter for the Evesham Journal. He used to cover all the functions that went on in the village as well as weddings and funerals. He used to travel around on his bicycle, dressed in tweeds and wearing a deerstalker hat and never seemed to be without a cigarette. Mrs Edwards was always, as mother called it, dressed up to the nines and always wore a lot of jewellery.

At the bottom of the top green was the cobbler by the name of Mr Hall. He was kept busy with all the farm labourers whose boots needing keeping in good repair in those days before wellingtons became the winter boot for footwear. He also sold laces, polish and dubbing. This was used by the farmers and the workers to waterproof their boots and so keep the leather supple for in the winter they would be constantly in mud and water and, unlike today, they couldn't afford to keep buying new footwear.

At the bottom of Foxcote Hill, opposite to the Village Hall, was the carrier owned by Sam Bennett who lived in the Fox House with his brother Harry, and sister Patty. Sam's son, also Sam, drove the lorry and bus which was kept in a large garage in the yard, the lorry being used fetching and delivering goods to and from the station and Tuesdays and Fridays to the market in Stratford. By this time the country was becoming more and more mechanised so produce and goods could be moved around quickly. The bus was a great asset to the village – it gave the people a chance to go to the market towns like Stratford twice a week, on the same days that the lorry operated. This no doubt will make you think that's impossible – how can one driver manage to do that. It is quite simple. The market produce was taken very early allowing the bus to leave the village at 10 o'clock with a return journey at around 1.00. This would give people two and a half hours to do whatever business they had to do. Also it would allow Sam to collect various small items plus the money for the produce sold at the markets. Harry Bennett was completely different from his brother. He preferred to stay in the background and just get on with whatever he was doing. He was very clever with wood for they had two orchards, one at the back of their property and the other right at the bottom of the village, right opposite Bennett Place. Not only was he an authority on fruit he also made ladders of all lengths from eight feet upwards to forty feet. They were made with ash and chestnut. The sides would be of ash, some four or five inches in diameter, split down the centre and the rungs about a foot long and about one and a quarter inches tapered at each end to about one inch. These would be turned on a foot operated lathe. Ladders would be reinforced with a quarter inch mild steel bar, the shorter ones having one at the bottom and one at the top and the longer ones would have one in the middle. They would be placed underneath a rung after they had all been morticed into the ladder sides. This was done by a brace and bit to a depth of around one and a half inches. The rods would then be notched with a cross at each end and passed through the ladder sides, have a washer over each end and then burned over so as to make a secure fitting. These ladders were never painted as paint can hide a split so making a ladder unsafe - no one would have wanted a fall from a ladder thirty feet up a tree whilst fruit picking. Sam Bennett did all the fruit picking and did have a lucky escape once when a branch gave way whilst climbing the ladder up a tall pear tree, the ladder twisted and Sam had to make an awkward descent unscathed.

I remember Harry making me a truck when we moved down to Bennett Place. He painted it green and put my name and date on with white paint on the side. That was in 1933. Patty Bennett ran the house and was a devout Church goer, never missing a service and had a hand in all the functions held in the village.

At the back of the Post Office and on the right down Featherbed Lane was the wheelwright shop. The wheelwright was a man called Jack Terry – one of four brothers who lived in the village. He lived at the bottom of Valenders Lane in the first of three cottages known as The Bevingtons. He was kept busy repairing broken waggons, trolleys and traps as well as making wheels of various sizes, depending on the type of vehicle. I spent many hours watching him through the many stages of making a wheel all done by hand with hand tools. The first stage was the hub – this was made from a square block of elm wood about a foot square which he purchased, like all of the timber, from the Timberyard of Mayos at Shipston who will be explained in detail in a later chapter. These blocks would come already cut to size. The first job was to shape the block like a barrel. This would be done with a variety of small hand tools and axes, drawknives and spoke-shaves along with rasps from coarse to fine. Once that was done, it would be clamped in a large vice and then drilled through the centre for the axle which had been marked out whilst it was in a square block. This would be done with a large bit depending on the size of the axle. These bits were kept extremely sharp for elm was a really hard, tough wood. They were about eighteen inches

Wheelwrights pouring cold water onto the wagon wheel after fitting the red hot iron tyre. Left of the picture, a third person is stoking the fire for another

long with a ring at the top for a wooden handle which was operated with two hands. Once this operation had been completed, it was then marked out for the spoke mortices. They would be drilled out to a depth of about one and a half inches with a bit size determined with the size of the spokes. He had a number of these bits of varying sizes hung up in his workshop. The next task would be to make the spokes, again the size and length depended on size of wheel. These were made out of ash, a straight grained hard wood that was ideal for the job. The rims were made of another hard and strong wood – oak. All these trees were native to Britain and could be found in all the deciduous woods. The rims were cut with the grain and in sections on a curve to make a perfect circle, all being morticed for the spokes once the wheel was assembled. It had to be fitted with an iron rim. These would be made

Repairs to a shaft of a hay wagon

by the local blacksmith. This was an operation carried out by two men. First a fire would have to be made on the ground, large enough for the rim to be placed on it. More wood would then be placed on top to heat the rim so that it became red hot. Meanwhile, while the fire was doing its job they would fill watering cans and a couple of buckets with water. Once the rim was at the right heat they would pick it up with special tools for the purpose, place the rim over the wheel, and then hammer it on. Once satisfied it was in the right position, they would quickly pour the water on to prevent it burning and cooling it down for as it cooled it would contract and so make a secure fit with no further fixings required. It would then be painted to match the vehicle it had been made for. The wheelwright's busiest time would be the summer when the farmers would be haymaking and harvesting for which they needed dry weather. This, of course, dried the wood and made it shrink. Many farmers would get the farm workers to douse the wheels with water in the evenings or even drive their waggons into the ponds if possible to prevent this but obviously there were times when breakdowns happen, such as wheels, the raves or other parts of the waggon needing attention for the farmers wanted it back in working order as soon as possible. Raves were the frames that fitted at the front and back of the waggons at an angle leaning outwards so that high loads could be achieved without falling off. In the quiet months of the year he would probably make a front and back waggon wheel for a quick replacement.

Across Front Street from the wheelwright's shop and part of the buildings attached to the Red Lion Public House was The Blacksmith Shop. The blacksmith whose name was Harry Hancox and his son, Lesley, did not live in the village. They came from Halford – a village some three and a half or four miles away where they had a blacksmith's shop. They came to Ilmington every Tuesday and Friday by bicycle and, like the wheelwrights, also had an audience of us boys watching the horses being shod and the shoes being made on the anvil. You always hoped you were the one getting there first to work the bellows to heat up the coke fire that heated the iron to make the shoes and watching with interest the way the old shoes were removed and the hooves being prepared for the fitting of the new ones. To make sure of a good correct fit, the shoes were always tried while they were hot. This created a lot of smoke as it scorched the hoof to show up any high spots which could then be filed down with a rasp and the shoe could be re-checked for a perfect fit. When satisfied, the shoe would be plunged into a tank of water to cool it before being nailed on, the nail ends being twisted off with a claw hammer and then clinched over with clinching tongues and finished off with a file. Shoeing was just one of the many skills undertaken by blacksmiths for they made the fittings for the waggons, trolleys, carts and traps besides gates and door hinges and various pieces of farm implements.

PLAYING GAMES, HOBBIES & PARTIES

PLAYING GAMES

Before the days of in-house television and even radio - wireless as it was called in the early years - children played outside together or individually. The main games for the individual were whip and top, the whips being a short stick with a length of thin cord or string attached and the top being in the shape of a mushroom with the end being slightly tapered with a boot hobnail in the end to make it spin. The way it operated you would wind the cord round the top then in one movement you threw the top whilst holding on to the stick. This made the top spin on hitting the road and before it stopped you would whip it again and so on for as long as possible.

Another game was hoop and iron. The hoop would be any size from two to three feet in diameter, either metal or wood. Metal was the best for you could propel it continuously with a small iron with a hook at the end by holding it against the hoop whilst running alongside, whereas with a wooden hoop you had to propel it by hitting it with a stick. Then there was skipping. You could buy skipping ropes that had wooden handles at each end and more often than not a length of suitable rope did just as well. Skipping could also be done with two stood facing each other with one turning the rope, with good co-ordination you could keep going for quite a long time. For three or more, two of you would stand apart and, depending on the length of rope, whilst they turned the rope a number of you would run in and skip on time. Both boys and girls could join in. What a good way to keep fit as well.

Another game played, mostly by girls, was hopscotch. This was done by a pattern of squares marked on the road surface with chalk and numbered one to ten or even more. The idea was to hop into single boxes then two boxes side by side you jumped putting one foot into the lowest numbered box and then the other foot into the next numbered box and so on. All this, without stepping on the lines. On reaching the end you turned round and repeated it back to the start. Providing you had not crossed a line, if you had, you would have to start again.

Another favourite game was chase and arrows, where one or two would set off and every so often make the sign of an arrow in the direction they were going. These were made with chalk and could be on the road, gate or fence on any surface that could be marked clearly and if you were changing direction you made a bent sign indicating the direction you had taken. The idea was not to get caught before you reached the point from where you had started which could often mean covering two or three miles all around the various lanes, alleys and fields. We must have covered miles over the years and a dead cert to keep obesity at bay. This game was also known as fox and hounds or even hare and hounds, either way it gave us a lot of pleasure as well as exercise. It was mainly played by boys but there were occasions when a girl or two would join in.

Another game anyone could join in was rounders. Two of you would take it in turns to pick one at a time to be in your team, then you had to decide who was going to bat and who was going to pitch and field. This was done by drawing a straw. The one drawing the long one would have a choice of batting or fielding. The fielding side would have someone at each corner – called a base - of the square, a pitcher and as many outfielders that made up the team. The batting team would line up one beside the other. The pitcher would then toss the ball. The batter would try and hit the ball as far as possible away from the fielders, then run as fast as they could from the base to base in an anti-clockwise direction, the idea being to try to complete all the way round before the ball was returned to the pitcher. The fielders' job was to collect the ball as quickly as they could and to throw it to the fielder at the base the batter was running to. If he caught the ball and touched down before the batter reached it he would be out. The idea was for the batter to complete the run, all the way round, thus scoring a rounder. This would carry on until all the batters were out. Teams would then change places and do the same over again until they were out. The winners, being the side with most rounders. This game caused a lot of excitement with a lot of shouting from both sides. The boys played football and cricket in the appropriate seasons.

HOBBIES

All boys in those days collected birds' eggs for it wasn't prohibited then. We would spend hours scouring the hedgerows, woods and roadsides during the spring and summer, looking for ones we hadn't got. I used to keep mine in a box that I kept in my bedroom, each one placed in cotton wool and labelled with the species. One of the largest were Mallard ducks when you are fortunate enough to find one, whilst some of the smallest ones were the Wren and the Blue Tits. I think by the time I left school I had about fifty. They were still at home in Bennett's Place when I left.

Another indulging hobby was stamp collecting. You could purchase albums and even stamps from all countries around the world and, of course, we used to swap with each other. Some of these stamps were quite elaborate in design and colour while others were quite rare and worth a lot of money, like the Penny Black.

Another popular hobby was the collecting of cigarette cards. The most popular brands were WD & HO Wills whose most popular and widely smoked cigarette was

Woodbines. While another brand, although more expensive, were Players manufactured by John Player. In years gone by cigarettes were sold in packets of 5, 10 and 20s for the cheaper brands but Players could be bought in 10s, 20s and round tins containing 50 which were mostly sold to the people who could afford them. The albums for these cards could be obtained from most shops that sold tobacco. Each set was of 50 cards, there being one card in each space. I used to collect the cards from Woodbines being that my father smoked them. He would bring home quite a lot of cards collected from his workmates, if they had no one to give them to. These cigarette cards were produced for many years and were of most interesting species and subjects. To name some of the ones I can remember collecting were wild flowers, British birds, dogs, horses and ponies, butterflies, moths, cars, trains, flags, garden flowers, flowering trees and shrubs. Not only were they interesting to look at but they were also educational for on the back of each card it told you about the flowers, trees and shrubs and gave both botanical name and common names and the family species and place of origin.

Of the hobbies that we had, I think that collecting cigarette cards was one of our favourites for we waited with great expectations and hope for father to come home from work with may be a card that seemed hard to get hold of or perhaps one to complete a set. I know by the time they stopped doing them, which if I remember correctly was in the early part of the war, we had quite a collection of them. I have no idea what happened to them for they were still at home when I finally left which is a pity for, a few years ago, on the Antiques Roadshow, someone had a few albums which were valued at quite a few pounds. Quite often in the summer, if we didn't go for walks, my younger sisters and I would go down the gardens and out onto the Armscote Road armed with pencil and notebook and sit on the garden wall of the cottage now called Quaint End. This was owned by Mr and Mrs Bridget and there we would put down the numbers of the registration plates on the cars that passed by. People lucky enough to have a car would go for an afternoon drive in the country with a picnic perhaps up the Campden Hill for the view on a clear day was and still is wonderful. They would come from all over, like Coventry and Birmingham, for the fresh air and, of course, the views. If we collected around 20 or more we would consider that really good for the two or three hours spent taking them.

PARTIES

Throughout the years we would probably go to two or three parties on a regular basis, like Empire or May Day where we had the crowning of the May Queen with her attendants all dressed up. She sat on a throne which was on a trolley, pulled by

Village Hall built in 1933

a horse which had been lent by a farmer and decorated with flowers and ribbons. They paraded around the village, finishing up outside the Village Hall. On the green outside Fox House the children would dance around the maypole, holding coloured ribbons. The children selected to do so had been practising for some weeks beforehand, ending up with a tea party in the village hall which had been prepared by the parents. Another party held in the village hall, usually in December, was the Sunday School party which was organised by the teachers with the food again being provided by the parents. After tea we would play games such as musical chairs, blind man's bluff and sticking the tail on the donkey. After which, the Rector would give out the prizes which were for good attendance. There were three prizes for both boys and girls, senior and junior. The first prize could be a Bible or a prayer book, a reading book for the seniors but the juniors would get a picture book or crayoning book and coloured pencils. It was all very exciting. I never achieved first prize despite having good attendance, but perhaps behaviour came into it, although I did get second prize on numerous occasions. I won a bible one year which I had for years but like so many things, it disappeared. My sister Myra had first prize one year of a beautiful bible which had a leather cover with gold letters and edges to the pages and full of coloured pictures which, of course, were religious and I know she had it still in later life. The one party we all looked forward to was the one given at Christmas by Lady Borwick at her home up Grump Street – Crab Mill which all the village children attended from the age of 5 to 14. Not only did we have a wonderful tea but under the large Christmas tree which was decorated with beautiful decorations, some of which were edible, were presents

Members of the Terry family with their hand bells

galore for girls and boys. They were handed out after we had played all the familiar games and been entertained by the Terry Family led by their father, Horace, who was one of the wheelwright's brothers. They played the musical hand bells. Mr Terry was also a keen Church Bellringer. After this came the appearance of Father Christmas, carrying his sack to the buzz of excitement for it was he that gave out the presents to each child who went up when their name was called out. Then to finish off, as your name was called out again, you went up and received from Lady Borwick, a brand new shinny shilling for the coming New Year. They were truly wonderful parties.

FOXCOTE ESTATE

Foxcote House was the home of Mr and Mrs Longsdon and their two children Robert and Phillippa. They employed both domestic servants to care and clean the very large house and most, if not all the servants, came from the village and lived in. There were cottages close-by where some of the workers lived plus the Catholic Church before the present Catholic Church took its place in the village. Being a large estate, there were a lot of estate workers. The ones that I remember were Jackie Pratley whom was the groom and lived in the cottage by the stables with his wife Mary who he met and married in the village. Then there was another of the Terry brothers, Phil, who lived in the thatched cottage which is situated between Grump Street and Frog Lane and was, I believe, the Carter who had taken the place of Mr Taggart Dumbleton when he retired. His brother, Fred Dumbleton, was the Manager-cum-Gamekeeper who also did manual work. Every year they held a sale of Ash poles which were cut each year in the winter months which is called coppicing. This process would be carried out by cutting the poles down to ground level. This would leave what was called a stole. In the spring this would produce young shoots to grow on for seven or so years before being cut down again. Over the years the stoles would grow to a diameter of up to four feet, so to be able to cut poles every year demanded a lot of ash coppices. Not only Ash was coppiced but Hazel and Sweet Chestnut was needed for various crafts. Hazel would be used for close weaved fencing panels of varying heights and, being a strong and flexible durable wood, it was also used by thatchers for holding the thatch on house and cottage roofs and ricks of hay and corn. It would be split to a thickness about the size of your thumb, cut into lengths of about eighteen inches, pointed at each end, as they were needed, were twisted in the middle and bent to form a staple and used to hold lengths of hazel down by pushing it into the thatch. All sorts of patterns would be done at the top of dwellings to give a secure and neat appearance whilst holding down the thatch. Chestnut a strong and durable wood also was used for fencing posts and also for the making of chestnut palings. This would be sold to companies that specialised in the making of this product. It would be split to a thickness of about an inch and a half, after being cut to length, then using special machines it would be joined together by galvanised wire top and bottom. Two strands, one underneath and one over the top were twisted, then placing another spur and so on until lengths of about six feet that were very flexible and would be rolled up for easy handling and transporting. Mr Dumbleton, whose son also Fred, worked with his father helping with the same tasks, one of which, in the roll of Gamekeeper, was the searching for and marking of pheasants nests. In spring and summer this was done by observation and the help of a good gun dog who, on finding a nest would set it by standing perfectly still with one front leg held off the ground. The gamekeeper would then approach the spot, call the dog off, by this time the hen pheasant would have left the nest, revealing the number of eggs. If there were only one or two the nest would be marked and left for more eggs to be produced. If there were seven or eight, he would take three or four, place them in a secure container, returning every few days to collect more until no more were produced. Over a period of a few more days, the remaining ones would also be collected. If, on finding one with a full clutch of about a dozen, they would be collected and during the season they would probably collect somewhere in the region of 200-300 eggs. As many as possible would be put under broody hens and bantams to be hatched, otherwise they would be put in an incubator which was heated by oil heaters in the early days and later by electricity. Partridge eggs were also collected with a single nest containing a clutch of 16-18 eggs. They were treated in the same way and once hatched, those hatched by natural methods would each have their own coup and run as with chickens. The chicks hatched by artificial means would be kept in the incubator inside until they started to grow feathers, then moved outside in their own pens. They would all be fed in the early days with chicken meal. As they grew they then were fed with kibbled corn and once they were growing well and their foster birds left them, they would be taken into the woods and kept in large pens that were sturdy constructions to make them safe from foxes. There they would be fed on corn and maize and given fresh water twice a day until they were almost fully grown when they would be released into the woods but food would still be taken out each day and scattered in the woods. This would encourage them to forage for their own food and so keep them as wild as possible as from the time they were hatched to their release, it was important that they had as little time as possible with human contact. Another of the many tasks the Gamekeeper had was keeping vermin and predators under control. Among these were members of the Crow family; these included rooks, magpies and jays. They all take other birds' eggs and young so you see the reason behind the searching for game birds. Other predators that included weasels, stoats and foxes were trapped and shot for they too took eggs and young. I first remember young Mr Dumbleton, having a motorbike and sidecar. The sidecar was a long box for the purpose of carrying the tools of his trade as well as the dogs for he always had terriers and spaniels. He lived in the village, first in a small cottage up Grump Street, later moving to a three bedroomed Council house down Featherbed Lane in Washbrook Place with his wife and two young girls, Ann and Dina, who I went to school with. He later changed his motorbike for a car but he still had his box and had it fixed to the carrier at the back. I remember seeing him park on the driveway by the side of our old cottage in Front Street, visiting his parents, with the dogs on the back seat and the box containing two rows of rabbits hanging on poles threaded between their back legs which had been, what is called. 'hocked'. This is done by making a slit between the bones of one of the back legs just between the hock and the foot, passing the other back leg through this slit, up past the hock then slitting it just above it, preventing it from pulling out. Another task undertaken and carried out during April was rook shooting for in April the young rooks were now big enough to leave the nest but not yet ready to fly. They would perch outside the nest and wait to be fed by their parents so if you heard shooting on an April evening that was the way of keeping the numbers down. They would go all around the estate to the various rookeries doing this providing people in the big house as well as the workers the ability to feast on rook pie This tradition that died out many years ago when the housewives found easier ways to feed their families for only the breasts of the rooks were used as the rest of the bird would provide very little to warrant plucking the whole bird. It would take quite a number of birds to make a family sized pie but they did it for the simple reason that it was free. The people who shot them were glad to get rid of the surplus and butchers meat took a toll on the average wage of the estate workers and farm labourers.

The seat in the tree on Foxcote Estate

The story I am about to reveal now in this chapter on Foxcote is one that over many years, has not only given pleasure but also of how it all came about. As children, mother often told us of stories of people in years gone by and this is one that had been told to her by her parents who were tenants of the farm up Campden Hill that was part of the Foxcote Estate. In the eighteen hundreds the owner of the estate was a gentleman by the name of Squire Howard who asked his daughter on her twenty-first birthday what she would like for her coming of age present. Her reply was that if you will accompany me Father I will show you what I would like. With that, she took him along the avenue to the entrance of the estate at the top of Foxcote Hill, turning right onto the Charingworth Road which ran along the side of a small spinney. After a few yards she stopped in front of a large beech tree with large spreading branches, some eight feet from the ground and said "Father, I would like a seat built up there" – pointing to the spreading branches – "so that not only can I go up there and relax and admire the view, but other people from near and far can do the same in the peace and quiet of our lovely countryside." So the seat in the tree was built with the steps leading up to it beside the spinney with a small gate in the boundary fence. Over the years there must have been thousands of feet climbing those steps to take in the view of the Stour Valley. I know, as children, we often went up there to see all the initials that had been carved in those branches, some with dates, others carved inside a heart, pierced with an arrow, declaring a courting couple's love for each other.

1939 - WAR

1939 was a year of many changes not only for one of my sisters but this country and Europe. In the summer month of July, both my elder sister and myself celebrated our birthdays. My sister's 14th and my 11th . For my sister it was the end of school and domestic service in the village of Armscote two miles from home and like most domestic servants she left home and lived in. It was surely a big step in life for young girls still in their childhood. Although she came home on her half-days there were others not so fortunate who could spend their half days with their families. There must have been a lot of unhappy homesick young girls in those days for being in domestic service their hours were long and the work hard. They had to start at the bottom doing the worst and dirtiest jobs like cleaning fireplaces, scrubbing floors and fetching coal and wood for the fires. For country girls there was little else in the way of employment so they had no choice and unlike those from the towns who had the chance of office work or being shop assistants. With my sister leaving home I was now the one to fetch the milk from Dowlers Farm up Middle Street. I not only fetched ours but also Mrs Hathaway who kept the little shop off the lower Green. For this I was paid 2d a week plus a couple of sweets. I did this before going to school and did so until I left three years later. On returning to school after the summer holidays I moved up to the top class and was taught by Miss Clark the Headmistress who lived in the School House just a few yards from the school. It also allowed me to join the Ilmington Scout Troup. The Scout Master was General Sanders who lived in The Grange which is up above Hill Farm. We used to meet once a week in the school. Our uniforms usually came from the boys that had left the scouts, mostly when they left school. Some of them carried on for a number of years. I still went to Sunday School and Church each Sunday and I remember walking home on this particular Sunday a few days before going back to school after the summer holidays. On coming down Hobdays Bank and only a distance of 200 yards from home I met Mr Moore who greeted me with the news Chamberlain had announced on the radio that our country had declared war on Germany for their unprovoked attack and invasion of Poland on 1st September. The British Government had given them the ultimatum of withdrawing their troops by 11.00 on the 3rd September or Britain would declare war and so we had no choice. Mr Moore said tell your parents as he must have known we had no radio. To us boys, we did not realise the seriousness of war, the cost of death and destruction to millions of people and towns and cities that would end up as piles of rubble. We could only think of war games and no longer of cowboys and Indians. Within a matter of days people's lives had changed from just going about with every-day life as normal, to what would happen next. It didn't take long for them to find out for the Government sent out leaflets on what to do in the event of air raids such as sirens sounding, the alarm and the all clear. Then there was the blackout for you were not allowed to show the smallest bit of light and street lights, neon lights etc were turned off. Drapers' shops like Smiths, a large shop that is now Debenhams in Stratford, did a roaring trade on the sale of blackout material. It must have been really hard for families on low incomes. Towns and cities had ARP wardens going round checking for any visible light, which would result in prosecution if it happened after a verbal warning. We, in the village, had what was called fire watchers but the local constable would go round checking. Most people would go outside and check their blackouts each night. I know mother used to. Gas masks were soon made available. They came in brown cardboard boxes with string attached to carry them by slinging them over your shoulder for we were given the instructions that they must be carried at all times and we practiced at putting them on, a regular basis at school. Anyone with small babies was given special ones where the baby was put inside while the mother had a pump for oxygen to be pumped in on the outside. Another change that happened very quickly was the introduction of identity cards. Everyone, young and old, had one each with an individual number starting with the head of the house down to the youngest. I could still remember the number to this day which was QFHK/1/5. The five being the youngest of five living in the house at the time for my two eldest sisters were living in domestic service at the time of registration. Being school children, we didn't have to carry them, only those over a certain age for anyone in authority such as Police, both civil and military, could stop anyone and demand to see the cards. While all these important items were being processed and distributed, all military reservists were being called to arms, such as Yeomanry for most Counties in Great Britain had these regiments who were similar to Cavalry. They were mounted on horses which were confiscated from stables and private owners but unlike the First World War where horses requisitioned were broken to harness for the job of hauling waggons, food, ammunition and other equipment needed by the Army, the horses that were needed now were ones used for riding. This reminds me of our Uncle Ceager who was married to one of my mother's sisters, Auntie Ursula. They lived in a large house with outbuildings and stables and quite a lot of ground including a lake which was in Oxfordshire near Rissington. Uncle Ceager, besides dealing in horses, also bought them for the Army who relied on them for the household cavalry and the Royal Horse Artillery. This meant he did a lot of travelling, not only in this country but spent a lot of time in Ireland. During the summer holidays we would often spend a few days there especially when father and uncle were working away. We had a wonderful time, being taken on the lake in the boat by our cousins, besides playing all the usual games. Besides the Yeomanry and other reservists being called up, men of certain ages had to register and later receive by post, notice of where to report for a medical. There were certain personnel that were exempt from the Armed Forces such as Police, Fireman and also young men who were doing apprenticeships. They were allowed to finish their term before being called up where their trades would be needed. Some agricultural workers could be exempt but many preferred to be like their friends and join up. Not only young men were needed but girls of 18 and over were needed in all three Armed Services, thus allowing the men to do the fighting while they filled in the rolls of office work, driving and any not too physical tasks. Other important jobs were taken on by the girls. The Women's Land Army was needed to replace all the men who had joined up. They carried out all the men's work including many who came from the cities and large towns and in all probability had never been to the country let alone seen real live farm animals. It must have been really hard and a shock to the system for farm work back then was a hard physical occupation with long hours and not very good wages. It must have been heart-breaking as well as back-breaking until they got used to it. Various hostels near the market towns were places where a lot of them lived while others lived on farms and also with people in the village. However, they all did a splendid job in helping to feed the nation for without them the food situation would have been far worse than it was over the next six years. Another task for the Women's Land Army that the girls filled was for the Forestry Commission, whose numbers of employed men had fallen due to the call-up. With the demand for home grown timber being greater than ever due to the fact that importing it from Eastern Europe came to an end .When the majority of Europe fell to the Germans, supplies from North America and Canada became more and more difficult with U-boats in the Atlantic, who from early 1940 were determined to starve us out of the war. So you see what a good job these girls did who were called the Lumbar-Jills for they took on with axe and saw, all the tasks of lumberjacks. Some may think on reading this, how could I have known all this when I was a lad and quite right too. I didn't know about the girls that worked for the Forestry until later and for those people of my age who are still around, how many would have known they existed. It's only in the last few years that the Women's Land Army has been honoured and allowed to take part in the march past the Cenotaph on Remembrance Sunday and given the recognition they deserve. No longer are they the forgotten army.

Another roll that girls did was the NAAFI which stands for Navy, Army and Air

Force Institute who had buildings on every military camp in the country that served tea, cakes, sweets, cigarettes. In fact they were military canteens who had set opening times, the most popular times being in the morning for about one and a half hours and in the evening from six till ten. They also had mobile NAAFI vans that went round the outlying units such as the RAF ground crews that serviced the planes that were dispersed round the airfield as well as the search light and ACKACK batteries. They were all round the big towns and cities and countryside, in fact where the military was the NAAFI girls were there also. Even Garrison towns had them. They all did a splendid job.

Around October, some six weeks or so after war was declared the Army came to Ilmington with the arrival of the Northumberland Fusiliers. Much to the excitement of us boys, they were billeted on every farm and large houses which had lofts in their outbuildings which had been cleared out on the orders of the Government. The Village Hall became the dining hall with huge mobile kitchens outside. Every meal time the troops were marched from round the village to the hall for their meals much to our delight for whenever possible we would tag on behind. At the time we didn't realise the seriousness of it all. The exercises they carried out up the hills and in the fields, it was all a game to us. I remember the times we spent in the field that is now the Sports Field watching them having weapon training, stripping down machine guns, cleaning all the parts, laying them out on groundsheets and putting them back together, time and time again, loading and unloading and placing them on tripods and pointing them skywards as if they were firing at aircraft. I don't remember exactly how long they were here but during the time they were, some became quite friendly with the locals. One of them by the name of Kelly Little, came back and lived here after the war and spent the rest of his life here in the village. I know in the early part of 1940 they were sent to France with other troops to help the French against the onslaught of the German Forces who had swept through Europe like the plague. They were by now slicing through France despite the French having one of the biggest armies in the world but, alas, one of the poorest equipped whose weapons and tanks were no match for the Germans. Having said that, we weren't much better equipped or prepared for war either. Unlike Germany who, under a certain little Corporal by the name of Adolph Hitler, and, despite the treaty made against them after World War 1, had been building up his armed forces since he came to power in 1933. It was during the retreat across France towards Dunkirk that one Fusilier by the name of Chris Wilson, was awarded the Military Medal. He had been billeted in the loft at Mabel House Farm and had become friends with my sister, Vera, who had returned home to recover from glandular fever and he had become acquainted by her visits to our uncle and auntie, the tenants of the farm. However, during the retreat he was manning a machine gun post during a heavy attack forcing the Fusiliers to retreat to better positions. He held the Germans off, allowing his comrades to get away until it was possible for him to follow suit. It was for this action, he received the Military Medal. They were among the 338,000 British and French troops rescued off the beaches of Dunkirk by ships and boats of all sizes - a lot of them manned by their owners, thus saving a force to recover and re-equip for further action later on. It must surely be the biggest rescue in the history of warfare. Those boat and ship crews were heroes, each and every one of them. They risked their lives to save a force that would soon become part of the defence of Britain, after the surrender of France, who did so to save further destruction of their country thereby leaving Great Britain to stand alone in Europe.

RADAR

During the mid thirties the Government became aware of the huge build-up of all the armed forces in Germany and, with the memories of their aggressive action that triggered the First War some 20 years earlier, their thoughts turned to what measures could be taken in the defence of our island. They came to the conclusion the threat would be from across the Channel. They were aware of experiments being carried out in the form of radial signals and so they turned their attention to the scientists who were engaged in this project whose names were Robert Watson-Watt, A F Wilkins and H E Wimperis. Working together over the following weeks and months of endless systems and experiments, one system was set up in a van, taken out to the country and tested, signals rebounding off certain objects from various distances. They then tried the experiment from different airfields around the country and found signals could be relayed back to a central point. Traces showed on a screen designed in the shape of a television with a point turning in a clockwise direction and indicating with a dot and bleep on the plane it had picked up. They duly presented these findings to the Ministry of Defence who, after further developments and tests, along with Sir Harry Tizard, decided that this was a major breakthrough for the defence of Britain. Orders were issued for the erection of masts and radio centres from the top of Scotland down to Lands End. By the time war was declared, and with these pylon-type masts and control stations in place, Britain had a system that could be monitored, manned and operated 24 hours a day, 7 days a week without having to rely on the Observer Corps who could only operate during daylight hours. They had only their binoculars and an instrument that told them the height and direction of the approaching enemy. This could be all too late (except for the anti-aircraft batteries) to get defence fighter planes in the air but with this system that could tell you from which direction, at what height and how many and what directions they were heading, we had an advantage. All this information from a distance of 100 miles away, gave the fighter pilots time to get airborn to reach the height needed to swoop down on the bombers as soon as they crossed the coast. Germany, like Britain, had spy planes that took photos of ground defences, such as fighter planes, airfields, gun emplacements and large buildings, for their intelligence people to study as targets to attack. They must have seen all these masts and control buildings up and down the coasts and just dismissed them as radio masts, which of course they were, but ones with a difference. They obviously had not yet developed the system that undoubtedly helped us to win not only the inevitable battle of the air but battles at sea and, of course, the War. However, there was one attack by Stuka JU87 dive bombers on one of these stations on the south coast, causing some damage that was rectified within a few hours after the attack. Whether the attack had been planned or whether the pilot just wanted to discharge their bombs and get back across the Channel, no one knows. If they had known, these would surely have been the first targets. This system was, of course, the great British invention by brilliant scientists of Radar which stands for Radio, Direction and Range.

THE NINETEEN FORTIES -
DESPERATE TIMES

The Government, like most of Britain after the fall of France and the evacuation of our troops from Dunkirk, knew that Germany would make us the next as we were the only country left to fall in their quest to occupy the whole of Europe. But, to achieve this, there were two obstacles in his path. The major one being the RAF. Hitler knew, before he could even think of invading across the second obstacle The Channel, he had to take control of the air and to achieve this he had to destroy Fighter Command who had fighter squadrons all round the south coast and up the east coast to Scotland. So, while the ground forces were working flat out with civilian companies to strengthen our coastal defences with gun emplacements, pill boxes, laying mines and stretching miles and miles of barbed wire with look-out posts and sentries manned and on duty twenty fours hours a day, while the fighter stations were on standby at dispersal points from dawn to dusk, day after day, week after week, ready to scramble and be air-born within minutes of the alarm bell being rung. In late July 1940, the Battle of Britain began and the fate of the country rested on the shoulders of those heroic, brave young men, many of them in their late teens and early twenties. The head of the German Luftwaffe, Herman Goering, thought to his cost, that his force would do the same to Britain that it had done to the air forces of Poland, Belgium, Holland and France but, as it turned out, he grossly under-estimated the planes at our disposal. Thanks to the designers at Hawker and Supermarine who had designed and built two wonderful fighter planes, the robust Hurricane and the sleek, agile Spitfire. Both could achieve speeds of well over 300 miles per hour, the latter being slightly the faster and on a par with the German Messerschmitt 109, the top fighter of the Luftwaffe, fitted with a Daimler Benz engine with a fuel injection system. British fighters were fitted with float carburettors which were at a distinct disadvantage in steep diving and climbing, resulting in stalling the engine which was a major fault to the otherwise superb Merlin engine, manufactured by Rolls Royce. Goering decided the best way to defeat the fighter defence was to destroy them on the ground, before they could get air-borne and gain enough height before making their attack on his bomber formations to stop them releasing their bombs on the grounded fighters and hangers. The slower Stuka dive bombers could also pinpoint ground targets as well as shipping in the Channel. These Stukas were fitted with sirens which screamed in spine tingling sounds when making a diving attack. As the first wave of bombers crossed the South Coast however, they were attacked from above by British fighters and taken completely by surprise. The German High Command had thought there wasn't any need for fighter escorts as they would be the ones creating the surprise. They lost quite a few planes on that first strike but, quite a number got through and attacked one of two airfields and found very few planes grounded. However, they did inflict damage to hangers and buildings. The ones that returned to their bases in occupied France reported the events, plus the fact that so few planes were on the ground, and that they had come under attack soon after crossing the coast. The German Senior Officers decided that they had been unlucky and ran into a squadron or two who were on patrol and the lack of planes on the ground meant we were short of defence fighters. When Goering was told, he couldn't contain his excitement and declared he would wipe out the RAF sooner that he had thought and reported to Hitler, who almost immediately started building up his forces along the Calais coast with ships and barges ready to invade once the threat from Fighter Command had been wiped out. The raids became more and more intense and his losses in men and machines grew but the losses he inflicted on us still did not affect the number of planes that we put in the air. Over the following two weeks or so, as the attacks grew with more bombers, so did the fighters Britain put up against them day by day. Finally, because of the bombers becoming easier targets, particularly through our pilots gaining more experience, Goering decided that his bombers needed better protection and so from then on they were accompanied by ME109s fighter escorts. Because of the fuel capacity being much lower than the bombers, they had to join them from their bases near the French coast, even then they only had sufficient fuel to engage our fighters for about ten minutes before they had to break off and return to base. So their pilots not only had to be on the look-out for our fighters but had to keep one eye on their fuel gauges. Even so a great many of them did not make it back and came down in the Channel and on the French coast while others only just made it back to their airfields but they did inflict heavy losses on our fighter numbers. The Hurricane being the main victim, good planes that they were, it became obvious to the Air Ministry that they were out-manoeuvred, out-climbed and out-dived by these superior ME109s and so with the knowledge that we could not afford the losses to our fighter numbers for, even with the numbers of the Luftwaffe casualties being higher, their plane strength outnumbered ours by about three to one. So a change of tactics was decided whereby the Hurricanes would attack the slower bombers leaving the agile and faster Spitfires to take on the ME109s, a tactic that proved extremely effective. And so the battle continued, through August in that very hot summer of 1940. With losses increasing on both sides, our experienced pilots were becoming both physically and mentally drained and with young replacement pilots fresh from training with many only having a few hours flying the Hurricane and Spitfires under their belts, times were looking grim. During the beginning of September, Fighter Command had a welcome boost. They had an influx of experienced Polish pilots who had escaped the Germans when Poland fell and who had a deep hatred of Germany and its people. However, the Polish had their own squadrons and their pilots were tenacious, brave and fearless fighters who contributed greatly in our fight for freedom, along with pilots from countries of the Commonwealth and even a few from the USA. With the production of fighter planes on the increase, we were beginning to replace some of the losses inflicted on us. Around this time, with the reports by the German Crews on the losses they were inflicting on the RAF, numbers that were totally exaggerated, Hitler had been monitoring events of the past weeks and steadily building up forces of men and equipment around the port of Calais, ready for the invasion of Britain. On the reports Hitler received he enquired when Goering could expect control of the air, to which Goering boasted that the defeat of the RAF would be complete within a week. Goering collected all his Luftwaffe commanders together and told them to prepare the biggest force they could muster over the next few days to deliver his boast to Hitler whose respect for him was diminishing daily. Hitler was running out of patience for he knew time was running out for favourable conditions in tides and weather for the invasion to take place. By now it was the middle of September and reports were coming in from our reconnaissance planes, which had cameras on board, and were returning from missions over France and Germany. Intelligence knew of the massive accumulation of planes being made ready for the biggest raid yet. Fighter Command Control Headquarters were monitoring events from early morning as they had done every day over the past seven weeks from information relayed from the Radar control posts all round the coasts. This particular bright and sunny morning, 15th September 1940, reports were coming in of massive formations of enemy planes building up over France and into Germany. These were being monitored by the WAAFS around a huge map of Europe who with markers and numbers indicating from where and how many and in which direction they were heading. With this amount of information coming in, the duty officer leading proceedings on this particular day, decided this was the time to alert Air Vice Marshall Sir Keith Park and Winston Churchill, the Prime Minister, who had been given regular reports of events during the past few weeks and had been staying in the underground bunker, under the War Ministry building in London, which was nearer to Fighter Command control HQ than Downing Street. Churchill had issued instructions that he was to be informed of any unusual events, no matter what time of day or night. For this purpose there was a special telephone line direct to him for such an occasion. The duty officer decided now was the time to use that phone. The Prime Minister on hearing the news was soon on his way to find the control centre a hive of activity with staff on telephones, WAAFS with earphones, working with their push-sticks, moving markers and numbers all along the south coast. While on the other side of the English Channel, Goering and his chief of staff were in joyful mood, gazing skyward as they stood on the French coast watching wave after wave of bombers with their fighter escorts up above them, heading for the English coast. Goering, thought this would be the day he could inform the Fuehrer that Germany had control of the air.

Meanwhile, back in England at Fighter Command headquarters, staff on telephones were alerting dispersal points on airfields within reach of the bombers heading in their direction and being scrambled in time to take up their positions ready to attack. On the ground, all the ACKACK batteries were poised to open fire as soon as the enemy was seen and in range over the Channel. Suddenly, the silence was broken with orders given to open fire to the crews all along the affected coast. This was mingled with the throb of hundreds of bomber engines as the spitfires and Messerschmitt climbed, dived, twisted and turned in dog fights high above the Kent, Sussex and Essex countryside, leaving thin white vapour trails as they tried to gain the upper hand. Far below land girls and farm hands paused for a while from the task of gathering the remaining harvest to gaze upwards to watch the ensuing battle and wait with baited breath to see if a parachute would suddenly open from any aircraft that was spiralling earthwards, leaving a trail of black smoke behind from its shattered engine. If a friendly pilot they would, rush to his aid if he came close by to help as best they could if he was wounded until military aid arrived. Or if he was unhurt, a pat on the back with a cigarette and a drink. If it was a ME109, a loud cheer would ring out and if the pilot escaped, he would be faced with a pitchfork or two. I remember one story that emerged later of a Polish pilot, having been shot down, and landed with no injuries. When faced with a farm worker, holding a fork, he greeted him in broken English with a cheery "Good Morning". Gesturing with upward motions and replying angrily, "Good Morning, my ass" and proceeded to escort him towards the village with the intention of handing him over to the local policeman with the pilot trying his best to convince him that he was a friend and not a foe. It was only on the arrival of the military that he was convinced that he really was a Polish pilot fighting alongside the RAF.

As the battle raged, Winston Churchill watched as more and more markers were being pushed around on the large map indicating enemy planes coming in and defending fighters from all nearby airfields brought into the fray by the busy WAAFS, turned to Air Vice Marshall, Sir Keith Park and said "Where are your reserves" to which he replied "There are none sir". Every serviceable aircraft had been used to stem the tide. In one raid, a lone German bomber made its way to London. Whether this was accidental or intentional no one knows for Hitler had made it quite clear that Inner London would not be targeted for he was still hoping to get the British Government round the negotiation table for a peaceful conclusion to hostilities. However, on having this news of the attack, the Prime Minister immediately instructed Sir Arthur Harris, the head of Bomber Command to make a raid on Berlin, which was duly carried out, despite another of Goerings' boasts to Hitler that no bombs would ever fall on the German Capital, words that would surely come back to haunt him. Hitler flew into a rage and in one of his ranting speeches declared that for every kilogram that fell on Berlin, 20, 30, or 40,000 Kg would fall on London. As the fight for air control over England continued, the losses of men and machines became more and more, while our losses increased, the German bomber crews reported the British fighter numbers did not diminish but remained strong. The simple answer to that was more and more were coming off the production lines in the factories. On 16th September some six weeks after the battle started, on this beautiful late summer morning, no sirens sounded around the coast while the pilots at the dispersal points continued with what particular thing they had been doing for the past weeks, to take their minds off combat the best they could. It remained quiet, no bells sounding or shouts of scramble, no engines starting - in fact the only sound to be heard was of the skylarks as they hovered higher and higher in the clear blue sky. With thanks to all those brave young men, the battle for control of the airways, now known as the Battle of Britain, was won. Hitler abandoned the idea of invasion and began moving troops and equipment from around the coast of Calais and to employ different tactics. Starting with North Africa, where the Italians were taking a mauling from the then British Forces, who despite being a much smaller force in both men and machines were far superior as an attacking force, inflicting heavy casualties and taking thousands of prisoners. Hitler, fearing that the Italians faced defeat, decided that part of the large Force withdrawn from France would be sent to back up the retreating Italians and formed what became to be known as the Africa Corps under their Commander, General Rommel – later to be renamed the Desert Fox for his cunning and clever tactics. Hitler was intent on defeating us and taking control of the Suez Canal as well as the vital oil fields which would greatly enhance his war over the course of the coming months. Meanwhile back in Europe, Hitler decided to try and bomb Britain into submission by attacking the docks and ports in and around the south coast as well as the docks in the east end of London, whose facilities for unloading vital supplies from across the Atlantic were more or less our hope of continuing the war. They were brought to our shores by the convoys of merchant ships with their precious cargoes of lease lend, a deal made with America and of course Canada, a country of vast raw materials and part of the Commonwealth. These daylight raids were again causing heavy casualties to the Luftwaffe, especially the raids on London Docklands as the ranges were beyond the range of their fighters so leaving the bombers more vulnerable. So these daylight raids were soon abandoned, giving our fighter squadrons a much needed break. From around October, subject to weather conditions, the German Luftwaffe started night-time bombing raids to escape our day fighters. Although we had night fighters they were not as effective and our defences relied on search lights and ACKACK batteries which were set up all round the country – in fact there was a searchlight about a mile and a half away from here on the Mickleton Road, right on the corner where the Admington Road joins it. The raiders' early targets were the London Docks, then the Ports of Portsmouth, Plymouth and Southampton with armament factories also targeted. The Spitfire Factory near Southampton suffered damage in one particular raid which disrupted production for a while but after a week or two it was soon back to normal.

By this time the evacuation of children from all the major towns and cities along with coastal towns all around the country was underway. Children were taken from their homes from the age of five up to thirteen, carrying their gas masks and clothes, and with luggage labels tied to the lapels of their coats with their names and addresses and the destination all written clearly on them by their parents. They were taken to the nearest railway stations and bus stations to be taken out of danger to the country. Every small town and village had billeting officers who were usually members of the WVS (Women's Voluntary Services) who had been out and about with other members to find people with room, willing to take the children in. If there were two evacuees from the same family they did their best to keep them together in the hope of causing less stress than if they were billeted apart. There were surely a lot of homesick, unhappy children around the country, while others took to it in their stride and loved the countryside. The majority that came to Ilmington were from Coventry with a few from London. The ones from Coventry had their own teachers. One was an elderly lady with white hair, done in a bun. She was quite slim and wore long dresses and skirts. Her name was Miss Rossiter who became known by us as Gran Rossiter, while the second was much younger with short dark hair by the name of Miss Bishop. They both stayed with a childless couple in Washbrook Place. Miss Bishop returned to Coventry after a short time.

Our school had three teachers with three classes with very little room left for more pupils so obviously, no need for five teachers. Most of the evacuees were aged around 11 so they would have all been in the top class, taught by our head teacher,

Miss Clark. So the overspill meant that different lessons were taken in the old carpentry room which was situated at the bottom of the footpath leading from the school, past the Church and in the grounds of Glebe Cottage. The single storey building was built with stone and had a thatched roof as did Glebe Cottage. Inside were five carpentry benches in a single row, spaced out to accommodate two boys between each bench with two boys to each one. At the far end was a fireplace with large floor to ceiling cupboards each side where all the tools were kept and where Mr Moyser, our teacher, stood and took carpentry lessons on Tuesday afternoons. He drove a little Austin Seven and came from Alcester. I can see him now at the end of the lesson, rolling a cigarette before dismissing us. The rest of the week, other lessons were taken, all verbal for there were no facilities for written ones. We had to sit on the benches there being no chairs – all these lessons were taken by Miss Rossiter who had a blackboard and easel. The evacuees, all girls, were billeted mostly with childless couples, couples with one child, or couples whose family had grown up. It would be wrong to say that all the children that came to the village were happy and content – far from it. Some were really unhappy while others were treated like skivvies and made to work hard with housework, gathering in coal and logs for the fires. This drove some to abscond back home only to be brought back again and moved to another home with the hope of better treatment. One girl, however, stayed in Ilmington and married a local boy and still lives here to this day.

It is now November with the bombing raids depending on the weather. If visibility was poor it gave the fire fighters, rescue workers and ambulance service a much needed break for the bombers stayed at home waiting for better conditions. My mind goes back to the middle of the month, the 14th if my memory serves me correctly. It was a lovely clear night. Mother and I were sat at home, father having gone up the village fire watching. It was about half past eight when all of a sudden the silence was broken by the sound of the air raid siren in Shipston, wailing out its warning for a period of two minutes, followed after a while by the sound of engines, lots of engines, throbbing in unison, directly overhead. We went to the back door, making sure the living room was closed, thus preventing any light showing. Mother opened the door and we gazed upwards, staring into the blackness but seeing nothing, only hearing the sound of these throbbing engines, wave after wave. Mother said they are after Coventry, which is only 28 miles away. After a few more minutes search lights pierced the sky searching to pick up a target for the anti-aircraft batteries to fire at. Our neighbours, like us, had come out but couldn't see a thing in the way of planes; only the throb of all the engines directly overhead, it seemed as though we were directly in the flight path. After a few minutes, everyone returned inside to get on with whatever they were doing. For me, it was time to get ready for bed which meant washing face and hands, then rolling down socks, turning up my short trousers – boys all wore them in those days – and washing my knees and brushing my teeth with paste that was in a flat round tin and was a firm block. You had to wet your toothbrush and rub it to get any on it. No tubes in those days. It was made by Gibbs and not very palatable. Finally, I had to comb my hair. That done, after kissing my mother goodnight, I was up the stairs with mum's words ringing in my ear – "Turn the landing light off and say your prayers" which we did from an early age. After doing this and putting my pyjamas on, I put out the light and drew back the curtains and the blackout to have another look at what was going on. The searchlights were still scanning the skies but the sight that hit me was one of utter disbelief – there was just one huge glow of red, orange and yellow as Coventry burned. They must have dropped hundreds, if not thousands, of incendiaries to cause a fire of that magnitude and to light up the target for the oncoming planes carrying the high explosives. I don't remember how long I sat there watching the destruction of a city and the cause of so much suffering before my very eyes, but I heard father come home so, thinking it must be later, I drew the curtains and climbed into bed. It was only during the course of the next few days that we learnt through the daily papers of the damage and destruction of the houses, buildings and the old and beautiful cathedral and of the near five hundred lives lost that night with hundreds more maimed and injured. It was obvious that the main targets were all the factories that were working round the clock producing all the things needed to continue the war. Although the hostilities had been going on for over a year, it had all seemed far away, but not anymore. From that night in November 1940 the war had come to the Midlands. A night that remains so clear in my memory and one that I will never forget. I must have slept soundly for I never heard the bombs that fell less than a mile away. A few days later, a few of us went down to where they had fallen in the hope of finding shrapnel and to see what damage, if any, had been done. We went down to the crossroads on the Armscote Road and turned left into Gypsy Halt, the road that leads to Berryfields Farm. We found six craters in a straight line from east to west in the field to the right of the lane and one in the corner of the field to the left. Also in this corner, we found a Fordson Tractor, just a few yards from the bomb crater. Whether it was there when the bombs fell or it had been parked there afterwards, I don't know, but there wasn't a scratch or mark on it, unlike the Elm trees that were farther away in the roadside hedge. Shrapnel damage could be clearly seen on the trunks and branches, some eight feet or so from the ground but we never found any shrapnel. I have often wondered how those bombs came to be dropped there for there were no properties in the close vicinity. Perhaps the crew didn't want to run the gauntlet through the search lights and the barrage of Ackack shells bursting around them or whether it was a case of getting rid of them and high-tailing it back home. Coventry, like other major towns and cities, picked themselves up, determined to carry on with their lives and to continue working with renewed vigour whether it was in the factories, offices and shops, even in the damaged ones, while builders worked around them, repairing the damage.

No town or city suffered and endured more during the blitz than London for they were hit, night after night, for a period, if my memory serves me correctly, of around forty nights without a break. People in their hundreds would make their way each night to shelters at their nearest underground station to spend the night on the platforms. Women with young babies and children, the elderly, as well as the day workers all tried to get what sleep they could not knowing what they would find in the morning once the all clear had sounded. Would they still have a home or just a pile of rubble to sort through in the hope of finding treasured belongings, a photograph, a piece of jewellery that had been left behind in the scramble to get to the shelter to find a place to spend the night. It must have been devastating for the ones that lost everything, to be left in clothes they wore and the few things they had managed to take with them. There were centres which had been set up in the Community Halls by local councils, to give shelter to these unfortunate ones and to provide them with food and clothing by the splendid dedicated ladies of the WVS. It was during one of these raids that Buckingham Palace received some minor damage, thus providing the Queen Mother's famous words of "Now I can look the people of London and the East End, in the eyes without a feeling of guilt." By some miracle St Paul's Cathedral escaped undamaged. I remember seeing a photograph in the daily paper of this famous landmark standing proud while buildings all around lay in ruins - a truly remarkable escape.

Despite all this loss of life and devastation to our towns and cities, the true spirit of the British Bulldog, although shaken, remained unbroken through it all. Hitler thought the affect of his constant bombing would break the British spirit and determination to carry on with the war and therefore urge the Government to seek talks to end it. In fact, it brought the people closer together and made them more determined than ever, to continue the fight against these dictators who wanted to rule the world. One of the hardships the population had to endure was the food rationing which started in the early months of the war. Everyone had a ration book for without it you could not get your allowed amount from the retailers who would cut out the appropriate coupons of each item, every week. The things that were really scarce were all things that were imported, like tea, sugar, coffee which was almost non-existent. Later it was substituted by liquid coffee called Camp Coffee which came in bottles and was not very nice! Bread wasn't rationed for the simple reason it had a short shelf life so it would be pointless having more than you could use within a couple of days. No freezers then. This was a big advantage of living in the country where most bread was delivered as I have mentioned earlier whereas town people had to queue often for hours to buy a loaf and often go elsewhere when the shop sold out. Milk was also not rationed but like bread, that too had a short shelf life, especially in the hot weather. I remember watching mother scalding our milk in hot thundery weather to stop it from going sour. Cheese was, of course, rationed but if you were a manual worker you were allowed extra. Coupons were also needed for clothes such as suits, trousers, jackets, coats, skirts, dresses but all garments were made under strict rules and regulations such as trousers having no turn-ups, jackets and coats – no pocket flaps, skirts without pleats. All these items had the utility label stitched to it and took a lot of coupons to purchase them.

RECYCLING

Recycling as we know it today, is not something new of recent years but back in 1940, during the first year of the War, the ministers issued leaflets and posters asking people to save all newspapers and magazines and any old pots and pans, scrap iron, bicycles. In fact all things that could be melted down. I remember cast iron railings surrounded the Churchyard from the Old School in Back Street, round to the clip clap gates into Berry Orchard and the vaulted tomb that stands on the right hand side of the path, leading to the entrance of the Church: these were all taken as were others all over the country. The old pots and pans could be taken to several collection points around the village. The newspapers and magazines became the responsibility for collection by the Scouts. For three weeks in each month we would go round the village with our trucks collecting from every house, including the two Public Houses and shops and take the paper to a large wooden building in the grounds of our Scout Master, General Saunders who lived in The Grange. On the fourth Saturday we would sort it into bundles, keeping the papers and magazines separate. This was then stacked near the entrance, ready to be collected by lorry. The Scout Movement would be paid so much for every ton but just how much, I never knew. I remember with good reason in late autumn, I was collecting from a family by the name of Johnson, who lived in Park Farm, Frog Lane. Their daughter, whose name I think was Susan and in her early teens, had been admitted to hospital with scarlet fever. I remember taking the bundle of papers from a lady at the door, put them in the truck and carried on collecting. A while later, I began to feel unwell and developed a high temperature. Mother confined me to bed and called the doctor who duly came out, examined me and told mother I had scarlet fever and that he would call for an ambulance to take me to hospital. It arrived about five o'clock the same day. The ambulance men wrapped me in a blanket, carried me downstairs, placed me in a wheelchair and took me out into the dark to the ambulance. It was the middle of December 1940. I was taken to the Isolation Hospital which was situated on the outskirts of Stratford about half a mile up a driveway off the Birmingham Road, a building all on its own far from any other dwellings, hence the Isolation Hospital. I remember having to go through two sets of front doors, the first into a porch, the second into a hallway. The wards to the right were for Diphtheria cases while the ward to the left was where I was admitted with scarlet fever. The wards were not over big where I was and there were about 10 or 12 beds with the occupants, all young boys. I well remember the next day, a nurse came to my bed carrying a small kidney shaped tray and took my temperature and then said, undo your pyjama jacket. On doing so, I saw for the first time, my body which looked as though I had been exposed to the sun and was suffering from severe sunburn. I was covered in a bright scarlet rash but, my gaze was instantly diverted to the large syringe she had taken from the tray with a needle that, to me, looked the same size as a knitting needle. Of course, it wasn't, although I had quite a mark in my stomach where she gave me the injection.

A few days later, a little boy of about two was admitted and occupied a cot next to me who had blonde hair, whose name, like mine, was John but everyone called him Jonny. I never knew his surname, but I know he used to cry a lot, poor little chap, he must have missed his mother. Although the nurses were very nice and kind to him, when I was allowed out of bed, I spent a lot of time playing with him to take his mind off her. For obvious reasons we were not allowed visitors. You could, of course, have things brought in. I remember at school, we were taught the French National Anthem and would sing it every morning after teacher took the register. To this day, I never knew why only the French and none of the other occupied countries so perhaps she had relatives or friends there but I do know she spent the summer holidays on the Isle of Man. Anyway, we learnt the anthem in English, not French, as we didn't have French lessons - you only had those if you passed the Eleven Plus and went to the Grammar School. The nurse would often ask me to sing it. Whether it entertained or amused them I don't know but little Jonny seemed to be calmed by it, for pleasure, I hope, and not from shock. My twelfth Christmas was spent in there and we did have a Christmas tree which we helped to decorate and so break the monotony. On Christmas Eve, my sister, Rita, who was in service with a wealthy family in Stratford, came and brought me a present which was a coach drawn by four horses. Although second-hand, it must have been quite an expensive toy when new. When the nurse told me to go to the window as someone had come on a surprise visit, I thought it was my mother but no, on the outside was Rita who had brought it along on her half day off. We managed to have a conversation through the glass which, in those days, was not double glazed. When she left, I stood and watched her go. When she reached the point of being out of sight, she turned and waived which I returned. Then she was gone and I felt very alone and homesick. I spent just over three weeks in there which seemed like an eternity. A few days before I was discharged, the little finger on my left hand became very inflamed and swollen in the corner of the nail and painful to the touch. The nurse who I told about it said "Let me see". She looked at it and said "I think you have something in it" and proceeded to poke it with a small pair of scissors that all of them had. After cutting the nail back as far as she could she said "There, whatever it is, I can't see it but it should work its way out now" and left me with a painful throbbing finger and thinking how could I have got anything in it in a hospital ward. During my stay in there, the air raid siren had sounded quite a number of times. We were under the instructions of nurses to get under our beds and stay there until told it was safe to come out. One particular night, we had hardly been under there when told to do so as the planes passed overhead when there were three or four loud explosions, not too far away by the sound of them. Whether they had seen a light or were after the railway station, I never knew but on looking back after all these years, did they really think those hospital beds would protect us? From a bit of falling plaster, maybe yes but from falling masonry, I don't think so but under the circumstances, they had no options. There were no shelters inside the hospital and we obviously couldn't leave the ward or mingle with diphtheria patients in the other wards. When the time came for me to be discharged we were now in the New Year of 1941. I was picked up by a Miss Hart, who lived up Frog Lane, and ran a taxi service who, despite being a Miss, dressed in men's clothes and had her dark hair cut like one and always seemed to be smoking. She never seemed to be short of cigarettes although they were in short supply and mostly kept under the counter for regular customers. So nearly a month after leaving home I was on my way back, clutching my precious coach and horses and with high expectations of what I would receive when I got there. But like the old saying, he that expecteth much receiveth nothing, well that is almost true for me for when I asked about Christmas presents, mother went to the shelves in the alcove next to the fireplace and took down this book for boys which contained adventure stories, handed it to me and said "This is from the Sunday School." It was third prize for good attendance. After saying thank you, I stood waiting to receive what I thought would be presents from her. She said "Right, let's have a look at that finger". "What about my presents?", I enquired, thinking she was playing a trick on me. The answer I got quickly dispelled any such thoughts. She said "There are none - Christmas is over and we're into a New Year now". Looking back, I doubt very much if it would have been any different if I had been at home for Christmas. Perhaps it had been the same for my sisters, a question that I will never know the answer to. That Christmas of 1940, I not only missed out on presents but also the parties given by the Sunday School and the one given by Lady Borwick at Crab Mill. Could it be like the song said, the little boy that Santa Clause forgot.

When I went up to my bedroom I noticed lots of white tape around the edges of the door and on the doorposts. When I asked mother what it was, she told me that when the ambulance men took me to hospital, she was told, under no circumstances should anyone be allowed to go in there and that the Council would be out the next day. They duly turned up first thing, dressed in white clothing. Once inside they put on head gear and masks, went into my bedroom and sealed the window and fumigated everything inside, came out, shut the door and sealed it completely with the instructions that no one could go inside for three weeks, when they would return and take the sealing tape off. This they did a few days before I came home and told mother to take all the bed clothes and boil them separately from any other item. I was now back in my bedroom once again as normal but I still had a very sore finger, despite bathing it twice a day in warm water and Dettol. I had to keep it in a finger stall to keep the bandage clean and protect it for I now returned to school and to fetching the milk again which, in my absence, had been undertaken by Violet Moore at Number Five.

My finger, over the next one or two weeks did not get any better. Mother said she thought it was a whitlow which, as far as I know, is an infection that affects the quick at the side of the nail. The nurse should not have used scissors that were not, of course, sterilised and could have spread germs to the affected area. So with no improvement and with the skin peeling off she said we would have to go and see the doctor. This meant catching Sam Bennett's bus that went to Shipston each Saturday morning at ten o'clock from outside the Red Lion Public House. The following Saturday, off we went to the surgery and saw Dr McMullen who, on examining it, told mother that it was badly infected under the nail and that the nail would have to come off. We had to return the following week and go to the Ellen Badger Hospital for 10.30. The following Saturday came around and again we caught the bus into Shipston, getting off at the plantation which is at the bottom of Telegraph Street. We walked up to the hospital some five to six hundred yards up the Stratford Road and reported to Reception, who told us to take a seat, a nurse would be out in a while and mother said "let me take the finger stall off – we might not get it back otherwise". She had made it by cutting the finger out of a leather glove. Funny as it seems, I don't remember being frightened by the thought of having to go into the operating theatre, probably the reason being my finger by this time was very painful and very swollen and it would bring some relief. After a while the nurse came out and said to take my coat and jacket off, also my shoes and then I had to get into a wheelchair. She wheeled me down to another room where she proceeded to put on a white gown and had to tie it at the back. It was from there into the operating theatre where another nurse and the doctor, who wore a green gown and apron and said "let's see what we can do to make this finger better". With that, I had to climb onto the operating table, laying back and gazing at the large bright lights hanging from the ceiling. Then a mask was placed over my nose and mouth with the instructions of take deep breaths. The next thing I remember before I came round was the moment he took the nail off for I screwed my face up at that precise second. As my senses returned, the nurse was in the final stages of bandaging my finger. Then it was back in the wheelchair and then to the waiting room where mother put my shoes and jacket on and with that done, the nurse put my arm in a sling with the instructions to keep it on for two days. It was weeks before my finger finally got better and the nail grew back and no longer needed the finger stall for protection.

ALLOTTMENTS

With the strict rationing, the Government decided that all children of school age would have free milk and being there wasn't any suitable milk delivery service at that time, our milk had to be fetched each day from Dowler's Farm. As Frank Everett and I were the two senior boys big enough we were given the job of doing this each morning after register. As this was well before milk bottles, we had to fetch it in a large oval delivery can which obviously had a lid but without the measures. With the amount of pupils at the school, each receiving a third of a pint, meant we had to carry just over two gallons between us and in the winter we had to put it beside the fire to warm a little before teacher gave it out at morning break. Each child had their own mug which was mostly enamel. I remember mine being white with a blue rim.

The war was not going well, especially in the Atlantic where the convoys from America and Canada were suffering dreadfully from the U-boats. These were hunting in packs and inflicting heavy losses of vital supplies of food and raw materials as well as the lives of merchant seamen who often did not have time to launch lifeboats before the ship went down. So unless they could cling onto any floating debris, they had little chance of survival as most of the attacks came at night. Even the ones that went down in daylight, survivors could not be picked up by any ship in the convoy, either merchant or escort, for

Pupils working in the school garden at the rear of Glebe Cottage. Photo taken when it was two cottages

they were under strict orders not to stop as this would make them easy targets for any lurking U-boats. Coastal Command sent out planes to search for survivors during daylight hours but the range not only from this side of the Atlantic but also from Canada allowed the whole area to be covered. So, with the need to grow as much as possible, the Government came up with the saying "Dig for Victory" and produced posters with the picture of a spade being pushed into the ground by a booted foot with these words on them. They were put up everywhere. They were even stuck on allotment sheds, together with leaflets encouraging people to dig up every available bit of ground, even flower beds and lawns in towns and cities, to grow more and more vegetables. Unlike today, vegetables and fruit were seasonal with the exception of some fruit which could be preserved, hence the need for big gardens that houses and cottages had as well as allotments. Here in Ilmington the six that I can recall – The Hulks, which was on the left just before the driveway to Foxcote House. Another between the top of Grump Street and Frog Lane, and one on Campden Hill, the Crowyard which is opposite the village hall; Armscote Meadows which is about three-quarters of a mile down the Armscote Road and the final one about the same distance down the Stratford Road known as Caley. When we lived in the cottage up Front Street, father had a plot up the Campden Hill. Although it was south facing it must have been hard work for it was on a very steep slope. After we moved to Bennett Place, he took a plot at Caley being more convenient and also much larger as they ran from the track at the top, down to the boundary edge at the bottom, the width of each one being from furrow to furrow the distance of some 16-18 feet. Later he took on more. He had the first two plots inside the top gate plus the triangular piece which is called a pike. This comes about when the field at one end is wider than the other. The old plot which was next to Uncle Harry's was then shared with him where they grew corn. Although these new plots were not as long it was a substantial amount to do by hand. Before I was old enough, my sisters had to help with light jobs such as weeding and potato planting and picking up. In the spring and summer with the light nights, father would say to mother before going to work "get them (my sisters) to bring my tea down" for he would go straight from work and work there until almost dark. But looking back now, I realise that he had no option. It would not have been possible to do everything on Saturday afternoons alone, being that people worked at their various employments Saturday mornings as part of the week. Farm labourers, especially those involved with milking, had to work depending on the amount of staff on alternative or even three week-ends. On reaching the age of eleven and with all my sisters having left school and in domestic service, it was now my turn to help. I must admit I was a reluctant helper. Each night with the exception of scouts night, after tea, I had to walk down there and do my allotted jobs while most of my friends were out playing. But I must say it didn't do me any harm. In fact, you could say it was part of my education for I was taught a lot that would help me later in life like working with nature. When war came it became more important to grow more. The soil at Caley was heavy clay but very fertile and it was vital that in late autumn and early Winter every bit of ground that wasn't carrying winter and spring crops was turned over by what was called "rough digging". My father used what was known as a Bretforton or Badsey fork for this task which had two tines with chiselled ends that were just over an inch wide. These did a really good job as unlike three and four tine forks, they did not become clogged which needed constant cleaning if the ground was on the sticky side. The idea of rough digging was to leave each spit turned up on its side in what was called a clat (large lumps), to let the winter frost and snow break it down for spring sowing. I watched with interest as father went to and fro from one side to the other in an unhurried rhythm that to me seemed effortless but it was surprising how quickly he covered the ground in a few hours. Winter was the time when there was little that I could do in the way of helping but for father, not only did he do the digging but as our plot ran on the inside of the boundary hedge, so each winter he had to cut the hedge. For this he used a trouncing hook which is a slightly curved blade with a fairly long handle and kept quite sharp and used with upward strokes for the side and sideways for the top. It made a really neat job. The spring was the busy time with preparing the soil for sowing or planting. For the small seeds, you needed as fine a tilthe as you could get by raking the soil back and forth. It was now you could see the benefit of early digging. Depending on the weather, March was the usual time to start the seed sowing and for the small seeds this was done with the help of the only mechanical aid used in the form of a hand drill. This little implement was a great help especially with the amount we grew. It was made up with two wheels that could be set between twelve to eighteen inches apart, depending on the width between rows required. For the size of seed sown as the drill was pushed, it turned by the cogs a spindle that ran through the seed-box which had a brush that rotated, pushing the seed through a hole in a disc that had holes of various sizes that could be set to the size of the seed being sown. The seed would fall down the funnel into the drill as it was pushed forward. Although you could sow peas with it, Father preferred to sow them by hand with the aid of a dibber, thus sowing them deeper and giving better protection from birds and mice. The ground for onions needed to be firm and to achieve this, father made a roller by taking a five gallon oil drum, filling it with sand, passing an iron bar through it, then fixing a length of strong wire to form a handle. Guess who had the job of pulling it up and down the plot to make it really firm and ready for the drill? Father always sent away for his seed at the end of the year, chosen from the catalogue sent each year by Dobies, the seed merchant. He always had 2cwt of Majestic, a variety of main crop seed potatoes. These were planted in April. Every year we had a load of farmyard manure from Mr Frank (Tiny) Hinton who had Yorke Farm, a big jolly man, hence the nickname. I am almost sure that this was in return for the vegetables that father gave him throughout the year. The manure we used to plant with the potatoes. All the years we had allotments, I never saw my father use a garden line. Instead, he used sticks for potatoes using three, each one being two feet six inches long, that being the distance between each row; one each end and the other in the middle. He had a really good eye for each row was perfectly straight.

It was my job to put the manure in the trench, then space the potatoes one foot apart and about four inches from the edge so that when he lifted the spit to cover them it did not move them. He continued to dig until he reached the sticks and so on. The ground that was used for this was where the winter greens had been and as they were in the ground for around ten months, the ground became quite compacted and lacking in nutrients, hence the generous amount of manure in each row. Our early potatoes were always planted in the garden for easy access. I was now approaching my thirteenth birthday and getting stronger so now was time for me to use a hoe in the fight to control the weeds among the crops that were, like the weeds, growing well., We still had to hand weed the ones in amongst the vegetable seedlings. Time consuming but very necessary for these weeds were competing for food and moisture with the crops. One Sunday morning, before I went to Sunday School, mother said she had a surprise for me when I came home from Church. . I couldn't concentrate on religious matters, thinking about what it could be. I couldn't wait to get home and ran all the way home to find out. On arrival, Mother said," look outside under the veranda" which ran over our backdoor to our neighbours at No. 3 and there, leaning up against the house wall was a BSA bicycle. What joy! For my first bike – I couldn't wait for my first ride on my very own bicycle but that would not be until Monday. My sisters had taught me to ride a few years before on mother's old one. I later learnt that father had bought it off Manty Sabin for thirty shillings. I only realised some time later, the reason for being given the bike was to get me down to Caley much quicker without the distractions I got to walking down there, enabling me to have more time working. From summer into autumn, we produced more than was required for our needs. So the surplus had to be dealt with in the most obvious way and that was to send it to Stratford Market. To do that it had to be weighed and put into boxes which were the property of Market Proprietors which in our case were Bullards. These were picked up from

Sam Bennett, the Carrier, then collected from his yard opposite the Village Hall. This I had to do with my bicycle. Dad would say on Wednesday or Thursday, fetch any number from two to six depending on how much he wanted to send off. If he told me on Wednesday, that gave me the chance to collect them on my way home from school, calling on my grandmother on the way home as now I had to fetch her water from the tap up Middle Street by Ballards Lane - Two buckets, six days a week. For this I received the princely sum of 2d a week. But I didn't mind for most Saturdays she would give me a slice of cake and believe me that was something to be savoured. My mother was a good cook but neither she nor anyone else could make cake like grandmother. If I had to fetch the boxes on Thursday, I had to go up after tea and take them straight down to the allotment. It would take me quite a time to do this for I had to sling them over the crossbar and the back wheel with string and had to walk most of the way for I could only ride downhill where I could freewheel. It was impossible to pedal with up to six boxes hanging either side of the bike and often as not father would be down there before and complain about the time it had taken me. Then it was all systems go to pick or pull whatever was going. It all had to be weighed which was done with a tripod and balance scales. The weight and your name written on labels tied to each box which had Bullards stamped on them were then put on the roadside to be picked up first thing Friday morning and taken to the sale yard to be sold. The carrier would later return to pick up more boxes, give the money the produce had sold for, to my Father who then had to pay him for the carriage. The system was changed soon after where the produce was sold by the box, thus cutting out the need for weighing. Your name still had to be attached to each box but it saved time. From the age of 11, each summer holiday was spent, five days a week, at Mickleton doing casual labour for a big market gardening firm by the name of Joseph Webb's who grew fields and fields of outdoor tomatoes. It was our job to eye and tie them. The eye shoots grew from where the leaf stalks meet the main stem. These were easily removed, then underneath every third leaf they were tied to the cane with raffia which had been soaked in water to make it pliable. Each tie was once round the plant and twice round the cane and tied in a reef knot at the back of the cane allowing a gap of about three quarters of an inch between cane and stem. I used two fingers for this which was to allow for growth. We were collected from the end of our road, both boys and girls, by a chap called Bernard Smith who lived with his parents in a cottage by the Lower Green. We all climbed in the back of the open lorry at around a quarter to nine and taken to whichever field was being worked at the time. School children from all around worked there. It was a massive operation. They employed a huge staff, both men and women. The women were employed in the dozens of glasshouses. Our neighbours in No 1, Mrs Handy and our cousin, Mrs Cooke from No 10 cycled there every day. I remember Mrs Handy who had light ginger hair and, in the hot weather, her face was as red as a rooster, even with a sun hat on. What with fetching the milk and Gran's water, waste paper collection for the scouts on Saturday mornings, besides helping out in the allotments, there wasn't a lot of time for play! From late July, it was time to bend the tops of the onions. This was done to increase the size of the bulb and start the process of harvesting. When the tops were turning brown they would be pulled up and laid out to dry in the sun before being strung with bag string. This was done so they could be hung in the shed for use in the winter. Each year we would hang 4, 5 or 6 strings depending on the length for you could have them as long as you wanted but the normal length would be from 18" – 24" for they were quite heavy. Every year we had large crops so were able to send the rest to market. For this we used proper onion nets and not boxes for they were easy to fetch and carry. I can recall one year, we had over 20 nets to send – a good return for the work put in to grow them. I have described the planting of the humble potato but to me it is the most versatile vegetable grown and plays a huge part in our diet for it can be cooked and eaten in so many ways. The time and labour taken in its cultivation was well spent. There is an old saying that if you have a piece of ground that needs cleaning up, then grow potatoes on it. The reason being the amount of time you are working the soil. Firstly you plant them as already described, then once they are up and growing, you hoe between the rows. In the case of heavy soil, you use a stock hoe which has a stronger, heavier blade that is used in a chop and pull motion, not the sliding motion of the draw or push of the Dutch hoe. Then as the growth continues you have the job of earthing them up as we called it mould them up. This is achieved by pulling the soil up each side from the centre of the distance between each row to form a mound. The reason for this operation is to prevent the potatoes as they develop from light exposure as this turns them green and unfit for cooking. Then, in the early autumn, I first had the job of cutting the tops off them and it was soon time to lift them. Father usually took a couple of day's holiday at this time for the purpose. He would dig them out and leave them on top of the ground to dry. Finally, it was my job to pick them up after school rubbing any soil off them, then keeping the very small ones and any with slug damage, separate for pig potatoes. The yield produced from the 2cwt of seed planted always depended on the growing conditions. A good season you could expect around a ton. This would be reduced by 5 or 6 cwt if the summer had below average rainfall. We depended more or less on nature for we had no access to water as the fields in those days had ponds to water the livestock which were fed by ditches and dew. There is, however, a way to help nature and the way to do this is by using the hoe. This saying was handed down from father to sons and gardener to gardeners over the years. When my father told me I thought another old wives' tale but when he explained the reasons for it, it really does make sense. If you use the hoe to move the top inch or so of soil, not only does it cut the weeds down but it creates a tilthe. The more you do it, the finer the tilthe to retain the moisture below. You can try this out for yourself by using your finger on a hot summer's day to scrape the top couple of inches off a pile of sand or fine soil and you can see and feel the moisture. So this was why I spent hours with the hoe, I even had days on my own down there with only the birds for company. When I had a break for refreshments, I would lie back and watch the skylark soaring high in the clear, blue sky, singing as they hovered then gradually descending still singing until the final few feet before stopping and dropping like a stone to their nearby nest. To this day, whenever I hear a skylark it always reminds me of a song my mother taught me and it goes "Skylark, Skylark, when you are up in the sky, Skylark, Skylark when you are singing so high. If among the angels mother you should see, then ask her to come down again to Dear Daddy and me." Then I would come back to earth and jump up to continue back and forth, hour after hour, knowing that father would have words if I had not covered the area he expected of me. This method could not be used with potatoes for once they had been moulded up that was it as far as cultivation went. You then had the top growth to shade the soil plus the manure and the depth of soil to retain the moisture and, of course, the heavy soil helped so it did have its advantages. Potatoes, being a vegetable that is relied on the year round, have to be stored and for this you need a frost-free building. This is essential as a frosted potato is rendered useless. Although it may look perfectly alright, when it is cooked it turns black and is completely unfit for the table. Council houses had no such buildings, so we, like the majority of allotment holders, had to store them in a bury. The way this was done, first a thick layer of straw is placed in a circle, the tubers piled on top and another layer of straw and finally soil piled up in a thick layer with a handful of straw out of the top for ventilation. The soil being tampered down to make it weatherproof. Carrots, another all year round vegetable, were stored this way if you had large crops, otherwise they would be stored in boxes or tea chests in layers with sand. Parsnips were left in the ground where they kept better through the winter and dug as required up to the time they went into new growth for then the centres would become woody. In times of hard frost and snow a number would be lifted and stored in a cool space.

When it came to harvesting the corn that we grew in partnership with my Uncle Harry, this was done by hand using a fagging hook and a stick kept for the purpose that had been cut from the hedge usually from ash, with a piece of branch at the end, cut to make a hook. This was used to bend the corn over cutting it just above ground level. A strip of corn would be cut about two feet or so wide with the length depending on the thickness of the crop, usually about eight or nine feet. Then using both hook and stick, draw the corn against your leg, moving backwards at the same time to make a sheaf. My job was to lay the bonds which were a dozen or so strands of corn laid on the ground so that when the men had pulled all the corn back from the strip they had cut, they would in one movement, turn on one leg and place it on the bond, I would then take both ends and pull it round the sheaf, twist the bottom round just below the ears of corn to prevent it pulling out. Once the bottom end had been tucked under, the sheaf was then stood up in a stook to keep them perfectly dry before being loaded on to Uncle's horse and cart and transported to be stored in the barn or in a rick in the yard.

In the spring of 1942 we were planting potatoes on Good Friday. That was the normal then, being as everyone had time off work over Easter. With all of the close allotment neighbours doing likewise, everyone was using their forks so I was left without one which I needed to put the manure in the trench. So father told me to go down to the shed at our old plot and fetch one from there, handing me the key with the instruction not to lose it and hurry up. So, having my bike, I rode the three hundred yards or so, took the fork out, locked the door and put the key in my pocket. Pushing my bike to the verge so I could get on, with the fork in my left hand, I stabbed the fork with the intention of sticking it in the ground while I threw my right leg over the bike but, being right-handed, I had no proper control of the fork. Instead of sticking in the ground, it went straight into my foot. It took quite an effort to pull it out. With father's words of hurry up in my head, I returned not daring to tell him what I had done so carried on working until lunchtime, which we went home for. I told Mother who immediately told me to take off my boot to reveal what was now the very blooded sock. Quickly removed to see what injury I had inflicted on myself, I think I was really lucky for the fork had gone into the toe next to the big one, missing the bone and passing right through. This was only revealed after it had been in a bowl of warm Dettol water. It was rather uncomfortable and swollen for a while but it gave me a few days off school and, much to father's displeasure, no help on the allotment.

CHARACTERS

Ilmington, like all villages and small towns, had inhabitants that, for certain reasons, became widely known for what they did in work and pleasure. The first that springs to mind and one that I have mentioned in earlier chapters is, of course, Samuel Bennett. He owned the Carrier business but, as far as I am aware, never drove. That was left to Sam Junior who, like his father, was not a very big man. They were only about five foot six or seven. Sam Senior had two orchards and grew varieties of apples, pears, plums and damsons. He single handed, looked after them and picked all the fruit. It was nothing to see him carrying a thirty foot ladder and placing it up a huge pear tree in order to pick the topmost fruit. The picking season started in August and continued until October. The early fruit had a short shelf life so would be sent to market while the later ones would be kept in a fruit store where they would be checked on a regular basis. Any that had defects were used or put in the hog tub. Kept in the right conditions, some varieties would keep well into the New Year when they would fetch a better price at market. The aroma that met you when entering a fruit store was a joy for anyone lucky enough to experience. Another skill that Sam possessed was that of pig slaughtering. During the winter he would be seen usually round about nine o'clock in the morning, calling to where his services were required. The pigs kept in those days were bred and reared especially for bacon so grew to whatever size the owners desired. The average weight was about twelve score, that is about two hundred and forty pound live weight. This would produce bacon and ham with a fair portion of lean to fat but some preferred larger animals of up to 18 or 20 score which had a much higher fat content. The silence of the morning would be broken by the squealing of the most unfortunate animal as it was taken from its stye and tied on to the pig bench to have its life ended as quickly and humanely as possible. Once this had been achieved, and the blood had been drained and saved for those that wanted to make black pudding the carcass was placed on a bed of straw with more piled on top and around. It was then set alight to burn off the bristles, and turned over to repeat the procedure on the other side. Now came the job of scraping the carcass once any straw had been brushed off. This was done after first pouring very hot water over and brushing vigorously with hard bristle brooms and scrubbing brushes. This was followed by someone putting more hot water on various parts while those around would scrape it using probably the head of a hoe. This was to remove a layer of skin and the stubble to leave it absolutely perfectly clean and white. No matter what colour your pig was at the start, it always finished up perfectly white. It was then hoisted up to remove the intestines along with the heart, liver, lungs and kidneys, all except the lungs which came out together with the heart. You then have to carefully remove the filmy membrane which adhered to the stomach. This is used to cover the faggots made from the offal before cooking them. The pig was then hung for a week before being cut up by Sam. The head was used to make brawn; the trotters (the feet) could be included in this or could be cooked separately and eaten with vegetables. The ribs, hand which is above and inside the shoulder were roasted while the shoulder and hocks were bacon joints. The sides and hams were preserved with salt, sugar and saltpetre. This was done in a salting tray or large shallow box with drainage holes that let the brine drain away. This mixture was rubbed in all over, making sure the hams were treated around the bones with great care. They were placed on a thin layer of salt with more sprinkled on top. The

The well-known character, Sam Bennett, entertaining his young audience on the step of his loft

hams and the other joints were piled on the top for two days, repeating it again and placing the joints in different positions. The bacon and small joints were left to cure for two weeks while the hams for three. It was then taken out and the surplus salt was washed off with warm water and hung up in a cool airy place to dry for a week or two. Finally, the bacon and ham that were to be hung in the kitchen, if the pantries were not large enough, would be placed in muslin bags to keep the flies off.

Sam, who was tea-total and a non-smoker had a passion for playing the fiddle. His knowledge of folk music and songs was remarkable. He played entirely from memory and for years played and led the Morris Dancers and the ladies performing square dancing, along with the school around the Maypole on May Day. His real party piece, for which he became well known, was the broom dance. He even went to America to demonstrate it on a Chat Show and I well remember him doing it on his 80th birthday held in the Village Hall.

Another well-known character in the village was Walton Handy or, as he called himself "the old "shupperd" (shepherd) in the dialect of Warwickshire and Gloucestershire and was never without his crook and sheep-dog. They even accompanied him when he did the famous broadcast at Christmas, 1934 from The Manor, owned by Mr Spenser Flower, whose son, Dennis, a real radio ham, had a studio. Of course, I never heard it at the time - being only six plus we didn't have a radio until years later. However, I had been told that he had to be faded out having gone past his allotted time and showing no signs of stopping. A few years ago, I heard a recording of it which confirmed that to be so. While he spent a lot of his time working for Mr Bell, the tenant farmer of the farm called "The Downs", he also helped out anyone needing extra hands at hay making or harvesting in the summer, and threshing in the winter. In the spring, Walton did what he loved and specialised in. At this time of year, he was in demand from farmers all around for the task of

*Walton Handy, the Cotswold shepherd
and his faithful sheepdog, Shep*

cutting the lambs tails off and depriving the males of their male status. To do this he would sit on a bench, in most cases the pig bench and the catcher would bring a lamb, sit it on the bench, leaning with its back towards him. Then the fireman would bring him a red hot iron, of which there would be three of four, and made for this purpose; it was all over in a second and cauterised at the same time. The tails were kept in a basket to be given out to whoever wanted them for they were destined to end up in pies and puddings. It took quite a lot to have enough and what a job the women had preparing them. I watched my mother doing it by scalding them in boiling hot water, then skinning them ending up with practically nothing, especially if it was a small tail. Although the bone had not developed, it was still gristle, I suppose hard times called for hard measures. It was food to put on the table. The sweetbreads were also saved for they were considered a delicacy, nothing was wasted. I can't imagine housewives of today going to that trouble if the same methods were still used.

The person that comes to mind next in this chapter on Characters was not a resident of our village. In fact, he had no permanent address, for he travelled from village to village over a wide area plying his trade. However, Ilmington is the only village of the many he visited that can honestly say he was born here. There is a quiet country road that leads to Compton Scorpion, a place that consists of a large farmhouse and a few cottages, one and a half to two miles away with two farms between there and the village. In the years I was growing up, this was a gated road, there being no roadside hedges to retain the livestock. It was along this road that Sonny Neal was born in what was known as the donkey field. Sonny had an older brother called Billy. Their parents were gypsies who are now called travellers who travelled by horse-drawn caravan. Their father was a tinsmith while their mother made clothes pegs. Of course, I did not know them but was told by my mother. I understand that Billy was the only one to follow his father's trade. I don't remember seeing him but Sonny was in the area quite often and stayed along the Berryfield Road, known locally as Gypsy Halt. Although being unable to read and write, he was intelligent and clever with his hands for he made his living sharpening scissors, knives, garden shears, in fact anything that had a blade. He did all this on a scissor grinder which he made himself from the wheels, metal rods and bicycle parts which he found at the village dump. In those days, before we had refuse collectors, villages and towns had dumps where they took broken bicycles, prams, pushchairs, pots and pans, bottles – in fact any item that no longer served its purpose. However, Sonny made his grinder in the form of a deep truck with brass bed-knobs at the top on each corner for decoration. It was sturdy, well made and clever in its design. To operate it he put it down on the back legs with the wheels being forward; this made it quite stable. It was strong enough for him to swing a 4 x 1 inch board between the handles for him to sit on for it was operated by his feet on a treadle similar to that of a sewing machine as he needed both hands to control the items being sharpened. It was fascinating to watch him using various grindstones on the spindle and testing items for sharpness by touching them with his thumb and slicing newspaper with the scissors. He charged from 2d to 6d for his services. He used to bring a can round and ask Mother for hot water he would collect after sharpening her scissors or knives but she always made him tea. He always called her" Mam"

A scissor grinder that is one the same principal of the one owned and used by Sonny Neal

and my father, Jack. If he came while father was at work, he always enquired about him. There were times, if he had done well, he would take refreshment of a stronger nature. I will never forget seeing him coming down Hobdays Bank one afternoon. He had been up to Biles Shop for a loaf of bread and had called in the Howard Arms for stronger refreshment but had obviously enjoyed considerably more than one or two - the path on this particular day was not wide enough so it had to be the road! The journey of a mile that day would seem more like three. I often wondered if he still had the loaf on returning to Gypsy Halt. It was only a few years later that I realised why Sonny used Gypsy Halt and why it was so called. The reason being it was central to three other villages besides Ilmington, all about a mile away and within easy reach from his camp saving the need for carrying his belongings from village to village and the putting up and taking down of his little shelter. One reason why Sonny stands out in the memory I have of him was his appearance. For someone who lived rough, he had neither beard nor moustache and his hair, what could be seen of it for he always wore a cap, was never long. Maybe he was bald, whilst his clothes were like any other labourer's and he was always well shod. He had a weather beaten face, the same as others who spent a lifetime outside in all weathers, although I don't remember seeing him a lot in winter.

Another person who stands out in the village was one of a family of eight children. They were the Garretts. Their father Frank lived in The Grange, (often called by the locals as The Mount). This is situated above and to the north west of Hill Farm and overlooking the village. He owned a factory in Birmingham that manufactured shot guns and cartridges. This was all before my time as were so many stories told to me by my mother. Later, in the early 1900s, the cartridges, called Crimson Flash, were made and packed in the building at The Grange where the Ilmington Scouts Troup stored the newspapers collected during the Second World War. Lesley Garrett and two of his brothers, Roy who has been mentioned in an earlier chapter and Aubrey who, with his wife, Hazel, ran the Bell Inn in the village of Armscote, were the only ones I knew. Lesley and Aubrey were involved in the production of the cartridges during the early 1900s, which although I have no proof, were sold to the cartridge makers called Eley. Lesley, who lived in the second and largest of the two cottages that lie at the bottom of the top green, on the short road that leads from Front Street to Frog Lane. His wife, Liz, whose maiden name was Cooke and

Leslie Garrett outside his cottage with his Model T Ford

sister Frances who was Roy's wife, were my second cousins. The Garretts were a talented family.. Lesley was the one that to me stood out with the early development of agricultural machinery; it was to him farmers turned in the event of a breakdown of mowing machines, binders or threshing drums, not only in our village but the surrounding ones also. He would travel in his car, the earliest one, I believe was a Model T Ford. He was a skilled agricultural engineer for he also owned the Village Cider Press which he converted from manual to one driven and operated by a steam driven tractor engine that he owned. In order to house it undercover when not in use, the doorway had to be raised. The conversion was done by using cogs, pulleys and levers for the press not only had to go forward but reverse as well. A very clever man. The cider making season was early autumn, around October or when the cider apples or pears were ripe and falling from the trees as cider fruit was never picked – it was too time consuming. Once it started to fall, the branches would be shaken until all the trees had shed their fruit. It was then picked up, placed in sacks, loaded on to a horse-drawn four wheel trolley then, on your appointed day, it would be taken up to Lesley's together with the oak barrels for the juice. Every farm in those days made cider, hence the need for appointments. The

Cider making - L. Garrett is on extreme right, loading press

process needed at least three men. To start with the fruit had to be put through the machine that chopped it. From there it was taken to the press and placed in layers on coconut mats which were about one yard square. The layers would be built up to the top of the press, then the lever was pressed and the cogs would slowly turn, winding the press down. It was a wonderful sight for us boys to see the juice being squeezed out and running through a fine mesh into a container from which it would be drawn off and poured into the barrels. If they were large ones, they were left on the trolley for on the ground they would be too heavy, once full. Once every drop had been extracted the press would be reversed and the pulp removed and kept to be fed to the pigs. Then the whole process would be repeated until all the fruit had been used and the juice poured into the barrels. A bung was placed in the hole and hammered home with a mallet and the barrels were stored in a cool outhouse to ferment and mature until the following summer. Lesley had a certain way of speaking that was unlike anyone else - his voice, soft yet clear and unhurried with a touch of dry humour. He was a dedicated Church man and like my father, a sidesman. This entailed taking the collection plate around the congregation during the hymn before the sermon, taking it to the Rector in front of the altar, who turned and blessed it before returning to their pews. To explain the sense of humour, this story was told to me some years later of a conversation he had in the Red Lion Inn over a beer which most men enjoyed, especially on a Saturday evening. These are Lesley's words as told to his fellow companions, "Never again will I eat green peas for my Sunday dinner before going to evening service, for no sooner you split one pea you have to split another!" From the age of twelve, I was asked if I would pump the bellows of the Church organ, played by Mrs Zilla Sabin, for morning service. This was similar to the bellows at the blacksmith's shop except that in order for the organ to operate you had to keep a small weight, like a plumb bob suspended on a cord, between two markers. The more you pumped, the higher the marker would rise. Once up to a certain level you could rest for a while. Mrs Sabin gave piano lessons, besides taking choir practice one evening a week where her husband, Charles, was Churchwarden and a keen member of the choir as was Hedley, their youngest son, who also played the piano. I blew the organ up to the time I had scarlet fever which was then taken on by another lad. However, it did not mean that I stopped my church going for I still had to go to Sunday School and then on to morning service. One Sunday morning Mrs Warren, our Sunday School Teacher, told me that Mrs Sabin wanted to see me after church. This meant staying for the sermon which I must confess did nothing to raise my curiosity into what Mrs Sabin wanted to see me for. Like most children, I did not find it easy to understand and rather boring. However, the resultant meeting would commit me to listening to the sermon for the next two years or so. It seemed that I had been waiting outside the church a long, long time as all of the congregation, together with the choir, had left. That left Mrs Sabin and the Rector still inside. Eventually Mrs Sabin came out, "Hello, do you know why I want to see you?" "No" I said, but is it you want me to pump the organ again". "Oh no," she replied "that's still being done by Dennis. I have been told by two people that you have a nice voice, would you like to join the choir as we need new, young people to swell our ranks. If so, ask your parents." I said that I liked singing and always enjoyed singing lessons at school taken by Miss Clark. "Good," she said. "If they agree we have choir practice each Wednesday evening at 7.30. You could come with Mrs Hall from along your road." So I became a member of the church choir which leads me to another example of Lesley's vocabulary. He always sat in the same pew across the aisle and opposite the choir. He told my father how much he enjoyed hearing me in the choir with the words "When that boy of yours sings, it's as mellow as a blackbird". Singing reminds me of the family that lived in the Bevingtons – Michael Bliss a singer whose wife, an attractive lady with red hair, and their son, also Michael who, like his mother, had red hair. He was the envy of every boy in the village for he had everything a boy could wish for. One bedroom was laid out completely with a Hornby train set, complete with tunnels, stations, in fact all the things a railway system has. Then his bicycle – how could I forget this as it was, not long after I had learnt to ride and before I had one of my own. On this particular day I was out at the end of our road when Michael came down the bank, stopped and after a while said, "Would you like a ride on my bike?" I jumped at the chance to ride a bicycle where I could sit on the saddle and reach the pedals unlike when I was allowed to ride my mother's by standing on them. Off I went downhill for two hundred yards, then turned right onto the Armscote Road and at this point, I realised Michael was on the back. Now the need to pedal to keep up the momentum was where it all went wrong. Having never experienced having a passenger and being a total novice, the next thing I remember, after seeing stars, was lying in the gutter and hearing the words, "Jump Up" from Mr Hall from No. 14, returning to work on his bicycle after lunch. I had a very numb and bloody top lip that became a very fat one the next day and for a week or so afterwards. This episode left me with a chipped front tooth which I still have today. Mr Bliss had a strong baritone voice and while he spent a lot of his time away, would always sing a song or two at the concerts that were mostly organised and performed by the Ladies of the Women's Institute. One particular song I remember, although all the words escape me, the ones that I remember were – 'She was just the sort of creature, boys that nature did intend, to go right through the world my lads without the Grecian bend. Nor did she wear a Gardenia I'll have you all to know that I met her in the garden where the pratiers grow.' I know not whether it was because we had no radio or it wasn't a popular song but I have never heard it since those days.

The final couple I feel are worthy of a mention are Mr and Mrs Lesley Bennett, (no relation to Sam) who lived up Grump Street. I have no knowledge of their background or where they came from but I do know they were connected in music. He taught the piano while Mrs Bennett gave singing lessons. Even in those days, our village had its share of musical talent, both professional and amateur.

VILLAGE & OUTLYING FARMS

Our village, like hundreds throughout the country, had farms and small-holdings which provided a fair proportion of employment to its inhabitants. The majority of farms were both dairy and arable. Starting at the top of the village was Hill Farm, whose tenants were Mr & Mrs Freeman, the grandparents of my closest friend, Geoffrey whose father Joseph and Uncle Alfred worked alongside their father. Hill Farm, as its name suggests, had its fields up above the farm to the right of the road that leads to Chipping Campden. Geoffrey and his parents lived along our road at No. 10. We spent a lot of time up there on Saturdays and school holidays. It was up there at hay making time that I saw, for the first time before power driven escalators were invented, a large tripod used for the building of a rick, once the rick was too high for the pitcher to pitch hay up from ground level. This method was used because of a lack of man-power when hay making was in full swing. Farms needed all the help they could get as labour was in great demand with the weather being crucial for the making of good hay. They needed to take advantage of that. It was usual to see women with wooden rakes, two or three warm drying days after a field had been mowed, turning the mown grass to speed up the process of drying as it wasn't all farmers who had horse drawn implements such as turners, rowers and rakes needed for making hay. It was a crop that the farmer depended on for winter fodder for his animals. There was no such thing as silage then. Collecting the hay by waggon was fine if you had the labour for it meant the need for two waggons and at least five men to load the waggons (two could do it but three would be ideal) one on the waggon, the loader, with a pitcher either side. Where at the rick, two could manage until the rick reached a certain height, you needed a third to stand at the edge of the rick and to take each forkful off the one unloading the waggon and pitch it up to the rick builder. A labour intensive and time consuming method, especially if each load had to be hauled from field to the rick yard at the farm which could be as far as half a mile away. Using the tripod, as I remember the Freemans doing, was a real labour saving way for two men could achieve this providing the rick was built in the same field as the crop. With just one horse, a sweep was used to collect the hay. This was made with wood in the form of a rake. It was about six feet wide with tines of about four feet, spread about six inches apart and slightly tapered at the ends underneath, with two slightly curved handles at about waist high of an average man. This was drawn along the rows by a trace horse until the hay was piled up to the top of the back rails. It was then taken to the rick where, under the tripod and with the horse still moving, the person holding the handles would lift them up until the tines caught in the ground where the sweep would turn completely over, shedding its load. The sweep was then pulled clear and the horse unhitched. The horse was now hitched to the rope that went over the pulleys and down to the grab, a device that as it was pulled, grabbed the hay and hauled it up the side of the rick to the waiting rick builder. He then had to pull it whilst the man with the horse was making it back up. Once on the rick it would be released. The horse would then be unhitched from the rope and the process would begin again until all the hay had been hauled up. The single horse would be hooked up to the sweep to fetch another load and the rick man left to build up the rick and so on until it was finished. It was on this farm that I saw a a binder in operation for the first time - a machine that cuts and ties the crop of wheat, barley, oats or beans, into sheaths. This implement was the equivalent of today's technology. According to the terrain it was being used on, a team of up to seven horses was needed to haul it on its huge wide wheel that was used to gear all the moving parts. The person that rode on the machine had to keep his eyes on all the various operations which made it impossible for him to control the horses. For this reason it needed someone else for this and who better than a young boy to ride the foremost*. This did not pose a problem in such cases where the farmer did not have a young school leaver employee for the majority of the harvesting was done during the summer holidays and the boys would take on this easy role for a few pence a day. After all, it wasn't often you got the chance to ride a horse round and round a field all day and get paid for it. It did not take an expert rider as long as you knew right from left and a few words of command, such as' walk on', 'come by', to turn right, and 'away' for left and, of course, when to stop. The horse used for this was an old stager that new the procedure inside out. These binders must surely have made hundreds or perhaps thousands of farm labourers think all their Christmases had come at once when they were developed and became available. Previously, it must have been a daunting sight to enter a large field of ripe corn that had to be cut with a scythe or sickle. However, even with the binders, there was still a need for the fagging hook, sickle and stick to cut a seven or eight feet wide strip all round the perimeter and the sheaths stood up against the hedge or fence, to prevent the team and machine from trampling or spoiling the corn on the first bout. That would be unnecessary waste. On Hill Farm and well off the beaten track, was a barn with an enclosed yard and an open fronted covered building with a hay rack and a manger underneath. This was called Hill Barn where cattle would be kept over winter. Although it was situated in a quiet, beautiful spot, my memories of it are not among the best I have of growing up. Geoffrey and I, on one occasion, decided we would go up there rabbiting. How we were going to catch these with a stick each and our dog, Nip, I have no idea, but up there we went and were soon playing around the buildings. While Nip was off hunting, suddenly, the silence was broken by the sound of barking. We followed the sound across the field to where she was jumping round all excited but what it was, we could not see for the grass was quite long. As we drew nearer we could see it was a cat, a very large cat that had a lot of white with black markings. It was stood up to its full height on straight legs with its back arched, ears laid back whilst hissing and spitting furiously and obviously very angry. It was standing its ground, having nowhere to go and no tree to escape up and with the barn all of 150 yards away or more. So with neither cat or dog giving way, I decided to step in and give the cat a smack with my stick. This, of course, was the wrong thing to do, for in the blink of an eye, this one very angry cat was clinging to my leg with claws and teeth and with only knee-length socks and short trousers there wasn't a lot of protection. It happened so fast and was over before even Nip could react. On looking down and seeing the blood, I don't remember feeling any pain. We decided to head for home, leaving Nip and the cat still squaring up. We made our way across the field, calling her as we went. She caught us up after we had gone half way across the next field, unlike me, with no injuries. On reaching home and telling mother what had happened, she didn't believe me for she said you caught that on barbed wire, even though there were long scratches on the back of my leg and quite a large hole in my grey sock. Yes, I can remember the colour and two gashes on the side of my leg which mother bathed with TCP or Dettol and then bandaged it. Not until sometime later when Geoff's father caught the cat in a rabbit wire, he told Mother that it was a feral and had been up around the barn for some time. It was obviously wild with its teeth and claws long and sharp and quite capable of inflicting the kind of wounds that I had. That finally convinced her. During the next year or two, Mr Freeman moved to Junction Cottage, a distance of about a mile and a half and was part of the old horse-drawn tramway that ran from Shipston and originally Moreton-in-Marsh to Stratford and like The Wharf, which is about three-quarters of a mile down the Armscote Road, served as stations. I used to spend as much time that I was allowed down there with Geoff. They had quite a lot of the old tramway with the cottage and Mr Freeman bought a horse which we used to ride and have great fun. Like all children then, Geoffrey, as he became older, had his jobs to do and one of those jobs was to chop the morning wood. One particular week-end, I had not been down so looked forward to seeing him at school on Monday. Kathleen came to school that day without Geoff. I thought he was ill with the flu or other ailments. "Where's Geoff" I said, "is he not well?" "I have to give this note to Miss Clark", she replied "I will see you at playtime". After what seemed like one and a half weeks instead of one and a half hours came round,

Kathleen said Geoff was in hospital. He had been chopping wood, as he had done many times, when a piece flew up and hit him in the eye. A few days later we learnt that despite all the doctors' efforts, they could not save it, and had to take it out. I did go down and see him when he came out of hospital. After a while he returned to school wearing a patch and then eventually he had an artificial one which had to be changed as he grew on a regular basis but he coped really well and we spent many happy times together. When he left school he served his apprenticeship as a bricklayer and later he worked as a self-employed builder, married and had a family and lived in the village of Armscote.

Harolds Farm, (now called Rowneys Farm) opposite the Village Hall, was farmed by Frank Firkins who was single and lived with his sister Ivy, who like Frank never married, and a Mr Van Helden whom I know nothing of his background or if he was any relation, but he was a smartly dressed gentleman and had a waxed, pointed moustache. What I remember most about him was that any evening, just after six, he would make a hurried walk down to the Red Lion, where he would stand in the small porch that had a sliding window which was known as the pigeon hole, having a quick beer, then dashed back up home again. This was a mixed farm which had fields up Foxcote Hill, along the Compton Scorpion Road and the Shipston Road, Nellands Close, where the Flower Show was held on August Bank Holiday Monday, while the produce was shown in the village hall. Windmill Hill, another of their fields, I well remember Mr Leonard Sabin fetching the horses in the morning for the day's work.

The Council smallholding called Wharf Farm was in Middle Street farmed by the tenants, Mr & Mrs Fred Everett and their two children, Hilda and Frank. They had a dairy herd of about a dozen cows and their fields were about a mile away down the Shipston Road with another one or two down the Armscote Road. It was quite a journey to fetch and return them twice a day for milking, during the spring and summer. During the winter they were kept inside during the worst weather.

Nextdoor was Manor Farm owned by Mr & Mrs Dowler who had three sons, Michael, the oldest, Christopher and David, the youngest. They owned a large herd of Red Poles, a dual purpose cow which produced good milk and beef. The cowman was Laurie Hughes, the eldest son of Mr & Mrs Hughes of No. 12 along our road. They had generations of these pedigree cows and Laurie knew every one by their names, along with the relatives within the herd, who to me looked all the same. Mike, the oldest son, worked on the farm but the two youngest were still at school. Others that were employed were Ernest (Coddie) Cooke who was a working foreman, Ernest Cook (no relation) and yet another Ernest whose surname is Downes. Although he was not a native of the village he moved here when quite young with his parents and older brother Leonard and sister Ethel. His father, being a policeman and came from the Birmingham area to take up his position as Village Bobbie. They lived in the end cottage that was behind the lower playground of the old school. Mr Dowler, who was quite deaf, travelled to Birmingham during the week by car where he had a business.

Also in Middle Street on the left-hand side was Burlingham Farm, owned by Mr and Mrs Jack Foster with their two sons, Ernest and Jack. Mr Foster's brother, Frank, along with Dickie Summers, worked for him. Although they had no dairy herd they had beef cattle and their ground was scattered all around from Foxcote Hill along the Mickleton Road,

House pic 1

the Compton Scorpion Road, Shipston Road, part of Windmill Hill, together with fields down Bald Addledon, so working there would give you changes of scenery.

Next to Fosters and opposite Dowler's at Manor Farm, was Middle Meadow where my grandmother, Fanny Potter and my Uncle Harry lived. This small holding was rented from private owners and had two fields down the Shipston Road, next to the Everetts. Being only 20-25 acres limited the number of livestock it could support which amounted to two short-horn cows and their offspring. Like the Red Poles, these were dual purpose animals, so once the young stock reached the age of two and a half to three, they were sold for beef. Most of the milk was put through a separator – a hand machine that was secured to the flagstone floor of the dairy and the warm milk straight from the cows poured into the hopper, then winding the handle the milk would pass through a number of perforated cone-shaped cups that

House pic 2

Uncle Harry (Rouse)

fitted inside one another. That spun round at great speed as the handle was turned with the skimmed milk coming out of one spout and the cream out of another. I watched my uncle do this many times and he would quite often give me a mug of warm frothy separated milk to drink. The rest would be fed to the pigs. The cream would be made into butter which was done by my gran with the aid of a butter church. This was a wooden barrel with a lid that was securely fastened and on its own stand, allowing it to turn over and over as you turned the handled in a nice steady rhythm. With the cream falling against the baffles it could take from five to twenty minutes, depending on the cream and weather before you heard the first signs of faint bumping that it was starting to turn. Gradually it would get louder until it was just a loud bump and splash. That was a satisfying sound. Then, off with the lid, lifting out the butter where it would be over the next few days, put on a rolling tray and squeezed with a ribbed roller to extract any water, salted, then weighed into half pounds and shaped with butter pats. These were wooden – smooth on one side and ribbed on the other to make a neat appearance then placed on grease-proof paper and folded up ready for market. There is nothing to compare with home-made farmhouse butter on toast. The buttermilk could be used for cooking, otherwise the pigs would benefit.

One of the fields would be used for hay which was needed for winter fodder – for this, Uncle needed outside help with both men and machines and horses which always came from Firkins and that meant waiting until such times that they were available. Man power came from relatives or anyone available so the need for plenty of good cider was essential for good cider encouraged good helpers.

Uncle always kept a lot of poultry for the production of eggs and Christmas Cockerels. This meant rearing your own birds. Every year in early Spring when egg production was in full swing, the hens would start becoming broody. On collecting the eggs, if one was sitting on eggs that had been laid that day or even in a nesting box without, as you moved her she would puff her feathers while clucking as they do when calling their chicks. He would then put her in a small coop of which he had for the purpose and sit her on a clutch of thirteen eggs. He would usually have three of four hatches a year depending on how many pullets he required to replace the old ones that were culled.

Farmers in those days rang their birds using coloured rings. These were coiled like springs, using a different colour each year. This would be done once the birds were large enough to tell male and female. The male birds were not rung unless another stock bird was required although these were often exchanged with other farmers to prevent inbreeding, the others being reared for Christmas. These birds could be sold live at market or if going to butchers they would be dressed ready for the oven, or rough-picked . This was removing the feathers, removing the entrails but leaving the head and legs on. By this method you could tell if they were young or old by the spurs on their legs and the size of the comb. I remember one year, about a week or so before Christmas, I accompanied my parents up to Middle Meadow, who with my Uncle, which they had done for many years to prepare the birds that were sold to butchers or privately. This was done by lantern light in the stable. The unfortunate birds had been put into coups and fattened up for about six weeks on barley meal and corn. They were then despatched and plucked straight away for a warm bird is easy to deal with than a cold one, the feathers coming out without too much effort. Having finished one, Uncle Harry brought this lovely black bird out of the coop, rung its neck, sat down, put it over his aproned legs and proceeded to defeather it. This done he got up, took it and laid it down on the straw bed with the others that had been done. Turning to fetch another when suddenly the one he had just put down, struggled to its feet, staggered in a drunken state round the stable much to my amusement and laughter. I don't think Uncle Harry found it funny or the poor chicken – it must have been sheer torture losing its feathers in a semi-conscious state but he soon did a proper job and put its misery to an end. My mother and gran had the worst job, for the next day they had to take out the intestines whilst keeping the giblets, ie heart, liver, kidneys, neck and legs and feet. These were used, back then, to make the gravy – the one day of the year the working class people had chicken. Some may be lucky to get a boiling fowl to make chicken stew for they were usually too tough for roasting.

The next farm, Hobdays, was owned by Mr Miles who had two daughters, Ena and Frances. Frances married a man named Parr who took over when Mr Miles retired and moved to the Old Rectory which had belonged to the Church. Whether he bought it, I do not know but he did keep a few beef cattle and also bred a few turkeys and chickens while the Parrs kept a few dairy cows. Their orchard went right through to the Mickleton Road with more ground along that road and shared the fields belonging to the Old Rectory. The oldest son of Mr & Mrs Bert Hall, who lived along our road at No. 14 whose name was Ron, worked for the Parrs until he joined the army at the outbreak of war.

The two Council owned smallholdings next to each other in Back Street were once a farm of 70 acres up to the end of the First World War. Then the Government made

Councils split the majority of the farms they owned to give returning soldiers jobs as self-employed farmers, thus these became two smallholdings of 35 acres. The original farmhouse is built with stone as were all the other buildings that formed the farm yard, had tiled roofs. The house was thatched and known as Mabels Farm House. It was allocated to Albert Wyton who was my Uncle, having married my father's oldest sister, Elsie. He had a few dairy cows and grew corn in a field he rented down the Armscote Road while Mabels Farm on the other side of the road was farmed by Mr Jack Sabin, whose fields were down the Armscote Road, including the field where our Council Houses were built. Having taken part of it for that purpose he was then left with a field of half the size. Across the road at the front and at the end of our row was another field which went to the Shipston Road. The Council also gave him the one opposite down to the Wharf. He had another along the Mickleton Road where he also grew corn. He had quite a herd of dairy cows that he grazed in the fields by us. You always knew when he was fetching them at milking time for he would whistle, non-stop from the time he left home on his bike until he returned with them, then the same on returning them to the field.

The farm below the two smallholdings in Back Street was Folly Farm, owned and run by two ladies – the Miss Peppilows who, so I am led to believe, took over the farm in the early 1900s to the dismay of the local farmers who said it would be most unlikely that two women would have the knowledge, let alone the experience to make a go of it, but make a go of it they did. Not only by growing cereals but also breeding top quality shire horses that were at that time in demand. They were still going strong at the time I was growing up and had earned the respect of bygone doubters.

The outlying farms and their locations are best described by the points of the compass and clock. So starting at the top of Campden Hill, that is west at twelve o'clock, that is the farm called The Downs and farmed by the tenants, Mr Bell on the Foxcote Estate. It is where the charity swedes were grown and delivered each winter to the village poor. Each household would get a sack of Swedes delivered by horse and cart. I have no knowledge of who bequeathed this charity but it was ongoing while I was at school.

Woodmeadow the next farm clockwise as I remember, was farmed by Mr Wilson, a farmer who was responsible for a miscarriage of justice which will be explained in a later chapter. Whether this farm was part of the Foxcote Estate, I am not certain but I do know is that it was farmed by my grandfather, John Joseph Potter and was where my mother and her brothers and sisters grew up. The farm did not grow cereals for it was unsuitable for ploughing. They did have a dairy herd along with pigs, sheep and poultry. I never knew my grandfather for he had died long before I was born but my oldest sister, Rita, used to talk about going up there when she was young. After he died, the tenancy went with him and that is when my grandmother moved down into the village and Middle Meadow.

Larkstoke consists of the Manor, Upper Larkstoke Farm and Larkstoke Cottage. The only occupant I remember was J Wilson, who farmed there but I have no knowledge of who lived in the Manor. I have a faint recollection of a man and his wife who came to the shop who lived in the cottage and that is all I remember. However, I know that William Cooke and his wife, Mabel, lived in the cottage on the Mickleton Road adjacent to the road up to Larkstoke and was called The Brickle and worked on the farm. The cottage was built of red brick but was later demolished and they moved to No. 10 along our road but he continued to work there. Stoke Wood was one of our favourite haunts as children. This old wood which has been there for hundreds of years was of vital importance to all those generations. I remember as I grew up how it used to be coppiced but we like the children of all those generations went there to play and pick the primroses and violets that grew in abundance plus the cowslips that grew in the meadows.

To the north of the village was York Farm. The house and buildings stand some 4-500 yards off the Stratford Road. The earliest farmer that I remember was a Mr Purser. He was quite elderly but had a son called Peter who later married Mr and Mrs Hughes' daughter Kathleen from No. 12 Bennett Place. Mr Purser's daughter was married to Frank Hinton and lived in the farmhouse with their two daughters, Joan, who is my age and her younger sister Monica. I have mentioned Mr Hinton in the chapter on allotments but not about his or Mr Purser's kindness towards the sports clubs of the village. In the years before the playing field, they provided the areas for the tennis and hockey clubs, both facilities were in the fields on either side of the drive. The grass tennis court was on the right complete with a high wire fence with a wooden pavilion and storage shed inside up against the hedge where the nets, balls and push mower and the line marker was kept. The reason I remember all this was because my father was, at that time, groundsman and I went down there with him in the summer. Depending on whether they were going to play, it could be evenings or week-ends, I was, you might say, the trace horse for I had to help with the mowing which was done with a push cylinder mower. I pulled while my father pushed. It had to be done once a week in the spring and summer and sometimes twice in good growing weather for it had to be kept short and often during the spring we had to use a roller as you can't play tennis on a soft surface. After mowing and before a match the lines had to be marked. This was done with a hand pushed wheel-marker and liquid chalk but unlike the mowing and rolling, father did this without my assistance. The hockey pitch was on the opposite side of the drive and was not so labour intensive being played in winter although there would have been cattle grazing during the summer and autumn. The job of removing the cowpats was mine at the start of the season. Once that was done there was little I could do although with matches taking place on Saturday afternoons every other week it was a quick lunch then down we had to go to get it ready for bully off at 2.30 or 3.00 depending on the time of year. Father would mark out the pitch while I carried out the nets and flags. Once the marking was done, I went round with the flags, placing one at each corner and then one on both ends of the centre line while father put the nets up. When the War started, I remember, people were called up into the forces so the clubs lost a lot of their members and although sport was still played with reduced fixtures, there was no need for a grounds person and I expect my father wasn't sorry for his allotments took on a greater need.

To the east of the village and standing about 300 yards from the Armscote Road was Mansill Farm owned by Mr William Prentice who kept beef cattle and grew cereals. Lying south east of Blackwell Bushes along the Compton Scorpion to Shipston Road and some 300 yards from Junction Cottage was the grounds belonging to the Parker Family who lived in a thatched cottage down the lane, now known as Ballards Lane. In Ilmington in my day, it was known as Parker's Alley. Mr George Parker, I believe, had lived there for a number of years with his wife, who I never knew but George, who was, I think, in his 70s lived there with his niece Nellie and nephew Herbert (Herbie) Parker. Although their Uncle George spoke with a local accent, both Herbie and his sister came from Derbyshire and spoke with a Northern accent. Apparently the land their parents owned in Derbyshire and was left to them on their deaths, was found to be on a prime seam of coal that was suitable for open cast mining. Herbie and Nellie had in all probability moved down here to assist their uncle with Nellie looking after the home while Herbie took on the outside work. Behind the cottage was a decent size garden and orchard while down at Blackwell Bushes was ground of around 11 acres which in the main were orchard where all the native fruit varieties were grown. Plums and damsons that seemed to do well as Herbie, so it was said, had a fondness for damson jam. Chickens were kept down there and he always had a pony. Among the various sheds there was an old railway carriage that was used for more secure storage, not forgetting the cat or two that farms had to keep the vermin under control. Herbie looked after his livestock really well. He rode round to Southfield Farm on his bicycle every day to fetch his cats milk. With the Freemans living closeby at Junction Cottage, Geoffrey and I spent quite a lot of time with Herbie, especially in the summer when I had a little time from my own jobs. One thing I remember from the days when Councils employed roadmen to keep the roads and verges neat and tidy, each village had their own length men - the length meaning the distance and area that was their responsibility. Each man had a wheelbarrow, a two-wheeled handcart together with a broom, spade, shovel, scythe, sickle and a rubber (a sharpening stone). Haymaking time was also the time when all the verges were mown, the old tram line that runs alongside the Shipston Road was quite a large piece of ground and produced a decent crop of hay which, together with the wide verges in the close area, plus what Herbie had from his own, produced enough to see him through the winter. At this time, Herbie would get Geoff and I to help him gather it with his pony and cart. I would go down early on Saturday morning and meet them by the gate which went into Herbie's orchard by the old tramway. Herbie would say in his Derbyshire accent, "you old ponies yed and I'll pitch up to guff". We would collect it all from the verges, leaving that which was in the orchard for Herbie and Geoff to collect in the evenings for I was needed down the allotment. Herbie was quite a character but also a shrewd one. What with the open cast mining and fruit orchard he also went round Shipston with his pony and cart, selling his fruit and vegetables that he grew. I have no idea what he gave Geoff but he always gave me six pence and half a dozen eggs.

To the south of the village, along the Compton Scorpion Road, was Southfield Farm owned by Mr Charles South and his wife, Joyce with their three children, Joy, Leonard and June, all of school age. They attended the village school and had to walk about two miles each way, winter and summer. Poor Len suffered terribly from chilblains during the winter months, so one could only imagine what it must have been like. The farm was in the main, dairy. They had quite a herd of shorthorn cows which were hand milked by Mr and Mrs South. Charles was also a keen poultry man and kept a flock of "Buff Orphintons" - a chicken known for the ability to achieve weights for hens of up to eleven pounds and the cockerels, more. Although this meant they were not such prolific layers as other breeds, they made excellent table birds and the reason why they were kept; the others were kept for egg production. There was a substantial walled garden where they grew all the vegetables they needed along with Charlie's famous marrows and rhubarb. The marrows, which were of the trailing variety, were cultivated to enormous sizes. To achieve this they were, on reaching about a foot in length, fed with sugared water. This was done by suspending jars of this liquid above each marrow and using soft string as a wick, inserted into the stalk with the other end held in the syrup solution. The fruit would then take this along with the other moisture and nutrients through the roots. At the end of the season when growth had ceased, the ones that had been fed this way would be taken inside, hung up and left to ferment allowing the sugar, both natural and supplement to turn to alcohol. By late winter the skins would become so hard that it became a perfect container and with the flesh having turned to liquid you had a casket containing marrow rum. The remaining marrows were stored and used during the winter. The large patch of rhubarb was not only grown for the table but large quantities were used for making rhubarb wine. Just outside the backdoor that opened on to the courtyard and next to the dairy, was quite a large outhouse that contained barrels of all sizes against the wall -each one containing home-made wine and cider along with the suspended marrows. Little wonder they always had plenty of help at haymaking time. This brings to mind one particular occasion after a season that had produced a good crop had been gathered in, the Souths invited everyone that had helped to a kind of harvest home. Father and I were invited, but I had to go on my own as father had the sick and divvy plus fire watching on this particular evening. Both had their headquarters at the Red Lion. Long before the days when employees who were unable to work through sickness or injury, there was a need to supplement their income. Unlike today, they did not receive sick pay. Therefore, clubs were set up whereby paying a few pennies each week the members would receive a few shillings a week for the duration they were off work. As you may guess the drinks flowed freely, not that I was allowed that much, just a small glass of cider but the food was good and plentiful despite the rationing. Mrs South was an excellent cook and, being a farmer's wife, had ingredients that the ordinary householders did not. The reason I was there was obvious in that although I couldn't do the manual work, I did lead the horse used with the sweep and waggons for Leonard South was a number of years younger. Just after ten o'clock most of the helpers were feeling the effect of the drinks and coming from Shipston and the village of Tredington, decided to make their way home as everyone had to work the next morning, despite it being a Saturday – no such thing as five day week then, everyone worked half day on Saturdays and some people all day. Phil Hancox, the oldest son of Harry, our blacksmith, also a blacksmith at Shipston, said to me "you go on and open the gate" so off I went on my mother's bike still unable to reach the saddle and no lights. I had barely got to the gate, unfastened and slightly opened it when they were there. Phil, being in front, hit my bike but luckily not me. The others managed to stop and said to me, "are you alright". "Yes", I said "but my back wheel is buckled." "Let me see", he said and with that, pushed it, making a rubbing noise. He jumped on it and started peddling. He went a few yards and said, "It's rideable, you will be OK" and off they went. I got on, standing on the pedals, just making it move, but no way could I ride it, not being heavy or strong enough like him. So I had to half carry and half push it on the front wheel, well over a mile home, arriving there much to mother's and my relief. She wasn't too pleased when I told her what had happened plus the fact that it was going to cost us to have it repaired. The next day, I took it up to Dickie Summers who did cycle repairs in his spare time. I collected it a week later with a few new spokes and the wheel turning straight and true at the cost of two shillings and three pence – the equivalent of about 12 pence in decimal currency. Father did all sorts of jobs over there in the winter from chopping wood to mending fences, mostly on Sunday mornings as well as Saturday afternoons. I went with him quite often, especially if he was shooting, being no shortage of rabbits. We always had a few which he shared with the Souths.

The next farm which was a little further on along the Compton Scorpion Road was Cathole that stands back on a sharp rise from the road. This was owned by Mr Bill Berry – a huge man with a round ruddy face who raised beef cattle and sheep. He travelled round by horse and trap and visited the public houses on the market days coming home rather the worse for wear. I remember seeing him coming out of the Red Lion, getting into the trap after a fashion and as he put his weight on the step at the back, the shafts would lift up as though it was going to lift the pony off the ground, much to the amusement of us boys. It was well known around the village that he didn't have to drive his pony home – it took him. He made home-made cider but according to father it wasn't very good for when the band went round at Christmas, playing carols, father told his fellow bandsmen not to drink it but just make out they were, and then when he fetched another jug, throw it into the bushes. That was fine until someone at the back was a bit late and threw it after he arrived with another jug. "What was that" he asked but someone at the back said "It's all right Bill, it's only a cat in the bushes, I think it was after a mouse". "That's what we keep them for" said Bill "Who wants some more?" "No thanks, Bill, we have a number of calls to make but thanks all the same and a Merry Christmas to you." Father said "we will go to Southfields now, where we will be sure of a decent brew without the risk of a bad stomach". Bill had two brothers, Tom and Jack, both farmers who lived in Blackwell, a village that lies two miles south east of here. Tom had two sons, Tom and Ben who worked alongside their father, raising cattle and growing cereals. They were the only farmers that owned a threshing drum that was hauled and driven by a steam tractor and operated by Ben, the youngest son. He was kept busy through the autumn and winter when most of the threshing was done and with it being the only one in the area, it was a case of booking well in advance. Ben made it somewhat easier by doing one village at a time, thus saving time on a lot of travelling. It still needed advanced planning and co-ordination on the part of the farms as not all farms had sufficient labour required for this but this is where the Land Army girls played a huge part in these times of war. For instance, at the time your corn was to be thrashed the War Agricultural would send out the girls from the Land Girls Hostel that was up the Darlingscote Road on the outskirts of Shipston and a few hundred yards from the War Agricultural Yard and Offices. The ideal number required for threshing was seven, although six could manage without counting the steam tractor operator – his job was stoking the boiler and keeping the water topped up to maintain the steam pressure and, of course, to lubricate all the moving parts. He was always first on duty in the mornings in order to have a full head of steam ready for the team to start. The team consisted of one on the rick, pitching the sheathes onto the drum where the bond cutter, armed only with a sharp penknife would cut the strings at the knot allowing the corn to fall loosely for the feeder to feed it slowly into the drum. This had to be done allowing the machine to knock out the grain as it passed down the drum. The corn would be separated from the straw, chaff and shavings by flails which then passed through a series of sieves, the corn going down the two chutes where a man would hook a sack onto the hooks then, lifting the shutter on one chute, allowing the grain to flow until one was full. He dropped the shutter down and opened the next one, then tying the top with string from the bond cutter, putting it on a sack-cart to be taken to the granary. This was the hardest job in threshing, needing a strong person especially having to take the sacks up steps. The chaff and shavings would drop out of the bottom of the drum where they would be raked out onto a large sheet and taken to the feed store to mix with the animal feed. The straw was deposited out of the back into a machine similar to the one that tied the wheat into sheaths when binding. The only difference being, it was tied one at each end making it into a bolting that was put into ricks for bedding or, in the case of oat straw, this was used for mixing with the hay and fed to the beef stock in winter.

The final farm in this chapter is Compton Scorpion which was one of the most isolated. It was owned and farmed by Mr and Mrs Ray Ashby. They had quite a mixed farm, having both beef cattle, sheep and a few dairy cows, plus growing cereals. Each Friday, he went to Stratford Market by pony and trap. You always knew when he was coming for he had a really smart pony, liver chestnut in colour and very fast. Just down the road from the farm were two semi-detached farm cottages, one being occupied by Mr and Mrs Westbury and their daughter Dillys. Mr Westbury worked for the Ashbys –as a labourer whilst Dillys helped in their house and in the dairy. The milk was used for butter, hence the weekly visit to Stratford. The second cottage was occupied by the Birch family. Mr Birch worked on the farm and their two children came to our school. Jack, the oldest, was a really big lad. In fact, I remember one instance when he had really misbehaved, and Miss Clark sent him down the classroom to the cupboard where she kept the cane. Here he was going to receive his punishment but Jack had other ideas! When told to hold his hand out, it remained firmly by his side. After trying a few times, without any response, she called on Mrs Davenport for help who also failed. When they tried to move his arms, he wouldn't budge. Enter Mrs Allchurch, the infant teacher but no matter how they all tried, Jack stood firm. No way was he going to have the stick. Instead, he spent the rest of the afternoon, stood up, facing the wall, not being allowed out to play and staying in after school with a hundred lines. I have no idea what he had to write or if he ever did, for it was a long way to walk to school from there and that was punishment in itself. Also working on the farm for many years was Len Taylor who lodged at Mrs Langston's at No. 11 Bennett Place and he worked there for many years. He originated from London.

To end this chapter on farms, I think it would be the appropriate time to mention the role of the War Agricultural. Soon after the declaration of war, the Government realised the need to grow as much of our own food as possible but with the young farm hands, joining the armed forces in the thousands, this meant a shortage of labour. Also most farmers were still very reliant on horses to cultivate the land and to grow more food, you needed more land to produce it. Farmers were now under instructions from Ministry Inspectors who visited farms to decide which fields and how many more acres could be put under the plough, plus what crops to grow. This meant fields that had been used for grazing and hay for perhaps hundreds of years, were now to be cultivated. The farmers had no options - they did it or risked losing their farms. The inspectors made regular visits to make sure these instructions were carried out. There were cases where some farmers failed to comply and were evicted and replaced by people who would. They were now working for the Government and at the beginning of the war, Agricultural Depots were set up all round the country equipped with tractors and implements plus the man power to use them. Their job was to carry out the seasonal tasks on the farms that had neither the tractor or implements to do it more quickly and efficiently. For instance, horse drawn ploughs had just one furrow, while the Fordson Tractor had two or three furrows and with the aid of spade lug rear wheels, they could cope with all types of soil. However, like the farmers the drivers had rules and regulations that had to be followed. They had to clean the mud off the wheels before leaving the field and were only allowed to travel very short distances on public roads with spade lugs fitted to avoid damaging the surface. They also had to remove the mud off roads to lessen the risks of accidents to cyclists and vehicles that might skid, particularly at night. .Because of the blackout, all vehicles had to have headlight covers with slots in to restrict the light that could be seen from enemy planes. To move the tractors around the farms and neighbouring farms, pneumatic tyres or hardwood blocks could be used. The tyres would have to take the place of spade lug wheels which would take a considerable amount of time to change so it was usually the blocks that were used for it was far quicker, even though each block was secured to the wheel with two bolts. The depots also had rubber tyre tractors and trailers to transport them to the villages in their area. In a previous chapter, I wrote about how we used to go down the lane at the bottom of our houses to visit our oldest sister, Rita, who was employed at Berryfield Farm. At the end of this track was a field that was covered in bushes and shrub where the Nightingales unforgettable song first fell on my ears. Well that field and their habitat too became a victim of war. The bushes and shrub was cleared by day and a huge machine, called a gyrotiller which had two rotating claws, each one having four heavy steel hook blades that ground out the roots and tilled the soil some 15-18 inches deep without bringing the subsoil to the surface. A clever machine – I remember lying in bed on the warm summer nights, listening as it droned and groaned and ground its way slowly to and fro across the field.

WIRES & WARRENS

Autumn and winter were the seasons for rabbiting. Not only did it supplement the meat ration but helped the farmers too by keeping their numbers down. I spent many a Saturday afternoon accompanying my father upon the hills overlooking the village setting rabbit wires in the fields without livestock, belonging to Mr Foster. Father would set any number, up to fifty or more depending on the runs that were in constant use. It was my job to carry the bag containing the props. These made from Hazel about as thick as a pencil and about eight inches long, pointed at each end - one end going into the ground and the other through the eye of the snare, holding it up to the required height. Father used to go round at around ten o'clock, after taking a glass or two at the Red Lion, armed with a torch and a stout stick. This was for the purpose of carrying the catch. This would also be done again on Sunday morning, often with me and Nip our terrier. We would also take up the wires. In the wooden shed that stood at the top of our back garden, father hung a four foot long by about four inches in diameter straight branch of an Ash tree that he had split in quarters. It must have been there for two years or more and then one Saturday afternoon in early autumn, after the root vegetables had been dug up and stored away for the winter, he took it down and cut it into nine inch blocks, then with the bill hook he split each quarter again. Then he made a cut with a saw about one and a quarter inches from the top and about an inch deep. On the narrow side this was then tapered from the bottom side making a perfect notch. The bottom was then tapered to make a really strong peg that would last for years. Father bought all his rabbiting equipment from a catalogue that specialised in game keepers needs. The wires were sold by the dozen and would come with the cords attached and in dark colours. The noose wire was strong and the colour of brass that never seemed to rust and was quite conspicuous. The old timers used to hang them up in the chimneys of the inglenook fireplaces to darken them and stop them glistening on moonlight nights, probably not only to stop the rabbits from seeing them but also the landowners and gamekeepers if they were doing a bit of poaching. Father used to put them in the bag of soot which everyone had from the coal fires and was used on the gardens after it had been kept for a year for to use it fresh would burn the roots. It was particularly good as a slug deterrent. The first ferret we had came about by chance. As I have mentioned earlier, father used to go to Southfield Farm on a regular basis. On this particular occasion he came across this white ferret roaming completely alone with no one else around so he picked it up and brought it home. He put it in a bag while he removed my now unoccupied rabbit hutch and put it round the back in between No.1 and our sheds. This ferret who I named Compton was the most quietest, friendliest one I ever knew. It had a perfect nature. I used to feed it every day and care for it. Whoever lost it must have missed it, but we never found out who that person was. Could it have been someone using it illegally who were disturbed and had to make a quick exit. Whatever it was, their loss was our gain. It was an excellent worker and gave us great service over the next two years or so until it died. I missed it a lot but these things happen and I suppose its part and parcel of growing up. Father said we would have another, and true to his word, he came home from work one day with another but this time it was a big fiche ferret that very much resembled a polecat with the same dark colourings. I was never allowed to look after him. Father said he wasn't to be trusted. Not long after, he brought another home, this time a white one, like Compton and a female which is known as a Jill. The males, I believe, are called Hobs. Father said he would have to make a larger hutch for them which he did but this time it had two compartments with a door to each one – one for sleeping and the bigger one for feeding. A short time after he took the big male out and put it into the smaller one and said we were going to have some young ones. I couldn't wait to see how many. Eventually they came out of their nest, seven of them, five white and two coloured. By the end of the autumn, they had grown to their full size and it was becoming a little overcrowded so father went up to the Post Office to see Mr Edwards. He was a reporter for the Evesham Journal as previously mentioned, to put an advertisement in the next two weeks, thinking it being early autumn, people would be needing some replacements or new stock for the coming season. Response was good for he sold five, two going to Percy Lines from Quinton which left us with two that father wanted to keep – the reason why I was to find out later. Father was very friendly with a man called George Tracey who was always called Bat by everyone who knew him. I never heard anyone refer to him as George. He worked in Mickleton but who for, I don't know, but I heard him mention the name of Smith-Bingham. On several occasions, however, he came down to see father in the Autumn of 1941 and said that the farmer who owned the farm that stands below Mickleton Wood, I think his name was Slatter, was plagued with rabbits and wanted someone to do something about reducing them. He asked whether father would be interested in helping him to do just that – the rewards being, to have what they caught except for a couple he wanted for himself. Father agreed without hesitating but said they would need more nets, the ones he had were not sufficient to cover those big warrens, especially those in the wood. Bat agreed saying that the ones he had would not make up sufficient numbers and said that they would share the costs which would be recovered from the sale of the catch. Father turned again to the catalogue to order the nets which duly arrived a couple of weeks later. The only day of the week that was suitable when both would be free would be Sundays, so Sundays were the days when Father would be up and ready to leave, bicycle loaded up with nets, graft, ferrets, four of them; three were in one sack slung over his shoulder and rested on his back - the big male in another over the other shoulder. He would set off at 8.30 with Nip and meet Bat at the bottom of Back Street where it meets the Mickleton Road, who was also loaded up. He lived up behind the old school in the first of three cottages, the third one which was occupied by the then Policeman, Mr Downes. It was a three and a half mile journey, not an easy ride for there were hills to negotiate both ways, the farm itself is situated just before you reach the village. There is a road that forks to the left off the sharp right hand- bend into the village. It is up there a good quarter of a mile. Now I had a bicycle of my own, I was allowed to go a few times over the present season of 1941/42 and the next one of 1942/43. My job was to help put the nets over the holes which could take up to thirty on the big warrens. It was vital that you covered them all which meant searching for bolt holes that were usually always on the outskirts of the warren and nearly always well hidden. Once this was done, very quietly, for you were not allowed to talk, silence was the key to successful ferreting for noise would make rabbits reluctant to bolt. If they didn't and the ferret stayed down there you knew that's when the hard work started, not for me but for the men for it meant digging. Once the ferret was introduced, it was a case of positioning yourself away from the front of the holes to the sides and top with a spare net in hand and listening for any sound below ground. The slightest sound would tell you that bunny was home. With any luck you would soon know if he wanted to leave. If it was your lucky day, a few seconds after hearing a sound, a rabbit would come hurtling out and be in the net and rolled up in a ball. Then you had to move fast and silent with net in hand you put your foot in the hole and making sure the one in the net could not escape. You placed the other net you had, over the hole and secure, taking the caught one with you. There were times when you would get five, six or more, bolt from a large warren. If the ferret, or if two were used, both came out, it usually meant there were no more in there. However, to make sure one was always put down another hole. There were two occasions that stand out in my memory when I went.

The first one was after we had done two smaller warrens on the outskirts of the wood with mixed success, we then moved to the larger warrens inside. After netting up, the mother of the two young ones was about to be used for the first time that day. All went well – we had one or two that came out but then nothing. After a few minutes there were no more rabbits coming out but also no ferret which meant she had either got some trapped up a dead end or she, herself, was trapped behind some. If that was the case she could be in danger of suffocating. This meant the 'liner' had to be used. This was a line used when a ferret, in our case, the big male would have a collar made for the purpose, was secured around the neck, not too tight but tight enough so that it wouldn't slip over the head. This collar had a long thin but very strong line attached to it, the line having a small knot at every yard starting at the collar. On releasing the ferret into the same hole the first ferret had been put in, you counted the number of knots as they disappeared down into the warren. Then when it stopped you knew how far and in which direction it was likely to be so you would start to dig across the direction of where the line was thought to be going and about a yard or two back from the length of line. This would be pulled gently at intervals to check that he had not moved. The one that wasn't digging would be holding this and both would be hoping that it wasn't caught up on a root which was the risk involved when among trees. After a while with the hole some four feet deep and avoiding any large roots, father took over to give Bat a rest and after a few minutes he broke through to the hole. After a bit of cleaning up, he said he could see the line, so proceeded to undercut the top of the hole in the direction of the line but still couldn't see anything and took out some more but still nothing. Then he did something that I would never do, he got down and put his left hand up the hole, only to withdraw it a few seconds later, not with a rabbit but the liner ferret on the end of his thumb! And ferrets once they get hold don't easily let go. To make them do this, you have to pinch one of their feet or blow directly into their face. He couldn't do the former for his free hand was holding him by his neck. After a few strong blows it let go. Bat took the ferret while father and I looked at the thumb. One of its canines had pierced the nail as blood was coming and must have almost met the bottom tooth. Although it must have been painful, he just shrugged it off and said that it's a good thing that blood came out, it would have been worse if it stayed underneath. Bat removed the collar and put him back in his sack and retrieved the line. Whilst all this was going on, the female appeared. She was quickly picked up and returned to her sack with the others. Bat then got down and put his arm in and brought out a dead rabbit, putting the graft in the hole to stop any escape. After a bit more digging, he took out four more. It was a fair reward for a lot of graft and a painful thumb. The hole had come to a dead end. On reaching home and putting everything away, mother made him hold his thumb in a basin of warm water and her favourite remedy – Dettol with the words to clean and stop any infection whilst drinking a well earned cup of tea before our much needed Sunday Dinner.

The second incident that comes to mind was at Mickleton Wood, on another occasion I went with them. We had started off again with two or three smaller warrens before moving into the wood to the larger ones. To save carrying the catch from warren to warren, they were hung up on the edge of the wood to be collected at the end of the day. After a quick sandwich for lunch, we moved into the wood with everything going well. It seemed as though we had a lucky break on our side when in a loud whisper Bat said, "there are two boys making their way back to the village from the direction of the catch" and with that he was gone with the words "I'll cut them off". Father and I carried on. After half an hour he returned carrying two rabbits and a satisfied smile. He told us who the boys were and said they were well known in the village for taking a fancy for other people's hard earned rewards. I often wondered if it had happened on other occasions. If Bat had not seen them they would have most certainly got away with it for it was only at the end of the day, when all the catch had been collected, they would be missed.

The word used for extracting the intestines was called "paunching". This was done by lifting the fur at the bottom of the stomach, inserting the small blade of a penknife under the skin and sliding it up to the ribcage making sure you don't puncture the inside. You will know soon enough if you do – your nose will tell you. Then, holding the rabbit by its front legs, insert two fingers below the ribcage, then with a downward movement, take out the unwanted insides. This not only stopped the meat becoming contaminated but also lightened the load for a dozen or more rabbits on a pole added a considerable amount of weight to all the other equipment that had to be transported by bicycle. If there had been a good day, there could be any number from two to three dozen. On these days Bat would come round with father to help. They would be hung up in the shed on the poles to be collected by the person that took all the catch he could get. That person was a man by the name of Mr Arthur Smith, a Birmingham businessman who had a cottage up Campden Hill where he and his wife spent the week-ends. His wife, in fact, spent a lot of her time here during the week. Their son, Norman, married Florence Biles, the eldest daughter of the village shop owners. Arthur Smith would call either on Sunday night to pick up the catch or Monday morning. If it was Monday, mother would have to tend to him for father would have gone to work. I had no idea what he paid for them but at that time rabbits were selling for one shilling and sixpence a couple – the equivalent of seven and a half pence in today's currency. There is no doubt he made a handsome profit for people in the large towns and cities were desperate for anything that would help boost their meagre rations and they would be willing to pay above the normal price. He continued collecting rabbits from father and anyone else in the village who had surplus each season during the war.

Another form of rabbiting that father employed was with the aid of a long net which was by far the easiest method with very little in the way of manual work. All that was needed was a mallet and a few four feet by one and half inch stakes. The net we had was fifty yards long by one yard wide. The ideal place was alongside hedges where the burrows were in or the edge of the grass fields or winter crops. About four stakes would be driven in the ground to which the top of the net was secured. The top of the net had very long thin draw cords to raise the bottom once in position. The net would be raised, the cord secured, then released to test the net had fallen to the ground without being caught up and then raised again and left returning in the afternoon, very quietly, so as not to disturb the feeding rabbits, drop the net down and then, moving in a wide arc in order to get behind them, walk towards the net driving the quarry into it. This method, along with snares, was the only way for one person to rabbit, for if ferrets were used in large hedges, you would need one person each side. In all forms of rabbiting, you relied on stealth, a little skill and a lot of luck.

LEAVING SCHOOL & MY FIRST JOB

This year of 1942 was a significant step up the ladder of life for me. We had been at war for almost three years and despite having America's help with vital supplies of machines and materials by sea, we were struggling to keep the enemy from over-running North Africa. Our forces fought hard to combat the continuing attacks on the Atlantic convoys by U-boats with the rising loss of life of these brave merchant seamen and ships with their precious cargoes. Although we were still getting air-raids they were not so intense as the blitz and to me, a real country boy, the war seemed a long way off as I am sure it seemed that way to thousands like me. But for me, that was about to change over the next few months for as summer approached I could think of nothing else but my birthday. Not for what I would receive or summer holidays but the fact that my school days would be over. From now on I would be getting paid for my labours but for that I needed a job and that was already waiting for me. Living more or less in the centre of the country and the countryside, we were surrounded by aerodromes that had been under construction soon after the war started which gave employment to local men and migrant workers from Ireland and the Commonwealth. So, by the time I left school they were operational. Even so, there was still much to be done. There was a gang of 12-15 men from the village and other villages that worked for a company called Henley Cables, who as the name implies was an electrical company who had the contract for laying cables all round the perimeter to provide electricity to each dispersal point where the bomber planes were stationed. One of these men happened to be my uncle whose name was Charles Carter known by everyone as "Trooper" being the nickname he was given after having served as a trooper in the Royal Horse Artillery during the First World War. Like all men working away from home, he had to take food with him plus what drink they required which usually amounted to a bottle of tea which would be cold by the time lunch was taken. (No thermos flasks then). This was where I came in for every military camp, naval base and aerodrome had a NAAFI canteen that sold tea and cake, cigarettes and sweets to the ranks below Sergeant and Petty Officers. The Sergeants and Officers had their own Mess. Henley Cables decided that their gang needed a tea boy whose job it would be to fetch the tea from the NAAFI. Through my uncle I became a tea boy. I left school in July as it broke up for the summer holidays but no holiday for me. Having left on Friday, I was to start in that role on Monday and so at 7.30 I caught Sam Bennett's bus at the end of our road together with Mr Hughes, George Hall and Aiden Williams, both 17, our neighbours. We were then taken five or six miles to Long Marston Aerodrome where I started my working life. Although you could hardly call it work, my job was to fetch tea, three times a day, the rest of the time I spent round the shed come store and foreman's office. There workmen were digging trenches with pick and shovel to a depth of over two feet by eighteen inches wide for the cables to be laid which came on huge drums - the cable being about one and a half inches thick. At each dispersal point the trench was some three and a half feet square with a spur trench leading towards the aircraft. Hard work, all done by hand, no mechanical diggers but they were well paid although I don't know how much they were getting per hour as I was being paid one shilling an hour – a fortune to my young eyes, eight shillings a day and four shillings for Saturday mornings. And then on top of that, I was getting a penny a cup three times a day during the week. I would fetch the first for ten o'clock when the men had what was then called lunchbreak. I had to walk a few hundred yards to the NAAFI where the girls would fill my large white enamel jug with hot sweet tea for six pence, so I was making over 100% profit each time. No wonder it was the best job I had ever had – such reward for so little effort. From ten o'clock until the dinner break at one, I spent watching the planes being serviced by the fitters without being able to get too close, and watching the electricians as they connected the large cables at the junctions using large metal boxes with special tools to cut and prepare the cable. Once it was all connected they would test it. It was then made water-proof by filling the box with hot pitch before replacing the lid. After a couple of weeks the men were working their way farther and farther from the NAAFI which meant it became too far for me to walk which would mean back to cold tea, so I had to take my bicycle but I brought it home Saturday lunchtime for I would often need it over the week-end. For a few weeks before and after my 14th birthday I had attended on alternative Sunday afternoons, Confirmation Classes, held in the Church Vestry taken by our Rector at the time, Revd. A J Mortimer, who lived in Back Street, opposite the Church in the fine Dower House that was the Vicarage. Our class of around six boys all similar to my age and a class of about the same number of girls attended the following week. After my birthday and on the Sundays we didn't have classes, we boys always went up around the hills after Sunday dinner. On this particular occasion we decided to go up through Hill Farm. There were six of us they were John Bryan, Jack Gaydon, Les Terry, myself and two younger boys, Colin Foster and Ray Bennett, not forgetting our dog Nip. We made our way across the fields finishing up at Hill Barn. What better place could there be for a game of hide and seek. After drawing straws to see who the seeker was, they had to face a wall and count up to fifty allowing the others to sort out suitable hiding places. Les and I ended up on top of a waggon load of hay in the centre of the barn waiting to be unloaded and stored inside for the winter. All went well with the occasional shout as someone was found. After several minutes it all seemed to go very quiet. I stood up to take a look through a hole in the roof where some of the stone slates were missing. No sign of any boys but I saw a man, some 70 yards off, approaching the double gates across the yard. Hey, Les there's someone coming I said. With that we came down off the hay, through a small door into the yard for I had to go across and release Nip before making a dash for the gate which we had entered on arrival. The farmer, a Mr Wilson, who I believe lived at Wood Meadow Farm, where my Gran had lived, recognised Les and said, Half a minute Master Terry, to which Les replied, I've got no half minutes to wait for you and with no hesitation on our part, high tailed it across the field, over the fence, catching up with the others half way across the next where we said, Did you see the farmer coming. Yes, they said and we shouted a warning. Well we never heard you and he knew Les and called for him to wait. A few evenings later there was a knock on the front door. Nip, as usual, barked a warning, Mother opened the door to find P C Perry our local constable standing there in uniform. It was obvious to me why he had come. After a few words, Mother asked him in. After explaining to my parents of his visit, he then proceeded to question me about the previous Sunday at Hill Barn. I told him exactly what happened which he wrote down in his notebook, after which he said Farmer Wilson had accused us of damaging the barn roof and was seeking damages through prosecution to pay for the repairs. I firmly denied this again replying that the roof was already missing tiles. On seeing Les the following week-end, he told me he had told PC Perry exactly the same story but being the first one to be visited he had to give the names of everyone that had been there on that Sunday. We were duly summoned to appear at the Magistrates' Court in Shipston one Saturday morning accompanied by a parent. Our individual statements were read out and confirmed as correct by PC Perry. We only had to state our name and age and heard the farmer's statement. I don't even recall him being there. After debating for a few minutes, they came up with the verdict of Unlawful Damage and ordered us to pay for the repairs. We had no chance to defend ourselves, being juveniles . The fines imposed were as follows: because I was the only one who had left school and had a job I was ordered to pay One Pound, ten shillings (or One Pound 50p decimal): the other three older boys had to pay seven shillings and six pence each (the equivalent of thirty seven and a half pence in decimal) and the two younger boys were let off - a total of Two pounds, twelve shillings and six pence in LSD. This part of my youth could have been different if my best friend Geoffrey's father, Joseph Freeman, who had worked on the farm for years until his father, who farmed it, gave it up, had been able to tell the court what he told our parents some time after that we had indeed told the truth and that the tiles had been off the roof a long, long time. To cap it all, Farmer Wilson, who was adamant that we had caused the damage, never had the roof repaired and after all these years, with Jack Gaydon and me the only two that are left, we were all the victims of a miscarriage of justice.

After being at Long Marston for around two months, all the trenches round the dispersal points had been dug so we moved some ten miles to the south west to the Aerodrome at Honeybourne which meant a longer trip. The way we travelled was towards Long Marston but instead of turning right when we reached the Broadway – Stratford Road, we turned left towards Mickleton in order to pick up the foreman who lived in a remote cottage about a mile from the village – quite a detour to pick up one person. From there we went on to Weston Sub-Edge and then took the Bretforton Road to the Drome. The Drome was about half a mile along there on the right hand side, positioned between that road and the one to Honeybourne. We were now in the employment of a company called Ward Electrics who did the same job as Henley Cables at Long Marston. The Drome here seemed much larger and had Wellington Bombers whereas Long Marston had Whitley Bombers. There seemed to be a lot to feast my inquisitive eyes on. For instance, the Bretfordton Road passed over the railway line from Stratford to Evesham and Worcester which passed through Long Marston where there was a large Royal Engineer Army Camp and Depot which had its own station to take the large quantities of equipment which passed in and out. This line ran up through Honeybourne so trains were constantly up and down. I spent a lot of my time on the bridge between my tea boy duties. Not too far from the bridge was the machine gun range which consisted of a twenty odd foot high wall, with huge buttresses at the back, each side had a sloping wall which was about four yards long at the bottom with a wall at the front of about five feet which served as a retaining wall where tons upon tons of sand were piled high against the back wall. Some 30 or 40 yards away at the front was a sturdy platform, over six feet tall where a gun turret was mounted which had two .303 Browning machine guns as they would be fitted in the nose and tail of the bombers. This is where the gunners were trained in the use of them, but without being able to traverse by ninety degrees either side as they could aboard the bombers, for obvious safety reasons by only firing straight ahead. You always knew when target practice was going to take place as a red flag would be raised above the range.

It was while working at Honeybourne I, along with countless family and relatives, were invited to my cousin Bill's wedding which was to take place at Toddenham, a village some three miles to the south of Shipston. This meant loading my bike onto the bus at twelve o'clock on the Saturday in order to ride the eight miles in time for the ceremony which was to take place at three. Not only was this the first wedding

I remember attending, but also the chance to wear my first long trousered double breasted Navy Blue suit, one that had been bought specially to wear for the first time when I was 'confirmed' on reaching the age of 14. It was like all clothes made during the war, utility, and requiring clothing coupons.

Honeybourne - a name that always reminds me of a significant chapter in our history. The war in Africa had been slow for the past few years until Hitler had sent his troops, later to become the Afrika Corps under the command of General Erwin Rommel (known as the Dessert Fox) to back up his Italian Allies. They had proved no match for the British and Commonwealth Troops, who were vastly outnumbered in man power, because the Italian guns and armour was altogether inferior. The Germans, however, were a very different story. Their troops were well trained and equipment such as weapons, transport and tanks were amongst the finest in the world. Add this to the brilliant tactician and guile of their commander and they were a force to be reckoned with. After the battles for Tobruk, a vital port, had ebbed back and forth under two or three British Commanders, Tobruk finally fell after being under siege for several weeks. Winston Churchill again replaced the Commander, and this time the General who was put in charge was Bernard Montgomery who, like Rommel, was a man for his troops and went among them, talking and encouraging and said there would be no more retreat – the only way to go was forward. The plan he had was formed around a small railway halt in the desert called El-Alamein. This was chosen for it was a perfect position for a defensive wall, having the sea on the right while on the left was an area called a Depression, a vast area of soft shifting sand that was impossible to cross with tanks and trucks. The only way the enemy could attack was head on. The defence of this line manned by three armies – the Australians holding the left flank, the British 8th Army (The Desert Rats) in the centre with the Indian and New Zealand forces on the right. The enemy made several attempts to break through, each time with the same outcome – failure, whilst taking heavy losses in men and machines. Rommel decided to fall back to recuperate and wait for reinforcements for his supply line was stretched to near its limit. His ships were under constant attack by the RAF. In the meantime, Monty, despite being under pressure from the PM to attack, stood firm and told Churchill he was in no hurry until he too had brought up massive supplies of American tanks and equipment including more troops that had been taken from the previous generals to assist in the defence of Greece which, despite this, had failed. This information was only disclosed after the war for the only source of what was happening abroad, came through the radio and papers. So one night towards the end of October in 1942, Monty launched a thousand gun bombardment on the German lines, firing thousands of shells of all sizes while, under cover of darkness, Sappers of the Royal Engineers crept forward on hands and knees with bayonets probing the ground in the search for mines. This was to clear a path to allow tanks and infantry to pass through, the path being marked on either size by white tape. However, this part of the campaign did not go as smoothly or quickly as planned for, just before dawn, only a small number of the attaching force had succeeded in making it safely through to safe ground before the pathway became a bottle neck. Luckily those caught up in it had not been seen by the German lookouts, or they were reluctant to use up precious ammunition although some tanks had been hit and been put out of action by the German's deadly 88 mm anti-aircraft gun that was used as an anti-tank gun with devastating effect. A few days later it was announced we had won the battle. The Germans had suffered heavy losses both in men and machines, and Rommel had defied Hitler's orders to stand and fight to the last man. He would not sacrifice any more men and being heavily outnumbered and outgunned, retreated to save what he could of his depleted army which he did under the constant pursuit of Monty's forces and attacks by the RAF. As it turned out, this was THE crucial turning point in the War, prompted one of Mr Churchill's famous speeches with the words of "Before El-Alamein, we never won a battle, after we never lost one".

After the gang finished at Honeybourne around Christmas time, we moved south to the Aerodrome at Shenington which is roughly midway between Shipston and Banbury. We now worked for another company who, if I remember correctly, was Eddison Swan, where the work was exactly the same. The drome was alongside the road from Shutford to the main road between Stratford and Banbury which it joined just above the famous, yet dangerously well-known Sun Rising Hill. The main part of the drome lay above the village of Upper Tysoe, a large village that spread beneath and between Sun Rising and lesser known, but still very steep and dangerous, Tysoe Hill. The village was split into three, upper, middle and lower. The east to west runway ran in almost a direct line between Upper and Middle Tysoe which must have been a bit unnerving for those in the flight path whenever the wind was blowing from the east or west for planes need a head wind when landing and taking off and there seemed a lot of flying in and out of Shenington. They used to do what they called 'circuits and bumps.' This was to give the younger and less experienced pilots more practice at landing and taking off. We had our office come store shed some seventy five to hundred yards past the west side of the runway. I spent a lot of my time watching them coming in to land, making sure I was well out of sight and danger for some of them had some hairy moments like coming too fast or too low and bouncing along the runway. I bet there were a lot of white knuckles among the crew although the co-pilot was a more experienced one who could take control if the need arose. As well as Wellington bombers coming and going, there always seemed to be other aircraft making visits like the Avro Anson a twin engine aeroplane used as a transport and carrier and sometimes carrying high ranking officers. Also,the twin engine, but slightly smaller, Oxford used to carry Government Ministers, and High Ranking Officers and Dignitaries. Occasionally a twin engined light bomber, the Bristol Blenheim and once, while I was there the twin engine Beau Fighter.

Another unusual but interesting site that we saw was human. On our way to and from Shenington after picking up our foreman, who came from the Birmingham Area and had lodgings in Shipston we went through the village of Upper and Lower Brailes where we picked up two brothers by the name of Ike and Cyril Smith. After picking up our foreman, who came from the Birmingham Area and had lodgings in Shipston. From Brailes we carried on towards Banbury where we came to a spot called Sibford Heath situated just before we turned left onto the Shutford Road leading to the aerodrome. About 300 yards before we made this left turn, were a series of sheds and chicken houses which were the home of the hermit, Theodore Lamb. The story goes, despite being an intelligent person, he was jilted as a young man and then chose to live the rest of his life in solitary isolation. He dressed in sacks and had long matted hair. The men referred to him as "The Bag Man". When we turned left you had a better chance of seeing him but if he was outside although you were much further away. I remember seeing him in Shipston with his bicycle that had no tyres and the chain being made tighter by running it over a well positioned cotton reel. With his usual sack clothing and home-made sandal type shoes, he was a scarey site for the very young. I did have the chance to meet him well before I left school for my sister Vera's boyfriend and future husband, took my parents and myself for a ride in his newly acquired car. We stopped outside Theodore's abode. He came out shaking his money tin. Once father had made a contribution of

An early photo of Theodore Lamb -
I only saw him when his clothes were hessian sacks

My first view of the experimental fast jet plane. The E28/39 at R.A.F. Edgehill (Shenington)

half a crown (two shillings and six pence or twelve and a half pence in decimal) he held quite a conversation for about five minutes. A pity we had no camera to take a souvenir picture. Shenington, as I have mentioned, always seemed to have more going on than the two previous aerodromes we had been to. One bright, cold day in February 1943 I was just killing time after dinner before going to the NAAFI to get the men's afternoon tea, when I heard a noise unlike any other I had heard. It was, as best that I can describe it, a low humming sound combined with a low whistle. On opening the door of the shed, to see where this strange noise was coming from, I saw this small yellow aircraft, coming towards me around the perimeter road. As it drew closer, I said to myself, it has no propeller at the front. On reaching the end of the runway, it turned into the chilly east wind and stopped, giving me a clear view of the back. At the end of the fuselage was a cylindrical tube with a faint orange and red glow within. There were no markings of any description on the wings, fuselage or the tail. After standing there for a few minutes, which I presumed the pilot was waiting for permission to take off, he opened the throttle and with flames and fumes which I can only describe as like the plumbers blow torch, it sped down the runway, faster than I had ever seen or heard before and was

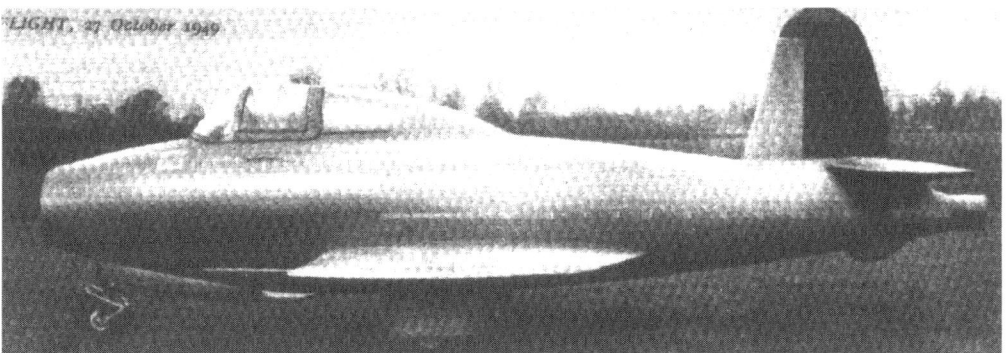

The view I had as it waited to take off

in the air and climbing at a ver fast rate of knots - a far cry from watching the bombers with engines opened up, gaining speed to haul themselves into the airt almost at the end of the runway. I stood and watched this strange little yellow aeroplane making several passes over the aerodrome at a few thousand feet, before coming back in, landing before making its way back to the hangers. I took out the Smith's pocket watch with its illuminous hands and figures that I had for my birthday from my parents which I treasured as the best present I had ever received, despite the fact that they were cheap and mass produced. It served me well and kept reasonably good time. It told me it was ten minutes past three, time for me to get on my bike and make my way round to the Shenington Road where the NAAFI was, a distance that took about five minutes. On my arrival with the tea, they asked me if I had seen the aeroplane and what was it like as they only saw it as it took off and made its passes for the noise had attracted their attention. After I had explained what I had seen, some of the older gang members remarked about it being some new fangled machine they are playing with while the two younger members wanted more details about the engine with no propeller.. Over the following few weeks the strange little aeroplane was coming out more and more but always in the afternoon. Often when the twin engines Hansons and Oxfords flew in during the mornings. It was then, that I thought, this was something special that was being tested and worked on with the the approval of the Heads of Government and Air Ministry. Little did I know or realise that this, in fact, was a development of a project that was to change aviation engineering of the future – the Jet Engine. To end this here would be like telling half a story of why something that was so important should be worked on and tested in a remote area like Shenington. One would probably say, without hesitation, security and may be that could be practically true but I and a few more could very well shed a little more light on another possibility. To explain this, I have to jump forward many years to 1996 – the year I returned to live in Warwickshire after moving three times in nine months, I moved to the village of Tysoe. Yes, the very village that lies below the old Shenington aerodrome (on which they now have a very successful gliding club.) My next door neighbour was a Mrs Megan Harris who had lived in the village on and off for many years, whose father had been the Parish Priest. In conversation one day the aerodrome came up and, of course, the little Gloster prototype jet plane that I had witnessed all those years before as a tea boy. She told me that the person behind the project who, of course, was Frank Whittle was great friends with the Marquess of Northampton who had a fine old house some two to three miles from Tysoe called Compton Wynyates. Despite the ancestral home being at Castle Ashby, near Daventry, he spent a lot of time there during the war. To save time on travelling,

Frank Whittle would stay with him to be close at hand as and when needed. Security was very tight then for Tony Lomas, a man who had spent his whole life in Tysoe, said as boys they would cycle up there at week-ends in the hope of getting a close- up view of this strange little aircraft but the military police would make them move on. It would be very satisfying to know the true facts. I have seen documentaries on Frank Whittle and his work on jet propulsion on television but there wasn't a mention of Shenington (known as RAF Edge Hill) or the work and testing carried out there. That was all carried out at Bentham and Farnborough, Hampshire. Shenington, as already mentioned, seemed to have a lot more going on there than the previous two aerodromes I had been on, not only with the jet project but it was the first one I had seen to be involved in action of a serious nature against the enemy. It was here that I witnessed bombs being towed on low trailers by tractor. These could be as many as five or six in single line, depending on the size of bombs and weight to be carried on each bomber.

It was now March 1943 and our spell at Shenington was coming to an end. Although we had spent the coldest months of the year high up on the Warwickshire and Oxfordshire border, where it would be rather bleak as I suppose all our bases were, being such vast areas of flat open spaces. I had found it so interesting and rather exciting that I had witnessed what I thought was the first jet propelled aircraft developed, produced at least in this country or even within any of the allied countries. Then far from the theatre of war as we travelled to and from Shenington each day, there was a chance to see the very person that a few years beforehand had been a feature story in the Sunday People - Theodore Lamb.

From Shenington, we moved North and a little closer to home to the aerodrome at Atherstone-on-Stour which is about a mile and a half south of Stratford. Still with the same company, Edison Swan, but the work for the men was different and for me too. The cables around the perimeter had already been completed. We would now be working away from the airfield, for during the war, military airfields like the rest of the country had strict blackout rules which made landing aircraft at night virtually impossible. There were landing lights on the runways that were used for aeroplanes that were in trouble, or for training purposes. So, to assist the crews, there were two circles of poles - the first one being a mile from the airfield, the second, a mile and a half away. Our gang had the task of digging the holes for the poles at the mile distance. This was too far from the NAAFI for me to fetch tea so, in order that the men had a hot drink and tea being rationed, (so out of the question), it was decided that at, lunch and dinner time, they would have oxo which was not rationed and could be bought at any grocery store for the princely sum of one penny each. They could be purchased singularly or in packs of six, twelve or twenty-four. Mother always had her groceries from Willersey and Mr Phillips always called on Tuesdays for the order and delivered them on Fridays. So it was easy for me and saved having to go up to the shop on Saturday afternoons. Of course, I still had to pay for them which cost five shillings and four pence a week. That was the easy part, for making Oxo you needed boiling water and being out in the country, that meant having a fire. So now was the time to put my boy scout learning into practice. I never had any problems finding kindling material or wood. There were plenty of hedgerows. It could be a little tricky if it was wet but I always made sure I had a few sheets of newspaper for such occasions which meant that boy scouts would have a little less to collect on collecting days. Once the fire was burning I then needed a billycan to boil the water. For that, I had to turn to the military, being that certain items of food came in tins such as jam. This came in round seven pound tins and was perfect for my needs, easily holding five pints. All I had to do was pierce two holes at the top with a piece of wire to form the handle to support it. I used my big enamel jug to fetch the water from the nearest source - cottages, houses or farms. For each brew, I used six oxos added when the water was boiling well and stirred in with a wooden spoon. To serve it, I used the enamel cup, and like the tea, I charged one penny a cup, so made the same amount of profit, On a few occasions, if we were anywhere near a public house, two or three of them, would, at dinner time, take a stronger beverage. The holes that the men had to dig were all marked with pegs and spaced about fifty to sixty yards apart. Each hole had to be a good four to five feet deep so to achieve that, a trench six foot long and two feet six inches wide, two men per hole had to dig it in steps. Being out in the countryside, away from the airfield, there were times that very little of interest was going on to satisfy my inquisitive eye. There were the usual farm activities but one incident I remember that comes to mind, we were working between the villages of Preston and Atherstone where two holes had to be dug across the corner of this field that contained sheep with lambs. For some reason, they had not been moved for farmers were informed and asked to move any livestock from fields that were to have the holes dug to avoid any accidents or injuries. This particular morning, on finding the sheep still in the field, the foreman told the four men, who had finished their previous holes, to carry on while he would go and see the farmer and ask him to move the sheep. The men opened the gate some fifty yards along the hedge, went through, making sure they closed it behind them and replaced the chain that looped over the post. They made their way towards the two pegs making the positions of the holes, scattering some of the sheep as they moved, when suddenly one of them shouted, "there's a ram heading this way – he doesn't look too friendly either!" On hearing this, I ran to the gate to get a better view of what was going on to see the men beating a hasty retreat towards the gate with the ram some fifty yards behind in hot pursuit. I took the chain from over the head of the gate to let four rather breathless men through minus their tools and closed it again just seconds before one very large irate ram arrived and there he stayed. There was no way he was going to let anyone near his flock. Sometime later the foreman returned with the farmer, accompanied by two sheep dogs and wearing a very broad grin with the words "No, he don't take kindly to strangers but there's no harm in him" – a remark that I think four of our gang would beg to differ. With that he opened the gate, went through with his dogs and said, "Come on you silly old devil, let's get you moved". The foreman later said that he had been given the wrong date for the stock to be moved. I didn't mind for it gave me a little amusement.

My father had worked on the airfield at Atherstone for McAlpines as a foreman over a gang of Irishmen soon after construction started shortly after the outbreak of war. Later he moved to Defford, near Pershore, Worcestershire for the same company but unlike Atherstone, where he used to cycle the five miles each day, he too like us was transported by bus. He had to leave home just after seven for the journey took almost an hour, having to make quite a few pick-ups on the way. After making this trip for well over a year, he was now back at Atherstone with the same gang and doing the same job as our gang only they were doing the holes for the outer circle. On a few afternoons when they were working within easy walking distance I visited them, after first making sure I wasn't needed as often I had to take messages for them to the office and on a few occasions to pick up various items. I remember one hot day in May, we were working near the village of Clifford Chambers where a batch of poles had been delivered but no protective creosote. Unlike telegraph or electric poles, the poles that were used for our job were not pickled. The bottom five feet of poles that went into the ground was given a couple of coats of creosote so I was sent the two miles back to the airfield to fetch some. On my arrival, the chap in charge said we only had it in five gallon drums which were far too big to carry on my bike. He said the only thing we had was an old paint tin with no lid. "That will have to do" I said. He poured out three quarters of a tin with the words "I won't fill it too full it will be less likely to slop over." So off I went towards Stratford. All went well until I had to make a left turn into the Broadway Road which is at the bottom of a small incline. So having to put my hand that was carrying the can on the handlebars to apply the brakes, I turned the corner and started to pedal when my knee caught under the tin. The next thing, I was on the floor, covered in creosote, all up the side of my face, in my hair and, of course, on my clothes. How that burnt! Luckily, it never went into my eye but the smell ! I ended up back on the site, one very smelly boy with no creosote, only what was on me and an empty tin, but otherwise unhurt. I spent the next ten minutes dowsing my face with water to ease the burning. The journey home couldn't come soon enough, to get out of the smelly clothes and into a warm bath but that didn't happen straight away. No such thing as running hot water then. First you had to fill the copper, well mother did, while I fetched sticks and small pieces of coal to get the fire going. That done, mother returned to getting the dinner while I got out of those smelly clothes and draped myself in an old mac that was many sizes too big. It served its purpose until I could get into the bath, which was some time later, after we had eaten and father had gone down to the allotment. As for my clothes, mother put them through the wash – I don't know how she did it but they came out clean and fresh without a trace of creosote. Luckily I wasn't wearing my jacket being a really warm day.

A few days after I had the fire started up to make the Oxo for dinner time when the foreman came over and said he no longer wanted Oxo. Instead, he said "I want you to go to one of those cottages and ask them for a cup of tea". I stood up and said, "You want me to go and beg a cup of tea for you". "Yes", he said. "I am sure they will if you ask them politely". I looked at him and said "I can't do that, for they, like everyone else, are on rations and it is not right to expect me to do that. I will not do it". "Alright", he said, "if you don't you will be out of a job". So the following Saturday, I picked up my last pay packet as a tea boy. The men, along with my parents, thought I had been wrongly dismissed from the most financially rewarding and easiest job that I would ever have. Looking back, it would have only been a short term occupation, not only for me but for the members of the gang which for some weeks had been reduced by two as Aiden Williams and George Hall had been called up into the Armed Forces.

MY NEW JOB

It was now almost the middle of 1943 and the news from the War was looking better on most fronts. The RAF and the USAAF were carrying out large raids on vital targets in both Germany and occupied countries. a matter of a few weeks before the papers and radio had reported the successful raids on the dams in the industrial Ruhr Valley but at a high cost for of the nineteen Lancasters that took part, eight failed to return and of these fifty-six crew, only three survived. This was the celebrated 617 'Dam Buster' Squadron whose leader was Wing Commander Guy Gibson who was awarded the VC and, as far as I know, one of only a few such awards awarded to members of the RAF during the War. While the Armies of the Allies were fighting in Algeria and Morocco during the winter of 1942/43, our forces in Italy were making very slow progress against the German Forces. The war in the Atlantic was now beginning to turn in our favour due to better technology and aircraft could now cover wider areas in their hunt for the U-boats that had played havoc with the convoys for so long. For me it was time to find another job.

We were now having our milk delivered in the afternoons by a girl that drove a blue van who told mother she needed help. Mother said I needed a job and asked would I be suitable. She said "I am sure he would – I will have a word with Mr Hicks this evening and let you know the outcome tomorrow." Two days later, I set off on my bike to travel the two miles to the village of Blackwell and Gables Farm for an interview with Mr Norman Hicks, the owner. On arrival I went through the wide entrance into a large courtyard. I knocked on the door of a large porch and waited. Out of the corner of my eye I saw movement through a large window on my right. A few seconds later the inner door opened and out stepped a lady of medium build and about five feet seven tall with black hair streaked with grey, done up in a bun at the back. This reminded me of a Roman Gypsy, whose olive complexion, now showing signs of ageing, would surely in her younger days have been one of beauty. I barely had time to say good morning, let alone introduce myself, when she said with a smile, "You must be John. Margorie said you would be coming – I'll fetch my husband – he's the one you want to see". With that, she turned and went back into, what I learned later, was the kitchen. After a while, a gentleman appeared. He, like his wife, I judged to be in his sixties with a round face and a neatly trimmed moustache. He was of medium height, well built with a figure, that despite rationing, showed good living and dressed in tweed jacket, undone, displaying an ample body, covered in a waistcoat which had a silver watch chain with numerous charms and coins hanging from it. "Morning Mr Hicks" I said, "I'm here to see if

I would be suitable for the job of assistant milkman". "Hello John", he said, "you look strong enough. How old are you?" "15" I replied. "Well", he said," let me tell you what it entails." With that,he led me across the yard to a building that resembled a garage that had double wooden doors and just inside and on the left of the entrance it turned out to be the dairy. Inside and on the right hand wall was a cooling device which resembled a radiator but with the channelled ribs running horizontal whereas radiators are vertical. This had a water pipe connected at the top of the right hand side and another at the bottom on the left hand side. Over the top was a large metal hopper with a brass tap. Along the top of this cooling device ran a channel with perforated holes at the front along its length while at the bottom another channel with a single hole in the middle. Under this was a double handed funnel that fitted into the top of a ten gallon milk churn. The funnel had two perforated metal discs that sandwiched a filter pad, all held in position by a spring metal clip. The milk was poured into the hopper, the water turned on, then the hopper tap and the milk would flow gently following the angled ribs into the churn below. Opposite this was a galvanised sink that stood on its own legs with a drain plug at one end. This was used for washing up the equipment with a metal draining board on the end that I would be using to wash up the churns and buckets used on the delivery. After showing me this he said, "The job's yours if you want it which will mean seven days a week for which you will be paid one pound, two shillings and six pence a week". Compared to what I was paid for five and a half days as a tea boy, this was a huge drop. Without hesitation I said "No Mr Hicks that is far below what I think is a fair wage. I will have to look elsewhere" and turned to make towards my bike. "Wait" he said, "how about one pound five shillings". I thought for a few seconds and said "alright", knowing that there were few options left so close to home. He said "you will start at 7.30 and finish about 5.00 or when the washing up is done". So the following Monday I became a milk boy. My fellow rounds person was Marjorie Land who I think was in her early twenties. She had red hair and originated from Canterbury. She lived in at the farm but she wasn't in the Land Army. When I arrived on that first morning the van was parked outside the dairy with the backdoors open. Marjorie was about to start loading and despite being quite slim she was very strong and would lift a ten gallon churn of milk and put it in the van. Now there were two of us, it made it that much easier. The milk we used for the Shipston round was from the night's before. Wwith some three hundred odd customers, we needed around four churns. This was, of course, before we had bottles. We each had a can, oval in shape, with a lid that had brass hinges while inside was a metal bar with the two measures, one half pint and the other a pint. Each can held about three gallons but we never put more than about two in –

that was enough to carry. We were usually in Shipston, having served our first customer who lived on the top of the hill two hundred yards past the level crossing that used to be on the Darlingscote Road, when the 'bull' bell sounded at eight o'clock at Mayo's Timberyard to start their working day. I understand the reason for calling it that was it sounded like a bull bellowing. As it was, like all their used saws and machinery driven by steam. It sounded again at five in the evening. Depending on which way the wind was blowing, you could hear it in Ilmington. I first became aware of Mayo's during the early years after moving to the new Council Houses and long before they were renamed Bennett Place. Their two teams of horses and timber waggons passed along the Armscote Road at the bottom of our garden on their way to collect the huge tree trunks that had been felled out this way. You could hear them coming from a fair distance away. You can imagine the sound that the teams of four horses made with their thirty-two large iron-shod hooves, plodding along the road. They would usually come along about half past eight before we went to school. Mother would say "Mayo's are coming – if you go down the garden you will see Joe Cooke." He was a distant cousin who was a carter for them. He lived in Shipston and occasionally you would see them when they returned loaded with as many as three huge trunks of our mature hardwoods like Elm, Oak and Beech while there could be four or five smaller ones of Ash. The waggons used for hauling these were designed and made especially for the purpose and entirely different from the waggons used for cereal crops for they had a body totally unlike the farm wagons. The front and rear axles were connected by a large hard wood beam down the centre with large cross beams that stood up above the wheels which were all the same size. They were about the same size as the front wheels of a farm waggon but much sturdier. At the end of each cross beam were square slots that held upright posts. These served two functions. First to be used as ramp slides to load the trunks and the second to help secure them once they were loaded. The loading was done by horse-power. First the waggon was drawn alongside the trunk, chains attached to it and then from the opposite side of the waggon, one or two trace horses would haul it up the slides and on to the waggon. This procedure carried on until both waggons were loaded. It was then a case of hauling it back to the yards in Shipston. Now you could understand why they needed a team of four for each waggon for these massive trunks would weigh over a ton each in their green state and then you had the added weight of large branches plus the heavy waggon. It would take a lot of power to haul them up the hills. Going down was an entirely different matter for no matter how big and strong these horses were there was only one in the shafts and no way could they hold back a load of four or five ton so to do this they used skids. These were iron channels about a foot in length, attached by a strong chain to the centre beam and hung on a hook when not in use. On reaching the top of the hill they would, depending on the severity of the descen, place one or two skids under the front of the rear wheels – simple but effective. Farm waggons also had these but light trolleys had brakes that were applied by turning a wheel at the front that applied wooden block brakes to the rear wheels. Mayo's also used a steam tractor to haul timber from distances that were often too far for horses to travel in one day. The driver for this was a man by the name of Jack Bramble. Another form of transport they used was a lorry used for deliveries. We often saw it coming along the Armscote Road loaded high with wooden crates, destined for the market gardens at Quinton, Mickleton and the ones in the Vale of Evesham. The driver of this was Mr Roland Humphries from Blackwell. It was while delivering milk in Shipston that I realised what a large and important company Mayo's was, for up to the time of the Second World War and the factory started by the Peak Engineering where Petiphers Garage is now, Mayo's along with the Shipston District Council were the largest employers in the town. They owned two yards, both of them up the Stratford Road. The one on the right ran from the Ellen Badge Hospital up to and including the large red-brick building. This was where all the steam driven machines and saws were housed while in the yard all the sawn timber was stacked including tree trunks all sawn length-wise in planks in various thicknesses, each one having spaces between to allow air circulation. This also helped with the seasoning for in those days, long before the practice of kiln dried timber, it is said that hard wood timber took around seven years before it was really seasoned. It was in this yard that the crates were cut and nailed together. It was an ongoing job. Great quantities were used by market gardens to distribute their produce. The second yard was on the opposite side of the Stratford Road and ran right through to the railway station. This was where the stables were plus other buildings which included an office. This, like the other yards, covered a lot of ground which they needed to store the amount of timber they dealt with. It was also within easy reach of the field where the horses were turned out. This field was known as The Brickle and reached by the lane that ran up to the rear of the workhouse. It ran right through to the Darlingscote Road. It was quite a sight, for you would often see a dozen or more horses grazing there. Now, it is part of the Tileman's Industrial Estate.

I think now is the time to mention the men that fell the trees for Mayo's. The gang consisted of three brothers and a nephew. They were Sam, Jim and Llewelyn (known as Butcher) Handy and Sam Freeman who was always known as "Nidgel". They all lived in a row of cottages on Flea Bank which is almost opposite our old cottage in Front Street. For Butcher this was about to change for around the time of King George VI Coronation in 1937, Mrs Coaton, our neighbour at No. 1 at that time, moved to a little cottage next to Biles Butcher's Shop in Middle Street. So Butcher, along with his wife and daughter, Edna, became our new neighbours. Shortly after they moved in, Mrs Handy's father, Joby Stanley, moved in with them. He was a nice, active man who did all the gardening and spent a lot of time riding his bicycle down to the allotments at Armscote Meadow. The Handys travelled to work in a small blue lorry which was garaged at the top of Whitehouse Lane. It could only accommodate two in the cab so the other two had to ride in the back. Each evening they would bring a load of wood back that was only good for firewood, take it up the lane to the back of their cottages where they had a saw mill and, once it had seasoned for a year or two, spent Saturday mornings sawing it up into blocks and selling them for a shilling (five pence) a truck-load. Aubrey Edwards and I had the job of fetching it during the autumn and winter. It helped eke out the coal. Jim was very clever with wood and had a workshop where he made among other things, wheelbarrows, including the wheels.

During the Shipston round I got to know a lot of people, like the Town Crier whose name was William (Bill) Hudson or as most called him, Toughen. He also acted as caretaker for the Shipston District Council and lived in the house that was part of their offices and yard situated on the corner of New Street and West Street. This was the time when Councils had their own workforce, both tradesmen and labourers and were responsible for both sewage and water. One of the biggest customers that I delivered to was Nasons, the Bakers. Mr Nason and his assistant, Arthur, a small man who was only just over five feet tall and a huge football fan who supported Liverpool, did the baking when Mrs Nason ran the shop and cafe. Their premises were next to what is now John Lyne's Hardware store. Their's was the smaller of the two Co-op stores that are there now. I used the back entrance into the bakery itself to deliver. The smell of new baked bread and cakes that met you as you entered really brightened the day for me in the worst weather. They used to have, on average, six pints of milk a day. We also delivered at least Marjorie did, to the Bell and the George Hotels. One piece of equipment I haven't mentioned, and an important one, is a plunger. As you will be aware, when milk stands for a while, the cream rises to the surface. So before refilling your can you had to remove the lid and with the plunger – a metal tube about a yard long, bent round at the top to form a handle while at the bottom is a round disk some five to six inches in diameter, perforated with large holes and riveted to a plate at the bottom of the stem to prevent any liquid from getting inside, while being plunged up and down quite vigorously to re- distribute the cream. This had to be done on a regular basis depending on how long between each refill. There were occasions when we would be short of milk. When this occurred we had to replenish from a milk parlour on the Darlingscote Road between Telegraph Street and Sheep Street that was owned and run by a Mr Haines. This had been arranged between him and Mr Hicks. We were always sure that this milk was produced that particular morning for, like all dairy farmers, there was a milk stand outside. Here the previous day's milk would be placed in churns labelled with the farm's name and address plus the quantity in each churn to be collected each morning by the milk lorry. Having picked it up, and dropped off the empty churns for the next day, the milk was taken to the dairy which was at Moreton-in-Marsh or Chipping Campden – I'm not quite sure which. Milk, like bread, was not rationed during the war for the Ministry knew that neither had a long shelf -life so people wouldn't purchase more than their needs (no fridges or freezers then). Housewives would scald the milk during hot thundery weather in the summer to prevent it going sour. The Ministry of Food also had inspectors that would turn up without notice and at any time on your delivery round and take samples to make sure the water and fat content were within the law. In other words, to make sure you weren't taking the cream or adding more water. They took two samples from any container, labelled each small container with the farmer's name, address and the date – sealed it, took one and gave us the other. This was taken back and put on the shelf in the dairy, where after a few days it would start to separate. Once this happened the results would be recorded and the previous sample disposed. We usually finished the Shipston round about 11.30, then it was back to Blackwell and the van unloaded. Any milk that we had left would be kept to one side. Then all the churns, cans, measures and plunger would be washed with hot water and soda, using a handled scrubbing brush made for the purpose, rinsed thoroughly a couple of times and then drained. The churns for the afternoon milk and the hand cans, measures and plunges for the Ilmington round, including the morning milk was already in the churns for that round. It had been put through the cooler by one of the milkers, mostly by Gladys, a Land Army girl. She was a big girl but a wonderful milker for it was all done by hand. Besides Gladys, who came from Crewe, there was Henry who came with the Hicks' when they moved from Basingstoke - he lived in. There was also Walter Brewer, who came from Shipston, and an elderly man who everyone called Uncle George. He was Mr Hicks' brother for he had the same features but with a much larger moustache, dressed the same and wore a pork pie hat just like him. He also lived in. No wonder they needed a big farmhouse for Jim, their youngest son, also lived at home. As far as I know, never got married and some years later, long after the war, he went to Argentina where he raised beef cattle and horses. He was a fine horseman and rode a lot in point to point races. Gladys lodged in the village. There were three more sons:

Jack, the oldest who owned and farmed at Aylesmore, a farm between the villages of Whatcote and Brailes; Willie who farmed in Hampshire and David who finished up owning Rowborough Garage and Filling Station on the Fosseway and a daughter, whose name escapes me.

The Ilmington round, not as big as Shipston, involved a lot more walking being many more alleys and no through roads where the van couldn't go. It still used to take some two and a half to three hours, which like Shipston, took longer in winter with snow and ice to contend with. That first winter was particularly bad for the footpaths, especially in Shipston, were treacherous and having to carry cans made getting about extremely difficult. We were lucky enough to stay on our feet although we came mighty close on a number of occasions. The van had to be fitted with chains, otherwise we would never have got round for this ages before road gritting took place. Even chains didn't stop us getting stuck a few times. Shortly after the winter we became more modernised. Instead of cans we now had bottles – glass ones – which made delivery much easier and quicker but involved more dairy work as not only did we have to wash the bottles but fill them by hand too. This was done with a jug. These tasks were mostly done by me. First, I washed them with hot soda water, bottle brushes and mops, rinsed in clean water and placed upside down in crates to drain. The bottles which were of four sizes, half pint, one pint, pint and a half and two pints, all with N A Hicks, Gable Farm, Blackwell in red letters printed on them. Once the crate was full, the tops had to be put on. This was done with glossy cardboard discs that came in long tubes which held about 500. These were pressed on by hand all round to make a secure seal. To open them, there was a perforated circle in the centre, allowing you to remove it when pierced. Each round had two batches of bottles enabling them to be washed and drained well before being filled for the next delivery. As the days grew longer with lighter evenings, after tea I would join the lads in Windmill Hill for a game of football. This was when it was a field and way before it was built on. It was on such an occasion that I went for the ball with John Bryan when I felt an excruciating pain in my right knee. It was so painful I couldn't straighten it or put it on the ground. I had to hop all the way home by which time it was very badly swollen. There was no way I could go to work or even get to the doctors until Saturday morning. Luckily for me, my two youngest sisters were now living at home, having given up domestic service as, in fact had all my sisters. Rita, my eldest sister was now in the NAAFI and stationed in Staffordshire, while Vera was living in Shipston and working in the office at the Peak, situated where Pettifers Garage is now. The Peak was a factory doing vital work, in fact I think they manufactured small armed gun barrels. My two youngest sisters also worked there but in the machine shop. They, being at home, meant that

Vera had to have lodgings as we had no room for three grown up young ladies. My two youngest sisters were picked up by Sam Bennett's bus which picked up workers round all the outlying villages. It was on this bus that my sisters helped me on Saturday morning to see the Doctor at the Shipston Surgery. I saw Dr McMullen who said I had to rest it for three weeks and to apply cold compresses three times a day to reduce the swelling. It was six weeks before I could return to work. Poor Marjorie had to do the rounds all by herself although she did have some help with the dairy work.

It wasn't long after this that Marjorie left and went back to Canterbury so we had a new land army girl by the name of Nora Morgan. She was a very pretty girl, 18 years old, who could drive and came from Birmingham. This, of course, initially meant the rounds took longer as Nora had to learn

My two youngest sisters, Elma on the right and Myra on the left, with their close friend Muriel Clarke at the time they worked in a small arms factory 1943/44

them and, of course, the area was also completely new to her. After a couple of weeks, she soon picked it up and for the next few months all went well until Mr Hicks decided that the Ilmington round could be done by pony and trap. Whether this was to save petrol I have no idea as petrol, like most things, was rationed. People lucky enough to have a car, but unlike now very few actually owned one, were allowed very little petrol. In fact, many cars owned by the better off were put into storage for the rest of the war. However, the pony and trap idea proved to be a bit of a disaster. The pony being young and new to the job had to be led from stop to stop and held while one of us did the deliveries. This made it more than double the time to complete the round and then the journey back to Blackwell proved to be hectic to say the least as every time we moved, the empty bottles rattled in their crates frightening the pony resulting in me having to lead it all the way back. Goodness knows where we would have finished up if I had tried to ride. There is no doubt the idea was sound as ponies had been used for decades on deliveries. It was unfortunate that our pony was so young and inexperienced to make it worthwhile carrying on. Given time, it would have paid off but I think Mr Hicks feared he would be left with no one to deliver his milk, so it was back to the van.

After a few months, Nora decided it was time for her to move on. For me it was a very sad time for we had developed a really good partnership and had hit it off from the start. After she left, Mr Hicks drove me round leaving me to do all the deliveries. I knew he was having a job to find the right person to fill Nora's place. After a few days, he sent Henry with me which helped as he delivered under my instructions and learnt the round well after a few weeks. One morning on arrival, Henry told me that a replacement had been found for Nora but there was a problem, the new girl couldn't drive. He said he had been given the job of teaching her and she would be starting in a week's time. This meant there would be no room in the van for me which meant I would be spending time round the farm. So, after finishing the dairy work of washing bottles and they had left for the Shipston round, and once the morning milk had been filtered and cooled, I would bottle it ready for the Ilmington round. The new Land Army girl arrived and, on our first morning, I thought she looked familiar. She was, in fact, the niece of Mr and Mrs Hughes who lived along our road at No. 12, who years before had visited them from time to time when they lived at No. 4. Her name was Gladys and must not be confused with Gladys from Crewe! was slim, blonde and good looking – in fact not the type of girl that would be in the Land Army but someone that would be more suited to office work. She had been married to a member of the RAF but had joined the Land Army when they had separated. For the next couple of months I did odd tasks around the farm. An example would be fetching mangols with a horse and cart, that were in a long bury in a field which was about three quarters of a mile away from the farm, and taking them to the barn where I then put them through a hand shredder before mixing them with meal to be given to the cows at milking time. Another task that I did, even when doing the milk round, was pumping the water into the tank that was installed in the attic. The pump was situated in the courtyard by the side of the house. The pump was there solely for this purpose as there was no spout to extract water directly from it. The water was obviously used in the house as well as the dairy and would often take twenty minutes or more to fill the tank. It was always a relief to hear it coming out of the overflow meaning the tank was full and you could give your arms a rest. This was long before a lot of villages had running tap water or mechanical pumps. One morning I well remember, Henry and Gladys came out to load the van when Henry took a pencil from his pocket and started writing on the garage door - "There! That is a date that will come every year but not the same as this year". He had written 1, 2, 3, 4, 5. That day's date was, of course, the 12th March 1945 and just two months before the war in Europe ended and for me, almost two years of being a milkman or should I say, milk boy for I was still four months short of my 17th birthday.

When the war in Europe came to an end on 8 May 1945, a day which became known as VE Day, Mr Churchill said in one of his many famous speeches that we should allow ourselves a day of celebration. This meant a day off, bonfires, street parties and church bells, woken from their long silence as they would only have been rung during the war if the Germans invaded. It was truly a joyous time, especially for the armed forces, the factory workers, shops and office staff alike but people in the country, farmworkers had to carry on. Bread still had to be baked and delivered, likewise milk, but everyone went about their work with an extra spring in their step and a smile on their face. It was an exciting time. By the way, the price of milk then was four pence halfpenny a pint, making a pint of milk per day for one week two shillings and seven and a half pence – 13p today.

Working in Blackwell I became friendly with the local boys. One family in particular by the name of Humphreys had quite a nice big house which had got a lot of ground and outbuildings where they bred pigs and kept poultry. One day they said their dog had given birth to six puppies but their father had told them they couldn't keep them, as they already had two dogs. He was going to sell them when they were old enough to be taken from their mother. If however, I would like one, I could go round after work and choose one – in fact having the pick of the litter. I couldn't wait to get round there and see them and after I had finished for the day, off I went. On seeing them, one stood out and caught my eye. Without hesitation I said "That's the one I would like". It was just like its mother with rough hair and markings of mostly white with two blue patches on its body. When I asked Mr Humphreys how much - he replied "ten shillings but they won't be ready to leave their mother for another four weeks". This suited me for ten shillings was nearly half a week's wages. I said that's fine but could I give them two shillings and six pence a week (also known as half a crown) otherwise I couldn't afford to pay it all at once. He agreed, and for the next four Saturdays I went round after being paid and handed over the money but the fourth time was the best for now I was going to take home my very own dog. All right, we had Nip but she was the family's dog and while we never had her from a pup, we still thought the world of her. As I carried the little bundle of fluff home inside my jacket, I wondered for the first time, what sort of a reception she would get, not only from Nip but from the rest of the family. I thought dad wouldn't mind but I wasn't sure how mother would take it for I hadn't told them before. Mother would be the one looking after her during the day with house training and taking her down the garden twice a day. I hadn't even thought of that – all I knew was that I had my own puppy and I was going to call her 'Patsy'. On arrival home, I opened the back door and said "Hello mum – I've got something to show you" and with that produced Patsy from my jacket. She took one look and said, "You can take that back from where you got it". Of course, that was out of the question. "We don't want another dog" she said "Nip will kill it". "No she won't" I said and with that I put Patsy down by Nip and said "Don't you hurt her, she is your new friend". Nip looked at her and as Patsy approached her she gave a low warning growl and with that I said "No Nip" and she just walked away. "Please mum", I said "she will be alright". "Well, we will see what your dad says about it" and so with father's approval, Patsy became part of the family. In those days, once a dog became six months old, you had to have a dog licence obtained from the Post Office for the sum of seven shillings and six pence, ($37^1/2$p) renewable every year. The only dogs that were exempt were sheep dogs owned by farmers and shepherds. Once Patsy became six months old, father started taking her along with Nip shooting and ferreting which she took to like a duck to water. He said she would, on finding something in a hedge, bush or form - that is the word used when rabbits sit out in the fields during nice dry days in tuffs of rough grass where they are hidden from view. She would stand there perfectly still with one front paw held off the ground. Sometime later I saw this for myself. I was down on the allotments in early summer, doing what I usually did, weeding. I had the dogs with me, Nip being that much older was lying down close-by while Patsy with her useful energy was hunting round to see what she could find. I happened to look up and saw her up by the hedge that separated the allotment from the field above, standing perfectly still in the set position, so I had to investigate. She stayed absolutely motionless as I approached. As I parted the long grass I disturbed a partridge that was sitting on a nest. As it disappeared through the hedge it left behind a site that I had never seen before or since – a clutch of 16 putty coloured eggs. I patted her and told her she was a good girl and led her away thinking that the bird would return and lay more as they can have up to 18 in a single clutch. I marked the spot where they were in the hope that she would have produced more eggs, when I returned in a day or so. On telling my parents when I came home, father and mother both said she wouldn't return now as she had been discovered. This proved to be the case for when I returned a day or so later, the eggs were still there as I had left them, quite cold. So rather than leave them I gathered them up and took them home where they were served up on our breakfast plates with some of our bacon ration. Even though Patsy was a terrier in looks, she was somewhat shorter than Nip by about two inches. She was a crossbred, her father being a Springer Spaniel so she had some of his genes, enabling her to set game. She was easy to train, I taught her to beg and if I said 'play' to her she would lift her front paws up and down as if she was playing the piano. She, like Nip, was really good company, always pleased to see you. No wonder they are called Man's best friend.

MY DREAM JOB

One evening on arriving home, mother told me that she had got me a job in the stables at Armscote for the Honourable, Mrs Stella Cardiff with whom my two youngest sisters had started their working life as domestic servants a few years before this. This was exciting news for me as I had always wanted to work with horses. I had wanted to be a jockey but, of course, that was never going to happen so this was the next best thing. The Head Groom was an Irishman by the name of Matthew Darcey, known by all as Matt. He was a first class horseman and a very good teacher. Mrs Cardiff was married to a serving Colonel so was away a lot. She had a son called David whose surname was Jackson by her first husband who was the major shareholder of the News of the World Newspaper. He had, unfortunately, died when David was quite young but had left his mother very well off besides leaving David a substantial amount in trust, to be inherited it on reaching the age of twenty-one. David was away at boarding school most of the time and only came home for the holidays. He, like his mother, loved horses so had ponies which I looked after and learnt to ride on. Mrs Cardiff had about ten or a dozen horses. She had show-hunters, point to pointers as well as driving ones. She did a lot of hunting, usually two or three times a week, starting with cub hunting in September, which meant an early start and then normal hunting where they usually met at a quarter to eleven and finished in the afternoons depending upon the time of year. When hunting finished around February, the point to point season was in full swing. In those days the meetings were held on Saturdays and Bank Holidays. There were always large crowds on Easter Monday at Spring Hill, near Broadway where the North Cotswold Hunt held their meeting. Father always attended this meeting. He used to set off on his bicycle around 10.30 with his packed lunch and bottle of beer, for the long hard uphill journey took around two hours and involved a lot of walking but he enjoyed it. Mrs Cardiff hunted with the Warwickshire Hounds and their Point to Point fixture was held at Chesterton on ground owned by the well known amateur rider, owner and breeder, John Thorne (of Spartan Missile fame). We had at least, while I worked there, a couple of runners. Mrs Cardiff always rode in the ladies race with mixed success for she didn't like starting and so lost many lengths approaching the first jump. Once over that she was fine. The times she finished second, she should have won if she had started with the others. All the transport that we used came from the next village of Halford and was owned by Percy Lomas. He had two or three cattle trucks which were used for all livestock to and from markets while the hunting and point to point was only used during the seasons.

Each year, on the day of the Warwickshire Hunt Meeting at Chesterton, our blacksmith, Mr Harry Hancock and his son, Lesley, who did all our shoeing and trimming even the horses that were pensioned off and lived outside, would come up for the day out. They, like me, would ride in the back over the top of the cab with all the gear that had to be taken. The cost of shoeing a horse then was five shillings a shoe, a pound all round. They made all the shoes in their forge and carried them with all their tools of the trade on their bicycles. They obviously had a pattern set for each horse hanging up in their forge. They would visit us at least one day a fortnight or more if we were racing. Then they would come up the day before and change the shoes from the everyday ones to racing plates on each horse that was running. Racing plates were made of light steel or aluminium and then replaced again a couple of days after. During the summer, the only ones left in were the show horses and David's ponies for he, like his mother, rode out nearly every day when he was home. The rest were turned out in the fields. We had two show hunters and a half breed hackney that was shown in driving classes. The hunters that were shown were in classes. There was a class for hacks, lightweight, hunters, medium hunters and heavyweight hunters. The classes being defined by what weight each class could carry and this depended on the build and confirmation of the horse. We had a heavyweight and a middleweight. The middleweight was six years old and a liver-chestnut mare by the name of Carmen Miranda - obviously named after the lady of that name who sang and acted and dressed in brightly coloured clothes and wore extraordinary head gear of coloured feathers and plumes and even artificial fruits. She was an extraordinary character. Our Hunter of the same name was well named for she was a showy character who was quite excitable but without any malice. At the shows, Mrs Cardiff would usually get riders that specialised in riding show hunters. David Tatlow, a Warwickshire man, was a well known one. They had the knowledge and ability of showing them to their highest potential. The judges would ride each contestant round the ring, sometimes twice before making their decision and awarding the rosettes accordingly. Although she was a nice mare, she never managed to win a class due to what I think was her excitable nature which unfortunately cut her showing days short which I will explain later. The heavyweight was an eight year old bright bay with black points, ie mane, tail and legs from below the knee and hocks. He was a striking individual who went by the name of Lord Godolphin. I only had the chance to sit on him a few times but it was an experience that I will never forget. I can only describe it as to the equivalent of sitting in a plush leather armchair or soft rubber ball. It's no wonder he swept all before him. We went to all the big shows – The Malvern, The Bath & West, Newbury and countless others and he won show after show. It is no wonder Mrs Cardiff was offered vast sums of money for him but she never sold him – he truly was a super champion with a wonderful manner and a great temperament. In fact he was a perfect gentleman in and out of the stable. Beside the loose boxes in the main stable blocks, there were three more boxes in a small yard at the back which comprised a small hay stall with an individual small building attached. This was where the chaff cutter was kept and where I spent hours cutting the hay into chaff which was mixed with the rolled oats. Before the days of all the commercial feed products this was what th horses were fed on. Besides the usual hay which, incidentally, was brought in by a specialist hay straw merchant, only the best hay was used which Matt inspected and approved before allowing them to unload it. It really was sweet smelling and all cut and trussed by a specialist hay tier like Mr Peachey who lived along our road at No. 6. At the end of this small yard was quite a large building called a Riding School. Like all the other buildings up there it was built of wood. The side next to the road and the far end were boarded from floor to eaves while the side that overlooked the garden and the front, which had a wide door, were only boarded two thirds the way up, allowing the light and air in. It was in here that our middleweight hunter, Carmen Miranda was put to stretch her legs while Matt was away for the day. It was a lovely sunny day in early summer and I could hear the sound coming from the garden of a lawn mower being used by Harry Wilkins (Tony's father) mowing the extensive lawns. Nothing unusual about that for it happened every week during spring, summer and early autumn. However, on this particular day, Harry appeared over the side and said "Can I give this box of grass to the horse". I said "yes" for we often gave them grass during the summer that was cut with the scythe. Thinking nothing of it he tipped the box of grass over the sides of the school which frightened her and being very excitable, she took off. With one mighty leap she tried to jump out at the far end but there not being enough clearance she hit her head on the cross beam with such force, it knocked her back on her haunches. She must have seen stars. She stayed there for a few seconds before getting to her feet and coming to me and putting her head over the door where I could see immediately the damage she had done to herself. She had broken the bone between the eyes and nose, being more or less skin and tissue, the only bit of covering there is I could see the pointed end of the bone and the steady trickle of blood down her white blaze. My first thought was get her out of there. I fetched her head collar from the hook on the side of the loose box, put it on her and led her into a loose box, where I took it off. Then I went down to the back door of the big house to ask Mrs Darcey, Matthew's wife, who was the cook and housekeeper, to ring the vet for Carmen needed treatment and would she also tell Mrs Cardiff. She said she would when she came home. The vet, who was John Thorne's brother, whose name I think was

Peter and practised near Leamington Spa, arrived around an hour and a half later, gave her an injection after examining the damage. He then cleaned the area with warm water and then dusted the wound with pink antiseptic powder, giving me the box and telling me to dust it with this three times a day as it would help keep the flies away. He also said that he would be in touch with Mrs Cardiff to discuss what further treatment the horse would need and left. I relayed this message to Mrs Darcey so that she could inform Matt and Mrs Cardiff, gave the mare some hay and water and left for home, wondering how they would react. Would they blame me for letting the gardener tip the grass in? On telling mother what had happened she said don't worry, you thought you were doing the horse a kindness. I am sure Mrs Cardiff and Mr Darcey will see it that way too. The next day as I rode to work I wondered what the outcome of the day before would be. Would I be held responsible for the injury to Carmen but thankfully my fears were totally unjustified as Matt told me that I had reacted in exactly the right way and that Mrs Cardiff had said that I was completely free from blame much to my relief. I was also told that in a few days the mare would undergo an operation. The vet saw no reason, other than a small scar, why she wouldn't be perfectly all right. A few days later the vet and an assistant arrived shortly after nine o'clock and unloaded all the equipment needed to carry out the operation which was to be held in the very place where the accident had happened and where a bed of straw had been put down for the purpose. Matt led her in where the assistant proceeded to place ties, strapped to each leg just above the fetlock.

Each one was then attached to a pulley from which was a long length of rope which, when pulled, would draw the legs together, helping to ensure her going down in the right position. Meanwhile the vet had placed a mask over her nose which was held in place by straps attached to her head collar. Once he started applying the anaesthetic we, that is the two gardeners, Jack Mallett and Harry Wilkins, Bill Foster, a groom who had returned after being demobbed from the RAF and myself, had taken up the rope and on the command from the vet of pull, just as her front legs started to buckle, this we did resulting in her going down gently and perfectly placed. Although I couldn't see the operation, being on the rope attached to the legs, I distinctly heard the crack as the jagged part of the broken bone was snipped off. I suppose the thing from start to finish took less than an hour. While the vet was finishing off, his assistant removed the straps from her legs followed by the mask covering her nose. Then the vet administered an injection to her neck and shortly after, she slowly regained consciousness, raising her head. Gradually she pulled up her legs to the normal lying position where she stayed for a minute or two before getting to her feet, still unsteady with Matt at her head. After a little while the vet said walk her round the school for a few times with the words she'll be fine. With that he packed up his gear and left after leaving another box of pink antiseptic powder as before to apply twice a day. He returned some ten days later to remove the stitches and a couple of weeks later you could hardly notice that anything had happened apart from a slight indentation and, with her hair growing back we were able to show her again but without her ever winning her class. During early December 1945 the War was over, the Japanese having surrendered in August after the Americans had dropped two atomic bombs on the cities of Nagasakii and Hiroshima in Japan with devastating affects and untold loss of life, horrendous injuries and burns from the blast and radio-active fall-out and with most of the buildings being of wood, vast areas were flattened and burnt. It was truly horrific. The pictures that appeared in the newspapers shocked everyone. With this country in the process of rebuilding and the armed forces gradually returning to civilian life, life in general was getting back to normal. Although rationing was still in place with the continuing shortage of the basics required, things could only get better. For me and the team at Armscote House, the hunting season was getting into full swing. I remember one particular day, there was a mid-week meeting in the village of Warmington near Edgehill and Banbury. Mrs Cardiff was, of course, attending. We, on the morning of the meet, loaded up two horses on Lomas' cattle truck, a really good point to pointer that Mrs Cardiff used to ride and one I looked after by the name of Mountain Knight, and Carmen Miranda. Then, as now, all point to pointers had to be fairly and regularly 'hunted' to qualify to run. This was verified as each time you attended a meet, the Master of the Hunt signed a ticket for each horse which had to be submitted to the Hunt Secretary before the Point to Point season started, towards the end of January. Matt, like all head grooms in charge of training pointers, didn't want their charges having all day hard hunting and no hunting at all after Christmas. Hence, the two horses going on this particular day and I with them, so I had to dress smartly in a brown hacking jacket, fawn breeches, brown leggings and boots and, of course, collar and tie. Not that I would be riding but to make sure the horses were well turned out. This involved, whichever horse was going firstit was saddled up correctly, firstly for rider safety as you didn't want any slip-ups such as saddle slipping and, secondly, it had to be comfortable for the horse. It was also important that the horse wasn't sweating as some could when enclosed in a horse-box and of excitable nature - such as Carmen - but on this particular day she was fine. Having the other horse with her helped and as she was the first to be hunted, she was the last to be loaded. On arrival in the village and finding a suitable parking place to unload, I, on a rare occasion was able to ride in front. The driver, having let the back down, it was now just after a quarter past ten and with Mrs Cardiff due after half past ten, I untied the travelling rug and folded it back over Carmen's quarters. Then passing under the horse's neck I fetched the saddle, bridle, saddle-pad and cloth along with a dandy brush and a rubber (a soft cloth) and a martingale. I then proceeded with putting the saddle on. The girth was already fitted to the offside of the saddle, so by undoing the rope of her head collar, from the ring on the horsebox, I slipped the neck strap of the martingale over her head and placed it at the base of her neck, then dropping the girth that was folded over the saddle down, I reached underneath, took the end of the martingale and pulled it through her front legs, holding it with my left hand. Now, I reached through with my right and pulled the girth while placing it through the loop of the martingale, clinching it to the saddle with leather straps, usually two, and pulling them up fairly tight. Now it was time to fit the bridle. First hooking it over my left arm and holding the reins in the left hand, I undid the head collar and let it hang by the rope while placing my right arm around the back of the head and holding her nose. Then passing the reins over her head, the bridle was taken up the front of the face, gently easing the bit in the side of her mouth. Now, taking the bridle over the ears, you fastened the throat strap, then the kerb chain. This is held by a thin strap from one side of the barred bit to the other by a link in the middle of the kerb chain, the chain being held each end by a hook on each side of the bit. This chain was only fitted on double bridles or bridles with barbed bits, each of these bridles had two reins. The bottom rein was only used to restrain a headstrong horse, as when pulled it tightened the kerb chain under the horses chin, thus making its head rise, giving the rider more control. Once all that was done, it was the turn of the nose band. You had to pass it through the other end of the martingale. This served two purposes. First it prevented the saddle from slipping back and also stopped the head from being raised too high. All that remained now was to pull the forelock from under the brow band, (the forelock is part of the mane at the front of the head). Finally now, I could take the tail bandage off, wipe her over with the rubber and brush her mane and tail with the dandy brush (this is a brush with stiff bristles). The time now was about half past ten so time to take Carmen out and walk her round to stretch her legs, then fully tighten the girth. This is always done a little while after saddling up as horses always blow themselves up when you first sinch up the girth. Next it was time to lift up the front legs, pulling them forward to make sure nothing was pinching. Then it was just a case of walking around and waiting for Mrs Cardiff to arrive in her pale blue MG car – pale blue being her racing colours. All the doors in the main stable yard, including the large doors of the barn, where her car was garaged along with various traps, all the field gates, also the doors into the property from Middle and Back Street were painted pale blue. She eventually arrived, came over and said "Good Morning John". She always called me by my first name –" is everything alright". I replied by saying "Good morning Madam, all is well." With that I pulled the stirrups down to the end of the leathers, took the end of the straps back under them and checked the girth one more time, pulled the rug off Carmen's quarters and gave Mrs Cardiff a leg up. She said "I will be back to change over between 1.30 and 2.00." "Very good madam", I replied and with that, off she went. While I had to while away up to three hours, normally the second horseman followed on behind the hunt at a leisurely pace to exchange horses but Matt didn't want Mountain Knight out all day being in training. As it was, Mrs Cardiff would only be out for an hour and a half or so. I went in the box to check him over – all seemed well. I went and sat in the cab and from my pocket I took out a race form results booklet which Mrs Cardiff had every week. As I was interested in racing, ,I used to have them when she had finished with them, usually about the middle of the week. They were in a form that could be filed for future use by people that studied form and there I wiled away an hour or so before checking on him again. I don't know where the box driver was, I had only seen him briefly after we had parked up. He was probably chatting to another box driver. However, I checked Mountain Knight over again. He was fine so I thought I would get him out and walk him round for a while to stretch his legs and to break the monotony. It must be rather boring standing in a box for a few hours, although he could see out. So this I did for half an hour or so. I put him back in the box and returned to the cab and there I stayed until twenty pass one when I decided to get him ready for when she returned. This I did, replacing the travel rug over the top of the saddle, took his tail bandage off and rolled it up. Then it was the turn of the bridle. This done and the martingale in place, it was a matter of waiting after putting the brush through his mane and tail. I waited a while, then took him out and walked him round at a quarter to two. Ray, the box driver appeared followed shortly after by Mrs Cardiff. After swapping horses, she told me she was only taking him for about an hour and had arranged for someone to take me back to Armscote as not only it would save the box driver a journey but he wouldn't have time to get there and back in time to meet her. I said "very good madam" and turned to take Carmen off Ray who had been holding her while I gave Mrs Cardiff a leg up. As I led Carmen towards the box to load her up, I could hear Mrs Cardiff talking to Ray, I presume telling him where to meet her and off she went to catch up with the hounds if she could. I took the saddle off Carmen and thought she looked a bit different now particularly splattered with mud which was still too wet to do anything with in the way of cleaning other than rubbing her down with a handful of straw. I took her bridle off and replaced it with the head collar. I then tipped some water out of the five gallon drum that we carried and gave her a drink which she readily accepted, tied the hay net up where she could reach it and put her travel rug on, closed the partition ready for when the other horse was loaded, tied his hay-net up and asked Ray if he would give him a drink. I didn't want to leave a full bucket of water which might tip over, leaving an empty bucket rolling round during the journey that would probably frighten Carmen, despite her having been hunting for three hours. With that, we put the back up and after a while he said he would get on his way and with that, jumped in the cab, started up and off he went, leaving me to wait for my lift. I looked at the time, it was twenty past two and I thought I should have brought my lunch for now I was beginning to feel hungry. However, I thought, if my lift comes now I could be back by three. Well, I waited – half past two came, then a quarter to three – still no one. By this time I was getting rather concerned thinking to myself if no one turns up by three, I will have to start hitch-hiking. Three o'clock came – not a sign. So, thinking out loud I might as well have gone with the box as at this rate, they will be home before me. So off I set making my way towards the main Stratford to Banbury Road thinking I'm more likely to get a lift there rather than sticking to the country roads. I eventually reached the main road, having not seen one vehicle, not even a horsebox which I expected to see. However, having reached the main road I set off towards Stratford with renewed hope, thinking there might be a chance of catching a lorry but it appeared that wasn't to be my lucky day. Having thumbed several vehicles without any luck, it seemed like I had walked miles. Looking at the time – I had been going for three quarters of an hour. A few more vehicles came by but none stopped. One or two blew their horns. I don't know why, perhaps being dressed as I was, they thought I had lost my horse and could see the funny side. Eventually, after covering perhaps a couple of miles, I heard the sound of a vehicle behind. I stuck out my thumb, more in hope than belief but to my delight it pulled up alongside. It was about the same size as an old Austin Seven, probably a bit bigger but a lot more stylish. It was in fact the only one I ever remember seeing, let alone a chance of a ride in one. I opened the door and peered in. At the wheel sat a middle-aged man with a round jolly face with a neatly trimmed moustache who was, as I remember, quite smartly dressed. He said "How far are you going. I am going to the other side of Stratford to the village of Wilmcote, where are you heading?" "I am going to a small village called Armscote" I replied "which is about four miles off this road". "I would be grateful if you could give me a lift as far as Pillerton Priors." "Of course", he said, "jump in". What a relief to sit down I thought. With that he put the car in gear and off we set. To make conversation and to satisfy my curiosity I said "Your car is one that I am not familiar with". He gave a wry smile and said "you are not the first person to remark on it. The make is a Swallow. They were made by a small company based in Coventry but like so many engineering firms, when the war started, they had to cease making cars and manufacture vital products to keep the wheels of war turning. It will be interesting to know if they go back to making cars again. I hope they do for it suits me in my job, its reliable and cheap to run." I never dared to ask him what his job was, I couldn't be that nosy even though I wanted to. By this time we were nearing Upton House the home of Viscount Bearstead - Within a half mile of the notorious Sun Rising hill where countless accidents occurred especially during the construction of the surrounding airfields where lorries carrying stone and other materials had brake failure. As most vehicle, if not all, had brakes that relied on cables and foot power. However, we negotiated it fine when he asked me how I came to be walking dressed in riding clothes as I was. I explained what had happened and said I was thankful for the lift for I had visions of walking all the way and arriving in the dark but now, thanks to him, I had a chance to make it in a little daylight. By this time we had reached Pillerton. He said, "Where do you want dropping off?" I said "by the Halford turn a few hundred yards ahead". As he pulled up, I thanked him again. "Don't mention it" he said, "I have enjoyed a bit of company". With that, I got out and said "it's a bit early but I wish you a happy Christmas - the first after six years of war". "Thank you" he replied and with that I closed the door and off he went with his little Swallow car. I don't remember ever seeing one again. Off I set once more but thankful I had only about four miles to go for the chance of getting another lift seemed very unlikely. I arrived back at Armscote just before five, almost two hours after setting off from Warmington. Matt was having a look round as he did every evening at this time to make sure all was well. He seemed relieved to see me. He asked what happened so I had to relay the story to him. The horses had arrived home shortly after 3.30 around the same time as Mrs Cardiff who had enquired if I had returned alright. On hearing that I hadn't he said she was quite concerned and to let her know as soon as I had. He said "Get off home, I will inform Madam that you are back and alright" so I picked up my packed lunch unopened, my hunger pains had long passed but was now looking forward to my dinner. The next morning Mrs Cardiff came out just after nine, rather early for her, for she wasn't dressed in riding clothes. She came in the stable and said "Good Morning Darcey". She always called him by his surname as was common in those days. "Is John here? He replied with "good morning madam, yes, he is in the end box saddling up ready to ride out". With that she came down and after exchanging good morning she said, "I am sorry for what happened yesterday. Having spoken to the person last evening on the telephone, it appears that there was a misunderstanding as to where you were to be picked up. She sends her apologies". I never knew who that person was who was supposed to give me a lift but I do remember the pay packet I received that Christmas. In fact, there were two envelopes, one brown, nothing unusual about that for my pay packet was always brown. They were made up every week by Mrs Oswald Smith who lived in Ilmington up Grump Street. The other was white with what felt like a card inside. Well it was Christmas after all. On opening it when I arrived home Christmas Eve, it was a card but inside was a crisp new pound note along with an equally crisp ten shilling one with the card written by Mrs Cardiff, wishing me a Happy Christmas. You can imagine my delight – 30 shillings – that was almost a week's wages. By then, my wages were 35 shillings per week, ten shilling more than I was getting on the milk round but it was still a six and a half day week. Sunday was only a case of cleaning out the boxes, giving the horses a quick rub down, picking out their hooves and oiling them and changing their top rugs for their Sunday ones and putting their head collars on with a blue brow band for Mrs Cardiff always did a tour of the stables with Matt and discussed every horse and what plans for them for the following week. On opening my pay packet there was a note inside informing me that from January 1st I would have an increase in wages by two shillings and six pence a week. More good news - perhaps it was compensation for the Warmington episode.

CHANGES IN THE LIFE OF THE FAMILY

The beginning of 1946 was a significant milestone for our family for my sister, Elma, who was twenty-two, had met and married an American GI who was stationed at Blockley. They met at the Saturday night dance held in the village hall every week - entrance fee one shilling, free to the Armed Forces - a very popular event.

You have attached this record to:
Cooke, Elma Jean in your tree "family"   Remove

Name:	**Elma Vanveghten**
Gender:	Female
Age:	22
Birth Date:	abt 1924
Departure Date:	30 Mar 1946
Port of Departure:	Southampton, England
Ship Name:	Queen Mary
Search Ship Database:	Search the 'Queen Mary' in the 'Passenger Ships and Images' database
Shipping Line:	Angle Sason Geboleum City
Official Number:	162134
Master:	S Algar

View original image

Sister Elma's departure - Shipping Line and Master of the Queen Mary

Name:	Elma VAN VEGHTEN
Date of departure:	30 March 1946
Port of departure:	Southampton
Passenger destination port:	USA
Passenger destination:	USA
Date of Birth:	1924 (calculated from age)
Age:	22
Marital status:	
Sex:	Female
Occupation:	
Passenger recorded on:	Page 173 of 175
Ship:	QUEEN MARY
Official Number:	
Master's name:	
Steamship Line:	
Where bound:	USA
Square feet:	
Registered tonnage:	
Passengers on voyage:	

Details of passenger list

People travelled from all around for the floor was excellent for dancing being, of course, Maple. While in early March my eldest sister Rita married her long time boyfriend, William (Bill) Randall. At the same time, Elma received through the post, notification of the day she would be leaving these shores for a new life, uncertain of what the future held. The letter arrived shortly before her 22rd birthday which was the 13th March. Her husband, whose name was Harold Everett van Veghten, but always known as Van had already left for the States to be discharged from the army. Before he left, he gave me American army clothes and a wooden case that he had made for his trade as a carpenter. On the lid of this case was a map of the journey he had made from America to Europe and then to England, very skilfully done.

His return to civilian life was in the small village of Poultney in the State of Vermont where he grew up. He spent the rest of his working life teaching woodwork at the

Elma's UK address and her new one in the USA

local college. When I visited my niece in 2001 she lived in the family home. The cellar to the house, (all American houses had cellars, although they called them basements) was laid out as a wood working shop with all the wood working machines which he worked on up to shortly before his death in the 90s. The day Elma left was a day I will never forget. Although it was a day that I was at work, I said my goodbyes to her before I left. The reason why I remember the date was that it was my grandmother's 86th birthday, 23rd March. She had to make her way to Southampton by train, having been taken to Campden Station by Mr Roy Garrett who ran the local taxi service. It was rather a sad day for us – it was like losing one of the family. That left just me and my parents at home. The place seemed empty without her for she was full of fun with a great sense of humour. However, life had to go on and we were left with our thoughts but we could hardly wait to receive news of her. We were all relieved on receiving that first letter over a month after saying that she had arrived safely after crossing the Atlantic. She left Southampton on 30th March 1946 aboard none other than the top liner of the day, The Queen Mary.

As time passed, we gradually got back to everyday life. Father was now working for a firm that was putting sewage pipes in the villages around as more and more Councils were switching to flushing toilets. Myra, my younger sister, had married in 1945 and was living in Shipston while Rita lived in Halford.

One day in June I arrived home from work. Mother said there is an important letter for you on the sideboard. I went over and saw this brown envelope, picked it up and noted that it was addressed to me, while at the top were the letters OHMS. Of course, I knew immediately what it was. It was a letter instructing me to report to a medical centre in Birmingham between the hours of nine and four in the afternoon, on a certain date to undergo a medical examination. This was to see if I was physically fit for National Service call up for the Government had brought in this scheme. Nearly all males on reaching the age of 18 were eligible for two years National Service. The only people that were exempt were, of course, those who weren't fit which could be anything from poor eye sight, loss of limbs or other disabilities and the ones that were serving an apprenticeship. In their cases they could be deferred if they so wished until they had completed it. The next morning

I took the letter and showed it to Matt. On the day I had to appear, I left home at 8.30 to cycle down to Snug Cottages, situated about 200 yards from the main road between Stratford and Banbury which is between Armscote and Halford to catch a bus into Stratford and from there another one to Birmingham – a distance of some twenty odd miles. On arrival at the Bull Ring, I made enquiries from a bus driver where this particular street was. He gave me directions, saying it will take you about 15 minutes walking or you can catch so and so bus. I opted to walk. On finding the place, I went inside where a notice said that all personnel report to the reception desk. This I did, giving the letter to the clerk of which there were quite a few. He ticked my name off in this huge register. Handing me a card with my name typed at the top he said "Take this with you through that door where you will be given further instructions". On entering the door I came into a room with a line of tables each side with a clerk behind each desk. On seeing a table with only the clerk in attendance I went over to him and handed the card to him. He took it and said, "Empty your pockets of all valuables, money, wallet etc." This I did. He made a note of each item, counted the money, took a small tray from one of the cupboards behind him, put everything in it, including the card with all the details on, replacing it in the cupboard and then handed me a large form that was folded in the centre and said, "Write your name and address in the appropriate spaces and proceed through the door at the other end" This I did; went through the door and found myself in a room. A man in a white coat was attending to the person in front of me. I waited while he completed the form, handed it back to the person in front and told him to proceed to the next room. I went over to the examiner,, gave him the form and waited for the next procedure which was the eye test. He looked into each through an instrument. Then I had to sit on a chair and read the letters on the card that was on the wall, one eye at a time. After that, he looked into my ears followed by my mouth, writing something down on the form, after each test. This done, I was directed to the next room which was quite large with cubicles and screens all round. There I had to strip down to my underclothes, putting all my clothes into a box including shoes, writing my name on a label and tying it to a button-hole in my jacket. This was taken by a medical orderly. My height was measured along with my weight and so I continued passing from one doctor to another, a total of seven in all until finally, ending up in another quite large room with tables and cupboards, behind all, bearing one of the following letters A, B or C. Again attended by orderlies I approached the table with C displayed on it and gave the orderly my name. He turned, went to the large cupboard, opened the bottom one and took out my box of clothes, placed them on the table, turned and opened the top cupboard and took out the small tray containing my personal items and asked me to check them off the list made when handing them in, ticking the box by the side of each item as I checked them. Having completed this I then had to sign the form declaring that I had received all items including money that I had handed in. This I did and on instruction, passed through a door carrying my possessions into another room with cubicles and screens with a chair in each. I got dressed, replaced all the items into my pockets, left the box outside as instructed and followed the arrows pointing to another door with a note on it saying All Personnel report to Reception Desk. I opened the door, went in the other room where a series of tables, each with a clerk seated behind and busy sorting papers or writing except the first one who sat at the desk with a notice on saying "Report Here". This I did, standing behind two or three others waiting there. As I got nearer I could hear him asking them their name and saying take a seat and wait until your name is called. My turn came with the same instruction. I went over and sat on one of the vacant chairs and waited as the names were called out one after another. I noticed that all the names called started with either A, B or C and then I realised that in this batch of personnel they were only dealing with surnames that started with one of these letters. Even then there were an awful lot of people in the surrounding area who fell into this category. If they, like me, were within a radius of 30 miles from Birmingham, my thoughts were suddenly interrupted by the sound of my name being called. I got up and went to a vacant table where I was handed an envelope bearing my name and told you are free to go. I said thank you and made my way to the door which said exit, went through and found myself in the main reception area which I had entered some two hours before for the clock on the wall was now approaching one o'clock. I went out into the street and made my way back towards the Bull Ring, passing several shops and thinking I hope there is a cafe nearby for I realised I was quite hungry. As I drew nearer to the Bull Ring I came across a cafe on the other side of the road. I crossed over to take a closer look, peering through the window. It looked clean with crisp, white tablecloths on the tables with the usual condiments in the centre of them. The notice on the door said hot and cold food served, sandwiches and cakes and I thought 'that will do me' I went and went up to the counter, a lady, who I thought would be in her forties, was talking to a younger one while she proceeded to arrange crockery – a milk jug and a small container, containing small white tablets that were saccharin sweeteners – sugar, like most things, were still rationed. On seeing me she passed it to the young girl who was, I think, about 16 and probably her daughter with the words –" that is for the lady and gentleman sitting by the window who has ordered a pot of tea for two, whose order will follow shortly". She turned to me and with a smile enquired what can I get you? "Can I have a cup of tea and what sandwiches do you have?" On hearing what she had to offer, which incidentally, was limited, I settled for a corned beef and pickle with a piece of swiss roll to follow filled with cream and raspberry jam, knowing that I would have a cooked meal that evening as we always did during the week. She said "that would be two shillings and four pence please". I paid her from the change I had in my pocket and sat down at a nearby table. I felt quite satisfied afterwards and enquired from the lady what time it was. She put her head round the door, turned and told me it was, nearly ten minutes to two. I thanked her and got up to leave. I put my hand in my pocket and took out the rest of my coins and put a threepenny bit under the plate and left, thinking if I hurry I would be able to catch the two o'clock bus to Stratford which ran every hour giving me plenty of time to catch the half past three to Shipston. I eventually arrived home around four thirty. Whilst on the bus from Birmingham I took the envelope, given at the medical centre, eager to know what it contained, opened it and took out the card which contained my name, address and various other information, and a stamp with pass on it and by the side A2. I returned it to the envelope. The next morning I told Matt that it meant I would be called up once I reach 18 which would be very soon.

In the meantime it was carry on as usual. Being the beginning of summer, the boxes were relatively empty as most of the horses were turned out with the exception of the show ones. So at this time of year it was common practice to give the boxes a spring clean, To achieve this, the horses that were in were moved from the main block, then it was a case of removing all the cobwebs, and with soft brooms, brush the back wall to remove the dust, remove all the bedding and swill the floor with a hard broom as a scrubbing brush. Then it was time to get the paint brushes out. The top half of the back wall was white so out with the whitewash. The bottom half was black – this was done with the blackboard paint which is a flat paint. The partitions and the front were also black but this time the wooden bottom half and the iron bars over the top were painted with a gloss finish. First, they were wiped down with a clean cloth to remove dust and dirt, then if needed they were painted. This year they were all in pretty good condition so I didn't have the task of painting them. When it was all done the passage, which was also white, was given a fresh coat, the windows cleaned inside and out. When finished it looked really smart and then it was back to the usual tasks like taking water, drawn from a tap, outside of the kitchen. This was done with a water tub on its own two- wheeled cart that could be let down onto the floor and removed if needed. There was a trough in the field, so it was used to carry the water over, topping the trough up with a bucket. This was also used for filling the horses' buckets in the boxes as there was no tap in the stable yard or the small yard up the back.When there was a full complement of horses in, carrying water could be as often as three times a day. Each morning water buckets were swilled out and fresh water put in. As each bucket held approximately three gallons, that was quite a lot of water so they were checked each day after lunch and topped up as required and then again in late afternoon.

The horses were certainly well cared for. When in full work they, had four feeds a day of rolled oats and chaff. Their first feed was early before I arrived at around 7.30. They were all tied up having finished their breakfast with Matt starting to muck out which was the first job for us grooms. This was done by placing all the clean straw around the outside of the box exposing the floor. All the waste material was put in a heap, then placed on a sheet, slung over your shoulder and then carried across the road and tipped in the area fenced for the purpose. Next the floor of the box was swept up and placed in the barrow, kept outside for that purpose together with the droppings which were picked up throughout the day. Then, a slight covering of the clean straw would be scattered over the floor. When the rest of the boxes had received the same treatment, each groom usually looked after two horses. It was time to strap them. This is the word used for grooming. Everyone had their own kit comprising water brush – this had soft bristles and was used for removing any dirty stains and for smoothing the mane and tail – and a body brush – an oval shaped soft brush with a strap that was slipped over the hand when used in conjunction with a curry comb. This was a flat metal plate about three inches square which had rows of teeth spaced about half an inch apart with a wooden handle. Right handed people held this in the left hand and with the body brush in the right hand the whole body using quite vigorous strokes. After every two or three strokes you would draw the brush across the curry comb to remove the dust and dirt from the bristles. Every so often you would bang one side of the curry comb on the floor to remove any debris thus keeping the brush clean. This was invigorating work and warmed you up in winter and made you sweat in summer but it had to be done – not only did it keep the horse's hair and body clean, it stimulated the blood vessels and toned the muscles as a massage does. This done, it was the turn of a moist sponge. This was used to wipe the ears, the eyes, nose and around the mouth, rinsed out and used to wipe the dock (ie under the tail). Then it was the turn of the dandy brush which I explained earlier to give the mane and tail a thorough brushing. This done, from your kit you took the rubber and wiped them all over. Finally, the last bit of the task, you took the hoof pick and picked out all the hooves. You could, of course, have in your kit an ordinary comb, usually made of aluminium, for the mane and tail but I always found it better with a dandy brush. On completion, if this particular horse was being ridden out first, you would put the first rug on to keep them warm in winter or, in summer, a light rug was used. Having done the second horse you would repeat the process and replace all the rugs with the exception of the top one for this was the night rug. Instead it would be folded up and put at one end of the passage on the manger for at each end there was a stall for a horse which could be housed there but would be tied up. The night rug would be replaced by the day one. It would then be time to saddle up ready to go out just before nine. In winter and autumn an exercise rug would be put under the saddle and down over the quarters. You could be out for up to two and a half hours depending on the level of fitness. On returning to the stable you would unsaddle and give them a rub down, then put their rugs on, fetch a little hay and then let them down, ie take their head collars off, and hang it up in the passage, then the same procedure for your second horse. The difference of the time you were out with the second horse depended on the length of time you had been out with the first ,but we were usually back before twelve for they would get another feed around that time, of oats. For me, once I had let my second horse down, I would be in the saddle room where all the saddles, bridle and other riding gear was housed along with large blanket boxes for blankets and rugs. After each use,the saddles and bridles and other bits were cleaned and put back on their brackets. The saddles were placed on a saddle horse. This was a wooden stand with the top made in the shape of an apex. This enabled them to be held firmly while you cleaned them. First you sponged them with a damp sponge, wiped them down including the straps. You then applied saddle soap which protected them and made them shine. Once that was done you pushed the stirrups up to the top of the leathers and pulled the leathers through the irons and pulled them down making a neat secure job. You then put them up on the saddle rack at the end of the saddle room. There were at least a dozen saddles all on the wall – saddles of various sizes – the ones that weren't used very often such as those used for showing and point to pointing had saddle covers on them but the ones in regular use did not. For the bridles they were hung up on a bridle hanger. This was in the shape of a four pronged grapple hook fixed to the ceiling in the centre of the room. It swivelled round which helped when three or more bridles hung up, save walking round. First you dipped the bits into the water then you followed much the same procedure as for the saddles. Then you hook the reins up by putting them through the throat strap and doing the buckles up then the nose band was wrapped round the cheek straps and buckled up. Then it was hooked over the bridle bracket with the brow band facing out making a really neat job. There was a row of these all along the one side of the saddle room except for where the door was that went into the garage but even so there must have been at least a dozen and a half of bridles of all kinds and with different bits. Then in between the bridles but lower down were the girths and the martingales. The girths were of various sizes all made with thin leather. They were made in such a way from one wide strip that was folded over to make three strips. They could be any width from three to four inches wide and very strong. The majority had three buckles at each end. These, of course, were for strapping them to the saddle to secure them. All the leather was treated at intervals with Neatsfoot oil to prevent it cracking and to keep it soft. It, like the saddle soap, smelt really nice. The opposite side of the saddle room was taken up by another door leading from three loose boxes, then a round cast iron stove that was used in the winter to keep a nice even temperature. Also Matt used to boil up linseed in the winter perhaps once or twice and mix it up with bran to make a mash – linseed being quite cold before being used. It used to remind me of frogs' spawn but the horses loved it. It was also used to warm the water to clean the tack. Over the top of the fireplace was a glass fronted cabinet where the tail and leg bandages were kept along with scissors, needles and threads – reels of black and light brown used for plaiting the manes when showing or racing. Also on that wall were all the rosettes, then further along were two or three sets of harnesses and then underneath that and at the end were the blanket boxes and baskets. The floor, except for in the fireplace, was made with wooden blocks which I think was oak, and was laid in a herringbone pattern which I had the job of sweeping and scrubbing a couple of times a year, usually in the spring or summer and sometimes in the autumn, depending on the state of the weather – I sat in there and had my lunch, while in the summer I would spend on the banks of the pond which is quite large and is situated by the side of the Blackwell Road and Back Street. I used to enjoy watching the Mallard ducks, the Moorhens and Coots – all permanent residents that nested all around. The Mallard ducks often nested in the thatched roof of the stables. One late spring or early summer I witnessed a site I would find hard to believe unless I had witnessed it first-hand. As I sat having my lunch in the sunshine, I saw this mallard duck standing on the grass behind the main stable block towards the end leading up to the back yard shouting or should I say quacking for all its worth. At first I thought it had seen a cat or something that was causing its concern but then I noticed movement up near the top of the roof. I stared at the place for a while and then I noticed another movement. Then I spotted what I thought was a bird at the entrance to what looked like a hole in the thatch. I sat and watched and waited while all the time the mallard on the ground continued with its persistent calling and then I spotted it again as it came out a little further and then I couldn't believe what I was seeing for there in front of my very eyes was not a bird but a small duckling and in between its mother's calling I could hear this faint chirp as it ventured out. I then spotted another behind it. The first one was now making its way very gingerly, half walking half slipping down the roof. I sat there transfixed, not daring to take my eyes off it, wondering what was going to happen when it reaches the bottom. Then after the first, the second one started down followed by another and another. As they continued down their slippery path, the first had reached the bottom. As I watched with baited breath I thought what's going to happen now as they continued to come down I counted eleven. After two or three more had joined the first one at the bottom their mother continued calling them and I suppose encouraged them. I thought how are they going to get down. They surely can't fly for they have no feathers, they are just little bundles of fluff and then I get my answer. One of them launched itself off the edge with tiny wings outstretched, it came down quickly and somehow gently and hit the ground and seemed to bounce. I sat there and stared in amazement as it got up and ran to its mother quite unharmed, who carried on with her persistent calling and gradually one by one until they were all down, perfectly alright. She then turned and led them towards the pond to join the others and to see them happily on the pond it was hard to believe what I had witnessed for jumping off the roof of the stables which was at least eight or nine feet, it must have seemed like a mountain to them for they couldn't have been much more than a day old. On telling Matt what I had seen he said that he had seen a duck on the roof on several occasions, possibly it was looking for somewhere to nest but all the time he had been there he had never witnessed what I had seen.

NATIONAL SERVICE

Life carried on as usual after I had my medical. Two of my friends had been summoned for their medical, one just before me – Aubrey Edwards, who lived at number four and the other, John Bryan, a couple of weeks after. I was surprised Aubrey had been asked to attend for. as I have mentioned earlier, he lost the four fingers of his left hand at the age of five which made him unfit for entry to the Armed Forces so he was exempt. John took his and passed. July came and, as my birthday grew nearer. I wondered how long it would be before I had any news. My birthday came and a week later I still had no news. Each night when I came home from work I expected Mother to say there's a letter for you and then just two days before the end of the month it came. I opened it, took out the letter, eager to see what it said. I was to report to Budbrooke Barracks at Warwick where I would undergo basic training for a period of six weeks. It also said make sure you have a stout pair of shoes. It also emphasised that no change of clothes were needed. In fact, the only things you could take besides what you stood up in was a toothbrush and toothpaste. All other gear would be issued and the date to report was the 15th August 1946 which was in 17 days time. The following morning I took the letter and showed it to Matt and asked him if he wanted to take it to show Mrs Cardiff. He said that wouldn't be necessary but that he would tell her. I also asked him if it would be alright if I left a week before. He said that would be fine and so the day came for me to leave the employment of the Hon. Mrs Cardiff. I must say I had enjoyed my time there and had learnt such a lot. So having said my goodbyes to all the other members, not only the ones that worked outside but the domestic staff as well who all said don't forget to come and see us when you get leave and so I collected my bike and made my way the two miles home. Over the following few days I called on my relatives and friends to give them the news but most of them knew anyway. News travelled fast around the village then for everyone knew each other, having lived in the village all their lives. Even those who had come to the village, for whatever reason, all joined into the closely-knit community. Of course, the population was smaller than it is now.

I remember one lovely warm summery day, I had been to see my grandmother, when I thought I would sit on the seat that is round the horse chestnut tree on the lower green and decided to do a bit of carving on the stick I had cut from the hedge on the way up. So I took out my penknife and started cutting the bark and taking out narrow strips in spiral down the left. Having done that I decided it was too long so I put it across my knee to steady it and started to cut through it. That was fine until I put extra pressure on it. Not only did it cut through the stick, it also cut through my trousers and my leg just above my right knee. That put a stop to my carving. I tied my handkerchief round it, having first putting it under the tap, where the the post box is now and after wringing it out, made my way home where mother bathed it with her favourite Dettol and put a bandage on it and telling me that I should have more sense at my age! However, after a couple of days it started to scab over and within a period of about two weeks it had healed leaving quite a scar which is still visible to this day.

The 15th August arrived – that was, of course, a big day in my life for like thousands of other 18 year olds all around the country we were taken away from home and pitched into a different way of life, away from family and friends, not knowing what lay ahead. At least you knew that you would almost certainly remain unharmed unlike the thousands that had served during the war years. Theirs was a completely different situation for they were sent to all four corners of the world where they risked life and limb almost daily. Yes, we could be sent far and wide in the event of trouble but that's what being in the Armed Forces means. On this particular morning I woke up to the sound of my bedroom door being opened. I opened my eyes. Mother was standing there with a cup of tea in her hand. "Here," she said," I thought it would be a little treat being this is the last morning you will be waking up as a civilian for a while". "Thank you Mum", I said, "what time is it?" "Quarter past seven" she replied. Normally I would now be leaving for work. As she left the room, she said, don't put your best suit on, wear your second best. " Ok Mum", I said. I drank the tea, dressed, went downstairs into the kitchen and washed, did my hair as I had done for years, went back into the living room where the table had been laid out for breakfast as normal. Mother asked would I like bacon and egg. "That would be nice" I said. It was usually reserved for Sundays. Afterwards, Mother asked what time I would be going. I thought about catching the ten o'clock bus from Shipston. Warwick is not very far and the buses run fairly regularly from Stratford. I wanted to leave in good time as I wanted to see Mr Webb about leaving my bike there as I didn't know when I would be back again but I believed it could be after six weeks. Just before nine, I said goodbye to the dogs, giving them a pat and said "cherio Mum, I will write you when I have settled in". I, took my bike from under the veranda and made my way round to the front, got on, turned right at the end of the road, down to the bottom of Hobdays bank, turned right again into Armscote Road, looking up the back garden saw mother standing at the back door, waving. I waved back and I shouted "Bye Mum" and made my way on the short journey to Snug Cottages. I went into the yard where they kept their lorries and coaches and found Mr Webb and asked him if I could leave my bike as I was off to join the army so I wouldn't be picking it up for a while. He said that would be alright but to take it down the other yard and put it at the back of the big open fronted building on the left. I thanked him, put it in and made my way along to the main road to wait for the bus. It duly arrived and I got on and made my way up the stairs to the top deck. Who should be on it but a lad from Shipston by the name of Reg Edwards who I knew well. He was the cousin of the three Edward boys that lived at number four. I said" Hello Reg what's on, no work today" for he was an apprentice bricklayer at the Shipston Building firm of Wards. "No" he said," I am joining the army and am on my way to Warwick". "Well, so am I" I said. Haven't you been deferred until you have finished your apprenticeship? "I could have but I have only another year to go so I opted to join up now and get it over with." He added we'll stick together and see if we can get in the same billet. We made our way to Warwick by bus. Arriving at the depot we got off, had a look round and saw a three ton Bedford Army Truck parked nearby with two uniform soldiers standing by the side. As we approached we could see one was a Sergeant, who asked whether we were heading for Budbrook – "we are" was our reply. " Well jump up in the back, we will be leaving after we have more arrivals coming in". We climbed into the back which already had about a dozen in. As more buses came in, more recruits joined us. Finally, with about two dozen aboard we set off on the short journey to the barracks. Upon arrival the driver came back and let the tailboard down. We all got out and were told to line up in two rows, then we were taken to this wooden building where two clerks sat behind a desk. You had to hand your papers to the first one who asked you to confirm your name; the second one checked you off in a large register and sorted through one of the long narrow trays that contained brown booklets which were opened at the front cover and placed on their ends in alphabetical order. On being handed one of these, we had to assemble outside and the sergeant who brought us in, told us to form up in three columns. Having put the brown books in our pocket, we then went a short distance to another building where we entered in single file. This time our group was a few more than those who came in on the truck. On entering the building there was a long counter. Behind this were a few staff and behind them were these wooden racks with piles of gear on them. As you approached you could see what was being given out at each station. The first you were handed three blankets, then a pair of towels and face flannel. At the next, you were given what we were later told was a small pack that was to become part of your webbing equipment. This was now issued for the purpose of carrying all the small things which were – a razor, shaving brush, shaving soap, tablet of lifebuoy toilet soap, a packet of razor blades, boot brushes, a tin of black shoe polish, a tin of brasso, a button stick, a block of blanco and brush, and what appeared to be dusters and a 'housewife' – this was we learnt later to be a sewing kit. Each item was called out as you were given them and having put all things in the pack, you moved to the next station where you were given a pillow, the colour which I remember so well was grey with dark stripes. I don't know what it was stuffed with but it certainly wasn't feathers. The last station you were given a knife, fork, and spoon and two mess tins. These were made from shiney metal with handles of steel that folded in, the smaller one which was used for tea, fitted inside the other, whose handle was then folded over it. Now with the pack slung over your shoulder and gathering up the rest, you made your way out and again we fell into three columns - Reg and I sticking together standing there with all the gear tucked under our arms. The Sergeant led us away from the red brick buildings to where there were a line of wooden huts on each side of the road that we were told were billets. We had now been joined by more NCOs. The Sergeant came and counted out blocks of 15 men and to each block he called one of the NCOs and said out loud "Men, this is Corporal or Lance Corporal so and so. He is your billet Corporal. He is in charge of you. If you want to know anything concerning the billet, he will tell you. He will also show you everything about laying the kit out and so on". The Corporal would then take the men in his block to his billet and so on. Reg and I finally ended up in the billet that had a Lance Corporal who, on the top of his arm, each side of his uniform, was a badge in the shape of wings of pale blue while underneath on his arm was a white badge of a parachute and below that was a single stripe showing that he was a Lance Corporal. He also wore a red beret and walked with a slight limp. We later learned that he had taken part in the Operation called Market Garden where members of the airborne divisions had been involved with in the Arnhem Landings some days after the Normandy Landings in June 1944. The objective was to capture the bridge behind enemy lines and hold it until relieved by the Seventh Armoured Division which as we all know now went horribly wrong. Instead of them holding it for the estimated couple of days, they held on for a lot longer until, with mounting losses from heavy counter attacks and many wounded, plus running short of food and ammunition, some managed to escape but many were captured. Our Corporal was one of those captured and being wounded in his leg meant he finished up in a German Military Hospital where he underwent an operation along with others who had received serious wounds. He told this to us over the weeks we spent at Budbrooke. He also told us that the walking wounded and other prisoners were sent to a prison in Germany to join other prisoners of war while the ones like him were left in hospital where they were eventually liberated by the advancing allies and the seriously wounded were shipped back to England for further treatment and to recover. Once he had recovered, he was declared unfit for a return to military action but remained in the Army to do the job he was now doing, helping with the training of raw recruits. As we entered the billet, to the right was a small room that separated it from the rest. The door was shut but a plaque on it stated we had Lance Corporal Howarth. The rest of the billet had 15 beds, 9 on the left and 6 on the right. There was a cast iron round stove in the middle. Opposite the Corporal's room there was a cupboard which had a soft broom, hand brush and dustpan, some various pieces of cloth and by the side of the cupboard was a fold up table. The beds were metal with a wire grill that was attached to the sides and ends with springs. The head was a tubular frame, likewise the foot but much lower. The mattress consisted of three squares called biscuits, stacked at the bottom of the bed – at the side of each was a two door metal locker with a top shelf while underneath was a clothes rail with three coat hangers. The Corporal said "choose a bed". Reg and I chose two together and under instruction put what we were carrying on the bed. He then told us to fall in outside with our eating irons (army slang for knife, fork and spoon). Together with the smaller of the two mess tins. This done, he said, "Right, now we are going to march to the cookhouse for dinner". "When I say right turn, you will turn to the right. Then he said "When I give the order to quick march you will step forward on your left foot while your right arm will swing forward from the shoulder." After trying it a couple of times we made our way to the cook house for our first army dinner. On instruction we lined up in single file. Once inside you took a plate from one of the piles and passed along the counter where members of the Army Catering Corps served up your food. One dished out the meat, the next the potatoes, then the vegetables and so on, finishing up with the gravy and at the end there was a basket filled with bread where you could help yourself if you needed it. At the end, you held out your mess tin for tea. Then it was a case of finding a table. Once finished you then returned to collect your sweet. After, you took your plates and rinsed them in several containers of hot water which contained some kind of cleaning agent, rinsed in more hot water and in cold, finally placing them place them in the large plate racks to drain. You would clean your cutlery at the same time, along with your mess tin. You then made your own way back to the billet. Once we had all returned we had to fall in outside again. We were then taken to another building to be issued with our uniforms. You passed from one storeman to another, collecting first a tunic, then trousers, three shirts, the same number of vests and underpants and socks. There was, of course, no measuring as if you went to a tailor. They must have got so used to dishing it out they could more or less tell what size you were by looking at you. The only measurements they asked you for were the size of you shirt collar, beret and boots and at the end, you were given a pair of braces. Then it was back to the billet where we had to put them on. This turned out to be quite funny for some were too big and for others too small, so under the supervision of the Corporal there was a lot of swapping between the men. If this didn't solve the problem for those with the wrong sizes, the Corporal took them back to be changed. Once sorted out, we didn't look too bad but the boots caused problems for a good many, especially for the ones that came from the larger towns and cities for they, more often than not, had never worn boots in their life. We who came from the country, had spent most of our lives wearing them, although in my case, during the time I was in the stables, the boots I wore were far lighter and made from softer leather unlike Army boots which were much heavier and stronger. Like all new footwear, they had to be worn in and this is what caused the problems. Over the following days there were cases of men having to report sick with badly blistered feet where the medical orderlies would pierce the unbroken blisters with sterile needles to let the fluid out and to bathe them with a saline solution. There were also foot baths that some had to visit where they spent time in shallow baths being told by staff which one to go in and told when to move to the next. They would spend an hour or more going around them which had different solutions. This was, of course, done to harden the feet. It also healed the blisters.

By mid afternoon we had to fall in outside. This time we were marched to another store room to collect PT kit ie physical training, which consisted of two pairs of blue shorts, three white cellular singlets – these were of cotton and had small holes in them and a pair of black plimsolls made from canvas with rubber soles. Then back to the billet where the Corporal gave instructions on how to get all our kit into the locker. This done, it was time for the bed. The biscuits were placed end to end followed by a blanket, tucked in all round, then the pillow followed by the other two blankets. After, it was time to be shown how our bed had to be made up for the day. The biscuits were placed one on top of the other at the foot of the bed, then the blanket would be folded from the head to foot and then spread over the top with the edges facing the head. The other two blankets folded in such a way that no edges could be seen from the bottom or the side and placed on top in a square roughly about twenty inches. In front of these would eventually be your best pair of boots which we had not yet received. On top of the blankets, your knife, fork and spoon would be placed along with the mess tins. We were then told to make up the bed as shown. He then inspected them and mistakes had to be remade. We were then told that we were responsible for our bed's area – this meant keeping it clean, also dusting the lockers and bed. The pillow was placed behind the biscuits. We were then shown where the ablutions were along with the latrines and also the NAAFI where tea cost a penny a cup and cake about three pence. You also received your cigarette allowance from there which was 40 – twenty expensive ones which were like Players, Goldflake or Senior Service and 20 cheaper ones such as Woodbines, Players Weights or Parkdrive. The dearer ones were four pence for ten and the cheaper ones half that. You could, of course, buy more but they cost the full price. The NAAFI opened three times a day from ten to eleven in the morning, twelve until two and six until ten but we recruits would leave at 9.30 as lights out was at ten o'clock, with reveille at six in the morning. Then it was dress, ablutions and making your bed up before breakfast at seven. Then it was on parade at eight. You would hear the Corporal call out "On Parade" a few minutes before eight so you would rush out and line up in three columns where you would be joined by men from the next hut making up the platoon of thirty men. Our platoon was D. Once we were all lined up we were taught to right dress, but on this, the first morning, we were heading for the sick bay where we would be checked over such as heart, lungs, reflexes, eyes and ears. Once all had been through, it was next door for a dental check. Anyone with teeth that needed attention would be called out when on parade on the day they would receive treatment. My teeth were OK so I didn't need any. After dinner we were taken to collect more gear, this time it was to be the webbing, such as ammunition pouches, belt, large pack, webbing straps, water bottle, bayonet holder. The small pack we already had. We also received a ground sheet. Over the following few days, we were shown how it looked when you were dressed in full kit. We were also issued with ankle spats – they held the bottom of your trousers at the same time as going round the top of your boots. We also had vaccinations. This gave me quite a bit of trouble for I developed 'vac fever' which caused the actual place at the top of your left arm where it was given, to become quite inflamed, swollen and septic a few days after receiving it. So I had to report sick every day to have it dressed at the medical centre until it cleared up. However, it didn't curtail my training programme as we were having drill sessions at least twice a day, sometimes more. In other words, we spent a fair amount of time on the barrack square doing what all service personal called "square bashing" where we learnt drill movements such as left and right turn, about turn, right and left wheel. This was done on the march where the inside and middle columns shortened their steps to wheel to the left or right. We were taught how to salute on the move as well as standing to attention, while another drill was "Open, Order, March". This was used when the platoon was going to be inspected. This was done by the front and rear columns taking two steps forward for the front and two steps back for the rear. All the drills were done by numbers which we had to say out loud. This was done so that we moved together but after a couple of weeks we still had to count but now under our breath. We were shown how to care for our webbing using the blanco we had been issued. This was done with a brush and water then laid out to dry. All the buckles were brass which had to be cleaned even the back, using the button stick. This was to prevent the brasso getting on the canvas which, when dry, would leave white marks and that would mean being punished – such as cookhouse fatigue usually after tea, like spud bashing (peeling potatoes) or perhaps being told to double round the square two or three times for the first offence. If it happened again ,your punishment would be more severe such as longer in the cookhouse, going round the square with all your webbing kit on. This was all part of service discipline. Once the Drill Sergeant was satisfied with Drill Progress, we were marched down to the Armoury to be issued with rifles which were kept in huge racks. You had to give your name and the last three numbers of your Army Number - my full number being 19027305. A rifle was then placed on the table where the NCO would read out the serial number which was recorded in a ledger where you had to sign for it. You were then handed the rifle which was now your responsibility. Your Army number was printed on the first page of your brown Army Pay Book, Part 1. This also served as an identity card for it gave your name, rank, the colour of your hair and eyes, your height and weight and any visible distinguishing marks, such as scars, moles or birthmarks. This little book also gave the results of various training results. The second part of the Pay Book was exactly that. It showed the amount that you were paid. Army pay then was six shillings a day. When first issued with your Pay Book, you were asked if you would like any part of your weekly amount to be paid to your parents, plus any that you would like to be saved and paid out when you were demobbed. I pledged seven shillings and six pence a week for my parents. This was paid through the Post Office and two shillings and six pence for my savings. Mother often sent me ten shillings. If you lost any of your issued kit, the replacements had to be paid for, which was stopped at so much each week. Pay Parade was Friday afternoon and again you were called in, in alphabetical order plus the last three numbers and in my case this was 305. On hearing this, you marched in, halted in front of the Pay Masters, stood to attention where the Pay Clerk stated the amount you would receive from the ledger in front of him. The Pay Master counted out the amount, placed it on the table and picking it up with your left hand, and making sure not to drop the coins, you took a pace to the rear, saluted, turned sharply to the left or right, depending on where the door was, and marched out where you made your own way back to the billet..

Having now secured our rifles we were taught how it was put together and the way the mechanism worked, how to remove the bolt and magazine and, of course, how to clean it. For this purpose we were issued with a pull-through. This was a length of cord of about four feet with a small loop at one end and a weight at the other. A roll of 4 x 2. a soft towel-like material, each piece measuring four inches by two which, when folded, was placed in the small loop and fed through the barrel from the breech, after the weighted end had been dropped down the barrel first, and pulled through. You were also given a small bottle of oil. This was occasionally used and then very lightly to the bolt. All these items were kept in a cavity in the butt of the rifle.

The next step was rifle drill. We had to learn how to stand at ease by having the rifle at right arm's length but angled slightly forward at the muzzle, feet about a foot apart with the butt resting on the ground by your right foot. Then with the command "Attention", you brought your right arm and rifle smartly to your side, at the same time raising your left leg and slamming it down by your right. Next, it was 'slope arms.' By raising the rifle with the right hand so that it rested close to your shoulder at the same time bringing your left arm across your chest with your left cupped hand holding the rifle butt, then taking the rifle across to your left shoulder at the same time placing your cupped left hand under the butt to support the weight of the weapon but still with your right hand across your chest and resting on the rifle; the final move was to bring your right arm away and back down to your side. All these moves like all the other drill movements were done by numbers, for example – the slope arms drill would be 1, 2, 3, pause, 123 pause, 1 Each movement being on one, while the two and three being a pause. It was a very easy way to get the platoon to work as one. We were drilled in these movements with relentless regularity but then as the saying goes, "Practice makes Perfect". We were taught how to present your rifle for inspection which could take place without warning so to avoid punishment for having a dirty rifle, we spent time in the evening, cleaning, polishing and keeping your kit up to scratch. We then had to go through the drill to fix bayonets which had been issued at the same time as the rifles. These weapons were now totally different from the old sword types that were issued during the war. They were now much shorter, about nine inches long, round and ending in a point. This was much easier to handle but still another part of your equipment that had to be kept clean. The final drill that we went through was how to salute on the move with a rifle at the slope. This was done by bringing your right arm as it came forward, across your chest and with your fingers outstretched you placed them against the rifle and with your head turned towards the Officer you counted five paces before returning to the normal swing of the march. To salute in the stationary position called 'Present Arms'was entirely different from the marching slope. You again brought your right arm across your chest clutching the rifle - this of course done by numbers – it was 1, slight pause, 2, 3, then bringing the rifle up and across to the front of you at the same time you slapped your left hand against the sling and the barrel 1, pause 2, 3 and then on 1 you turned the rifle with the magazine at the front, pause 2, 3, then on 1 you brought your rifle down so that your right arm was at waist level at the same time, picking your right leg up and slamming it down at right angles behind your left heel – this sounds more complicated than it actually is.

The standard British Rifle at the time was the .303 Lee-Enfield Mk 4which was a versatile and reliable weapon and most effective at around six hundred yards. The flip-up sight at the rear had a scale from 300 -1000 yards with a slide that could be set to these distances which had to be calculated by the individual. For shorter distances the sight was down flat enabling you to sight it through a small hole with the front sight. We had to learn on instruction how to load the magazine which held ten rounds which were in clips of five. This was for quick and ease of loading and was done by pulling the bolt back, then, placing the clip in the top of the magazine, you placed your fingers under the magazine, at the same time pressing the rounds down with your thumb out of the clip which fell away. Rounds had previously been placed in the clips in a precise way to avoid the risk of 'jamming'. It only took a few seconds to load ten rounds. You then slid the bolt forward and locking it in position which pushed a round into the chamber ready to fire but first you had to apply the safety catch. This was a small lever which prevented the trigger from being used by locking the mechanism. We also had to learn the light machine gun known as the Bren Gun. This had a magazine that held thirty rounds which, like the rifle, was 0.303 of an inch which could be fired with single shots as well as automatic, which, when fired in this mode for any length of time the barrel had to be changed on account of it becoming extremely hot. For this reason, each barrel had a wooden handle. It only took a few seconds to change it. This was a very good weapon which could be fired from the shoulder or hip, despite it weighing about twenty pound. Like the rifle, it was extremely accurate, up to 600 yards from the prone position with its short bipods in use. It could also be mounted on a tripod against aircraft and from where it got its name, mounted on a Bren Gun Carrier –a tank like vehicle with tracks and open top. The other weapon we were instructed on was the Sten Gun which I believe came about in the Second World War when a large quantity of nine millimetre hand gun ammunition was captured. It was made entirely of metal and like the Tommy Gun was only effective at short range. It could also be used for single shots or automatic in short bursts. Personnel didn't care for it much. It was a two handed gun but your left hand had to be in the correct position to prevent damage or loss of the end of one's little finger from where the empty cartridge cases were jettisoned - the short barrel being encased by a perforated cover to protect your hand from the heat when firing on auto-mode. We eventually got to fire these weapons at various times during our primary six weeks training which, I must say, I enjoyed. This was the only time we were handed live ammunition being that blanks were used in rifle training while for the Bren and Sten Guns we used empty magazines. At the end of the first month of Army life we had been fully kitted out, having now been issued with our great coat. Fortunately for us these had buttons that were not brass, saving us the chore of cleaning but we still had to fold it in such a way that the buttons showed at the front and the half-belt fastened also at the front and hung up facing the front. Our kit was completed by our best battledress.

PT was a vital part of our training. This was all done under the supervision and instruction of PT Instructors. This involved working in the gym on apparatus like the vaulting horse, horizontal bar, and climbing frames that were fixed to the walls. All these exercises were done to improve your fitness, together with standard exercises such as bending, stretching and floor exercises. Later in our training, we would have runs from one hundred yards sprints up to a three mile cross country. Then there were the assault courses which consisted of obstacles from scaling high walls, climbing rope nets, swinging by rope over water with the object of landing at the precise moment on the other side. Get it wrong and you would finish up in the mud and water. Also crawling through drainpipes, under barbed wire on your stomach, using your elbows and your legs to propel you forward. Later we did this course in full kit. Another part of our training was route marching. This started with short ones, gradually increasing up to eight and ten miles with probably a ten minute break at half way. The final test came in full battledress with your rifle slung over your shoulder where you had to cover four miles in one hour. At the end of our six weeks, we had a passing out parade and for the first time since joining up we were allowed out by means of a 48 hour pass. It also gave us the chance to take our civilian clothes home and the opportunity to wear our shoes again. We were issued with our pass on Pay Parade which gave the time you could leave, which was around tea-time, and the time you had to report back by which was Sunday at midnight. I was one of the lucky ones, being so close to home with a good bus connection it only took about two hours at the most. For those that lived far away, they spent a lot of time travelling and, because of the cost, many stayed on the camp and visited the local towns. Free travel passes were allocated twice a year for every four months service you were allowed longer leave to ten or fourteen days. You were notified by lists on the company noticeboards when you were due. A month's leave for each year, was in fact pretty generous as civilians then, were lucky if they had a week annual holiday with the majority only having bank holidays and Christmas. For each long leave you had, you received a few shillings for your keep along with the appropriate ration coupons for the majority of food was still rationed. My first leave was ten days at Christmas 1946 and the New Year of 1947. That first leave is still vivid in my memory for that leave was extended by fate. Then, as now, a National Hunt Meeting was held on New Year's Day at Cheltenham which my father, along with other people, visited annually with Norman Smith. He, as mentioned before, was the son of Arthur, the Birmingham businessman and was married to the eldest daughter of Mr and Mrs Biles. I was given the opportunity to go as one regular was unable to. I, of course, jumped at the chance for it was a chance to see, for the first time, professional jockeys and trainers applying their trade. An added bonus was a former inmate of the stables at Armscote running in a hurdle race for the first time since being sold a few months before my call up. The horse's name was Fergus and was ridden by R Black. I couldn't resist having a sentimental bet of a shilling or two. He went on to finish fifth in a large field of novices. It was good to see him despite losing my money. However, he went on to win a few races over the next couple of years but I never recovered my lost shillings. That evening, I, along with two of my friends, Aubrey Edwards and Frank Everett, went to the village of Wilmcote which is a couple of miles north of Stratford, Aubrey drove us as he owned a van which he had bought through Taylor's Garage in Shipston where he worked as a mechanic. Our attraction at Wilmcote was the dance held in the village hall but first we had to take refreshment in the local where we had a few glasses of cider as this was cheaper than beer and more affordable. We made our way to the dance around 8.30 where the atmosphere was one of joy and happiness as you would expect for we all looked forward to seeing the New Year in. All went well, enjoying the dancing until late in the evening around 11.00 I began to feel unwell. I tried to pass it off thinking it would pass but I had to tell Aubrey and Frank who suggested, we go outside and get some fresh air for a while and see if that will help. It was quite warm inside plus all the cigarette smoke! Although being a fit young man that should not have had an effect on me. They asked if I wanted to go home but not wanting to spoil their night, I just sat in the van for a while. I must have dozed off for the next thing I remember was waking up to the sound of the National Anthem being belted out with gusto. I saw little reason to celebrate for I was now quite feverish and I just wanted to get home and to my bed. By the time we reached home the house was in darkness for my parents had retired and I quickly followed. In the morning I woke up, it was light. I could hear mother filling the coal bucket but I felt too ill to get up so waited until she came in, then banged on the ceiling to attract her attention. She came to the bottom of the stairs and called up. I told her I didn't feel well and could I have a cup of tea which duly arrived. The look on her face told me she thought I had over celebrated. But on telling how I felt and the back of her hand on my brow, it quickly dispelled that idea for she said "You have a temperature, I think you are in for a dose of measles.

I will have to call the doctor out. You won't be going back" I was due to be back by midnight on the second January. When Dr McMullen came out, I was diagnosed with German Measles which meant I was isolated for three weeks, being contagious I would not be allowed to travel let alone report back to camp. The doctor gave me a certificate confirming my condition which mother sent to my Commanding Office. So December had once again proved an unlucky month for me for only six years before I had spent the festive season in the Isolation Hospital with Scarlet Fever. This time, however, I would be home. By the end of my isolation period I was given a clean bill of health for which the doctor declared me fit to travel. I returned to a new camp located between Stourbridge and Kidderminster. On reporting to the Guard Room I was informed by the Guard Commander that I was to be detained for being AWOL (absent without leave). Despite explaining the situation and protesting my innocence he said I was on the list as an absentee and therefore I had to be detained until such time I was given the all clear. After two or three hours he told me I was free to go and collect my kit from the stores. I was now back in Army life.

THE WINTER OF '47

Less than two weeks after my return to camp, news came that we were to be posted. This time it was northwards to Sherwood Forest, famed for the legendary Robin Hood but instead of encountering bandits, now it was ammunition. Tons of it, all sorts except the large shells for the big naval guns. We found ourselves a short distance, a mile or two from the village of Edwinstowe and not too far from the famous major oak reported to be the oldest tree in the forest which according to the story, Robin used for storing food. It was said that 7 men could get inside the trunk so we tried to equal that but the most we managed to squeeze in was five. It was a magnificent tree but today it is fenced off from the public to protect it from the amount of visitors it attracts, for the old tree is propped and braced to preserve it for as long as possible. The time we were there it had steel braces to support the large branches.

During late December 1946, the weather had turned cold with north easterly winds, flurries of snow and sharp frost and so the move to our new camp was a journey through snow covered fields, trees and hedges in the countryside while towns and villages alike were shrouded in a blanket of snow. It certainly made a pretty picture looking out from the carriage window as the large engine huffed and puffed its way north belching out smoke of grey and black as the fireman shovelled more and more coal into its hungry fire to maintain the steam pressure. They earned every penny they received but it was a job they had to do if they wanted to achieve the childhood dreams of being an engine driver.

We arrived at Sheffield and were told to get out. This took a while for we were in full kit and carried all our belongings in our kit bags and packs plus our rifles. We had to fall in on the platform in three columns, then with kit bags on one shoulder and rifle slung over the other we had to make our way to the exit in single file and once again line up in three columns. There the officer in command told us that we had to change stations, a distance of about a mile and a half as I remember, and one that I would become familiar with. We had to march as best we could under the conditions and be wary of the trams. On arrival at the station our kit bags were once again loaded into a covered goods van. Once we were all aboard we set off again on the next leg of our journey. This time our destination was the town of Worksop in Nottinghamshire. It was on this journey we ate our packed lunches which consisted of one sandwich of cheese and another of bully beef, ie corned beef and a slice of slab cake. On our arrival we collected our kit bags and made our way to the station car park where a fleet of three ton covered trucks were waiting to take us on the final leg of our journey, but not before we had a welcome cup of tea provided for us by the ever reliable mobile NAAFI vans and NAAFI girls.

On reaching our new camp it, like everywhere, was under a deep layer of snow but it didn't hide what was to be our billets. No such luxury of wooden billets of our previous camps but corrugated Nissen ones. Once we had lined up a Sergeant counted us off where a Corporal took us to our allotted billet. On entering there were the usual row of beds each side while in the centre stood a cast iron stove with a bucket and hand shovel, poker and rake. We selected a bed where we dumped our kit, fell in outside again and marched to a large wooden building to collect our bedding. This took two journeys; first the mattress and pillow and then the usual three blankets. We were then told that we would be allowed a bucket of coal a day and that the compound would be open between four and five each day for the billet orderly to collect our ration where an NCO would take our billet number and tick it on his chart. This was done to make sure you could only receive your ration. The compound was fenced in and the gates padlocked, otherwise it would have surely been raided.

On that first day we were taken to the dining hall for our first meal – a hot one which was welcomed for it was bitterly cold. Over the next few days we became familiar with our surroundings. Each morning, breakfast was taken between seven and eight and then it was on parade at 8.15 for roll call where the Sergeant used to say "Fall out the sick, the lame and the lazy" which usually brought a few chuckles. Quite a few suffering from colds and other ailments would be off to see the MO who would say 'medicine and duty' or 'confined to bed'. For those with flu, confinement was in part of the medical centre, where you would be cared for by male orderlies of the Medical Corp. Despite the atrocious weather, we still went out into the forest, checking ammunition which was housed, like us, in small Nissen huts with the ends covered by tarpaulin sheets and secured at the bottom. The ammunition was stored in boxes either wooden or metal depending on what calibre. Smaller ammunition would always be in wooden while the large could be in wood or metal. Certain civilians had access to the storage area for there were estate workers and farm workers, living within the vast area of Sherwood alongside farms and large country estates, such as Columber Park. The storage bunkers that were built of brick concrete and covered in soil which was then grassed as camouflage were all placed in the areas near the roads where there was busy civilian presence. These bunkers had doors but no locks for they only contained larger calibre ammunition which, of course, were no use to anyone, whereas all the small ammunition was stored in remote areas.

We were taken out in Bedford trucks which had snow chains fitted but still would get stuck especially in snow drifts that could be as deep as five or six feet which meant a lot of shovelling and pushing. There were times when it was just impossible to get through without the help of a snow plough. This was a truck with a blade fitted to the front. It we were lucky, the NAAFI van would come, where, for a few pence you could have what the Army termed as tea and a wad (bun or cake). The winter dragged on. February was particularly bad – frosts and snow, in fact it was so bad each afternoon we were given a rum ration. This, I suppose, helped the circulation in keeping us warm. Many occasions through those weeks my friend, a north country lad by the name of Nichols, had what I am not ashamed to admit, two dinners and I know we weren't the only ones. The evenings were mostly spent in the hut, writing home or visiting the NAAFI, depending on the funds. Once a week, going to the Camp Cinema, depending on what was being shown. Being in the forest there was a lot of wild life but oh dear, how they suffered. Rabbits were eating the bark and shoots of shrub bushes and trees to try and stay alive but many succumbed to the harsh conditions. You could pick up their bodies completely frozen. They were just skin and bone. Pheasants and partridges also, like the rabbits. Their natural food being beneath the snow and ice and like the rabbits many of them suffered the same fate – starved to death. The deer suffered too but not as much for they could move about plus the wardens and gamekeepers taking out hay by tractor. They also took grain for the birds but many couldn't make it for they hadn't the strength to fly. The only ones to benefit from all this were the foxes. Even then there wasn't much in the way of food on those skeleton bodies.

March came but we were still in the grip of winter. We still had those icy cold winds from the north and east with days where the temperature never rose above freezing. Not until towards the end of the month did it show signs of relenting its grip. The temperature began to rise – a welcome relief. Now it was sludge time. Ditches gradually started to run again getting rid of some of the surface water. The ground beneath still frozen, some of the snow still remained in the middle of April where the big snow drifts lay. Nevertheless, to see the emerging shoots of new grass springing up and the new buds appearing on the trees and hedges gave us the welcoming sign that spring was at last on its way. People could try and get back to normal for that winter had disrupted the whole country. The rebuilding of the devastated towns and cities that had suffered so badly in the war had to stop from Christmas up to the present thaw. Transport was disrupted, power lines had been brought down by the sheer weight of snow, ice and wind. It had been what you might call a torrid time.

Through the years of my life I would say that the winter of 47 was by far the worst that I can remember. Yes, the one we had in 1963 was almost as severe but in my opinion the biting cold winds of 47 were worse. Or the winter we had in 1980 and 1981, another bad one that started early in December. At that time I was living on the Hampshire Surrey border where you would think that being that much further south it would not be so harsh but we had a lot of snow and temperatures were way down below freezing for days on end. Now that it was well and truly spring in 47, I enjoyed another ten days leave, after which it was back to the same routine for we seemed to be on a never ending stock take mission. By the time we were into summer I had served a year for King and Country; the time had passed quite quickly. One morning in July, after roll call, the Sergeant informed us that a certain number of us were being posted and said that if our name and last three numbers were called out we were to remain there while the rest were dismissed to pursue their normal duties. Having had my name called, I remained with the others who numbered around 30 or so. We thought that the story tales that had been going round the camp that we were going out to trouble torn Palestine were not just idle gossip but fact and we would now be having our over-seas inoculations and then going on 14 days embarkation leave. However, our hopes of seeing another part of the world were dashed when we were told that instead of Palastine, we would be going just a few miles away, still in the county of Nottingham to a camp about a mile from the town of Worksop. We had no idea of the reasons for our move to a camp so close. We still had a Sergeant and two Corporals who moved with us but we were all going to be under the command of the existing Camp Commander, Captain Brandt. After settling in and being shown around on the day we arrived, the information why we were there was told us at morning roll call. It seemed to us that what they said our role would be was just to find us something to do and help pass the time. Our task was to guard the perimeter road entries to the forest of which there were about eight or so in the area that we covered. Duty times to start would be fours hours on and twenty hours off which was for us a doddle! The procedure was that about an hour before your guard duty began, nine of us would dress in our second uniform with webbing, belt, braces, ammunition pouches plus bayonet and, of course, rifle. Then you would be inspected by the Guard Commander who would pick the one that he thought was the best turned out. Whoever was chosen was called "The Stick" and would be dismissed to return to barracks. It was seldom won by the same person twice running. Then you would climb aboard the three ton Bedford and taken to your point of duty. Mine was just off the Great North Road which runs from Nottingham to Doncaster and very close to the road off it which leads to Retford. The road into the forest passed through a big stone archway which was joined each side by a huge wall to a lodge where an elderly couple lived

Members of our billet in Sherwood Forest

who were extremely kind to me. Each time I was on duty there, the gentleman brought out tea and biscuits or, if it was the afternoon shift, it was tea and cake. I often thought, if they did it for every daylight shift it must have been quite costly. We were under instruction to allow military vehicles and personnel in but civilians were only admitted if they had a legitimate pass. There were quite a few who lived in and worked inside the forest while others worked outside so when the road was quite busy it helped to ease the boredom. However, you had to remain alert for you never knew when the orderly officer would turn up for he could be in any army vehicle, day of night so if you didn't want to be put on a 2-5-2 that's a charge or in Army slang a "Fizzer", you challenged everyone that wanted to enter. There were on occasions when military drivers, especially ones on their own, would slow down, then accelerate away and roar with laughter when you had to jump out of the way – a dangerous thing to do really but it was easy to report them. There were a few regular offenders but you only had to take the number of the vehicle and report them. In the main they stuck to the rules but there was one incident that occurred at the next station to me. A soldier, whose name was Mitchell, was on duty when a civilian male approached on his bicycle. When challenged to halt, he gave back a few choice words to the fact that he was fed up with being challenged to show his pass and rode on,to which Mitchell responded by pursuing him and sticking his bayonet in the man's rear tyre. Naturally the man didn't take kindly to this action and promptly gave the startled Mitchell a fourpenny one while saying he would have to walk the five miles home. For his action, Mitchell sported a real shiner for the next few dayts. As for the cyclist, I never heard of him refusing to show his pass again but if this had happened during the war, security was so tight, the man would, without doubt, have suffered a far worse fate than a punctured tye. But then in all probability it would have stopped!

We continued on guard duty over the next two months and with all the free time that went with it, as finances allowed, we would go into Worksop to the cinema or just to look around and have a cup of tea in one of the cafes. It was on such an occasion I remember, on a Sunday evening, that four or five of us were just wandering around when we bumped into a similar number of young ladies. Naturally, we got chatting and as we walked I got talking to a nice looking brunette and arranged to meet the following Saturday evening with a visit to the Worksop Palais where they held a dance as was the case everywhere then. Saturday came and as I walked down into the town I thought, would she really turn up or would I, on the very first date I had made with a young lady, be stood up. I arrived at the appointed meeting place and waited anxiously for I was in plenty of time. After about five minutes, no sign, then after another five minutes which seemed like an hour I was beginning to think that it was just an idle promise made in haste and that I was going to look a real fool in the eyes of my mates. As I waited I asked a gentleman the time, twenty five to eight he said, looking at his watch. I thanked him and thought, Oh well, she is only five minutes late – that's not so bad after all. Isn't it said that it's the woman's prerogative and with that thought, my spirit rose as I said to myself, I will wait a while longer, hoping upon hope that she would turn up. Then my eyes fell on this figure walking some 200 yards away. As she approached I knew then that my first date had arrived and I breathed a sigh of relief. As we made our way to the Palaise, we spoke of our families and I told her where my home was. She, whose name was Joan Chambers, came from Manton, a place right on the edge of town, where her father and brothers worked down the local mine while she worked in a local shop. This particularly Saturday night dance was the first of many over the course of the following weeks and as duty allowed, Sundays we would meet in the afternoon and go for walks along the canal or out of town, then take tea in our favourite little cafe. I must say, those week-ends were looked forward to by me. It gave a welcome relief from the camp and the repetition of army duties but like thousands of other relationships formed by members of the armed forces with local boys and girls, we knew that our friendship could be broken at any time for military postings and this is precisely what happened to Joan and I. For around mid to late October in 1947, news came that we were once again being moved on and so it was with a strong sense of sadness that I walked into town on that final Saturday to meet Joan in our usual meeting place and to dance at the Palais du Dance for the last time and tell her that this was to be our lasting meeting. It was a long, slow journey as I walked her on the now familiar route to her home where we had a long and sad parting but we knew we had no choice and we spoke of the happy times we had spent together.

SAVANAKE FOREST

Once again we found ourselves on the train and heading for the County of Wiltshire and another forest close to the town of Marlborough. Savernake, like Sherwood, was another ammunition storage area where it, like all ammunition storage places, would have been a hive of activity during the war but now after two years of relative peace they were being scaled down, although the Military Chiefs and the Government were wary of what the communists of the Eastern Block wanted. We, in the west, didn't trust Stalin which proved to be right when a while later we had the cold war but for now all was well and so we carried on with our normal duties. We were looking forward to Christmas when those south of the border could enjoy a few days at home with their families and friends while those from the North went home to their families for Hogmanay. The winter of 47/48 was nothing like the previous one with much higher temperatures which also brought more rain but it was better than days of freezing winds, snow and ice. With the arrival of spring in 48 and the lighter nights coming, we used to have games of football in the camp between ourselves. It was during one of these that my right knee gave way exactly in the way it had some four years before. So the following morning, with the help of billet mates, when the Sergeant after roll call, said fall out the sick, I joined them. On seeing the MO my knee was now more like a balloon. He took one look and said I would have to go to hospital and would probably need a lengthy stay depending on what treatment I would receive. A medical orderly eventually helped me back to the billet for I now had to pack all my kit with the exception of my toiletries and clean laundry which I put in my small pack, not forgetting my writing pad and envelopes for I would have plenty of time to write home and to my sister in America. Having packed every item into my kit bag and large pack, the billet orderly had to take it to the stores. He then had to return and do the same with my bedding and then, with his help, I returned to the medical centre to wait for transport which duly arrived and I was soon on my way to the Military Hospital at Tidworth (Hampshire). After being admitted, I was taken to a ward which, as I remember, had about 15 or 16 beds but only around 6 of them were occupied. The orderly took me to a bed that was ready for me with sheets and pillowcases where I was instructed to get undressed and put the pyjamas on that had been placed out ready, get into bed and the MO would be round to examine me. After putting my clothes into the locker again with all my other bits, I got into bed and waited. I soon got into conversation with the occupant of the bed on my left, the one on the right was empty. He said that the MO had been round earlier so he didn't think he would see me until the afternoon, as dinner usually came round any time after twelve. The MO came and after his enquiry of how it happened and a brief examination, he said I had to rest it and have cold compresses several times a day to try and get the swelling down. After he left, I asked my neighbour, the reason he was hospitalised. He told me he had been in there three or four days with a carbuncle on the bottom of his foot which had been lanced and was now on Penicillin and with that he threw the clothes back, swung his leg round for me to see for it had no dressing. It was big, at least an inch and a half across and quite a lump, with a neat clean hole in the centre, showing that the Penicillin injection he was having daily was doing its job. I asked him how he had passed the time away, he said that a paperman came round each morning and he and the old soldier in the bed opposite, took it in turns to buy one and invited me to join in, which I agreed. He also told me that the WVS ladies came round a couple of times a week with books which could be borrowed, library style along with writing pads, envelopes and stamps. He also said that the old soldier had taught him to play chess. I don't remember what the old soldier was in for but he had been in a while and was mobile and over the next few days, on getting to know him and engaging in conversation, he said he would teach me, if I wanted to. I had never thought about playing chess although I remember newspapers having chess puzzles in them when I was at home. So I agreed, thinking if it helps to pass the time for I had no idea how long I would be hospital bound. As the days passed I continued to have the cold compress treatment but there didn't seem to be a lot of improvement to my knee. After a couple of weeks, when the MO came around on his regular visit, I told him that it was still very painful and he said, we are still undecided what treatment we can give you as it is not cartilage trouble which can be treated by surgery. There seems to be a lot of fluid in and around the joint but the decision will be made in a day or so. A day or so later, the MO had decided what could be done and so, on the day that things of a more positive nature were about to happen, the orderleys arrived for the routine bed-making followed by one wheeling a wheelchair. I was given a gown to put on and taken down to the theatre and with not having had to be starved from the night before, I knew the treatment would not be under anaesthetic. The MO said they were going to take the fluid away, not by draining but by a syringe (if you saw the scene today you would swear it was one from the carry-on series of comedy scenes made some years later for the needle was at least the size of a sock needle used in those past times by the ladies to knit these garments and I was to be on the receiving end of the fearful instrument). It still makes me wince to this day when I felt him inserting from the outside of my knee under my kneecap and then withdrawing the plunger and filling the syringe with red fluid. He then unscrewed it from the needle, and emptied it and then went through the procedure again – he must have taken half a pint of fluid out – for me not only the fluid from my knee but also from my brow and I can assure you that I would not wish to go through the experience again but at least I now had a knee more or less back to normal but my treatment did not end there for I could not flex or straighten my leg or flex the muscles from my calf to my thigh due to the intense pain on trying to do so. The next morning the MO said that I would now have therapy for that reason by sitting on the edge of the bed and swinging my leg from the knee. This I must say was all right in theory but painful in practice for the higher you tried to achieve this the higher the level of pain. I had to do this three times a day. The other treatment that I received at least once a day was the electric current. This consisted of a box about the size of an early battery charger. From the box were two thin cables which had, at the ends, been connected to pads that were placed to the muscles each side and above the knee. It was then plugged into the electric supply, switched on and then with a plunger about the size of a candle which you then inserted into the box which sent the current down to the electrodes to your leg which flexed the muscles. This was done by whosoever was receiving the treatment for the farther you pushed the plunger in the stronger the current and muscle flexing and not least the pain you were inflicting on yourself. Once the orderly had set it up on the first occasion it was just a matter of him bringing it, turning on the current and letting me do the rest. Each session lasted about half an hour. I had now been in hospital a month and at last my knee was showing signs of improvement for I was now able to put it to the floor and put a little weight on it. My carbuncle bed neighbour had been discharged but more injured personnel had been admitted and discharged but the old soldier was still there. I call him the old soldier because he must have been in his late 40s, early 50s and so far as I could see was a regular, but I never knew the purpose of him being there but we spent many hours playing chess during the time I was confined to bed and after. I had, on three or four times been visited by an officer from our Unit to see if there was anything I needed. The only thing I needed beside a knee that was well again, was money which was the main purpose of his visit. I would be given a certain amount somewhere in the region of a pound while the rest of my pittance would be placed into my savings. Now with my knee improving I was able to go to the ablutions, have a shower and visit the cookhouse for my meals. Imagine my surprise on one occasion when who should be there dishing up but Ralph Turville, one of three brothers from Shipston whose father had a boot and shoe repair shop on the corner of Old Road and West Street. Although my knee was some way off being one hundred percent, the walking wounded were aloud out to go into the town of Tidworth to the cinema or to look around the shops and visit the cafes. Two or three of us went down on two or three occasions dressed in our wounded soldiers uniform of sapphire blue jacket and trousers, white shirt and red tie. It was a relief from the confines of the hospital and with it now being the beginning of June with warmer days and lighter evenings it certainly made a welcome change. After being in hospital for six weeks, although having a slight limp, I was discharged with a note to the Camp Medical Officer who I had to report to. The note said I was to go on light duties so at morning roll call, when the Sergeant said fall out the sick, I did just that. The one thing I must not do was to take part in football or cricket. So over the next few weeks I had a real easy time. Now, in July 1948 I was approaching my 20th birthday and with that I thought, like countless others of my age, that my two years National Service was rapidly drawing to a close. It came as no real surprise around the last week of July when at Roll Call one morning our Sergeant announced that if your name and last three numbers were called out you were to fall out and wait further instructions. This done we were told we were once again being posted - this time to another Wiltshire camp at Calne. We were dismissed with the order to return to our billets, pack up our kit and then after dinner assemble inside the main gate. From there, we were transported by truck through the countryside to what was to be our home for the next couple of weeks. Calne, like the three or four previous camps which I had been posted to, were all connected to ammunition depots. However, the one at Calne differed from the others for they were located in forests and covered large areas whereas this one was underground in a web of tunnels. After settling in we were asked if we would like to have a tour. All agreed as we had little to do to pass the time. On arrival, we had to pass the tight security of military police and surrender all cigarettes, matches and lighters, in fact all things that could cause fire. Little wonder that military fire fighters were on duty twenty-four seven for there were bays of ammunition of every calibre with the exception of the large naval shells. These were obviously nearer to the naval ports. After spending two weeks or so at Calne we were on the move again. This time for the last week of our service we were posted to Blandford Forum in Dorset which, as I remember, was a holding camp for Army Personnel awaiting demob. This was where we handed in our webbing equipment and told we could keep one pair of boots, our socks, underclothes and a uniform. We could also keep our great coat but would have to pay a small sum which would be deducted from our final pay day which would be the day we were demobbed. I chose to keep it for in the two years of service, I had grown and filled out so none of my pre-army clothes would fit any more. After mother had got to work with the dye and change the buttons, I would have a good cheap winter overcoat. Once we had handed in all our surplus equipment we packed what was left in our kit bags and waited for further orders. To pass the time and being summer what better way to do this than taking in the sea air and soaking up the sun in nearby Poole. What could be better than spending time strolling around the harbour, having an ice cream and when funds allowed, having fish and chips in a fish bar and getting paid to do so. At last, on the afternoon of the 19th August we were told that we were to be discharged the following day and to parade outside the guard room with our kit at 07.45 hrs. Next morning,after breakfast, and with our blankets returned to the store, we gathered outside in columns to wait for further instructions and as the CO appeared we were brought to attention being still in the forces. After being stood down, he proceeded to tell us where we were heading and the procedure that would follow on arrival at our destination which is called the Home of the British Army, the garrison town of Aldershot. He wished us well in Civilian life and hoped that the time on National Service had given us a lift in life and taught us responsibility, comradeship and independence. With that he dismissed us and we were soon on our way by truck in order to catch a train to Aldershot. On arrival at Aldershot we were met by a Staff Sergeant and soon on the short journey to the Demob centre. It was then a matter of moving from one area to another and choosing your demob wardrobe. I chose a grey herringbone suit, a white blue striped shirt with two collars, shirts in those days were not buttoned all the way down and the collars were held in place by front and back studs; a blue tie, a green pork pie hat which I gave to my dad – I never wore a hat, having lost a brand new one when I was at school and mother would not buy me another to lose. Of course, I had to wear a beret in the Army. I also chose a pair of Oxford style brown shoes being that I already had a pair of black ones and finally a gabardine mackintosh. This was parcelled up in thick brown paper and string. The next port of call was the paymaster where you had to hand your brown pay book to a clerk who then checked it off in the ledger, hand it to another clerk who took out of a file your pay book part two with more paperwork and pass these to the paymaster. He then read out to you what money you were to receive, less any deductions, ie loss of kit which had to be paid for and any purchases such as the great coat I was keeping. That was only a few shillings. In all with my pay savings, gratuity pay and subsistence allowance, you can imagine the shock and sheer joy that went through me on hearing the sum of £57 and a few shillings. He then counted it out onto the desk in front of me. I will never forget seeing those crisp white five pound and one pound notes as he put them down and the coins on top. He then asked me if I wanted to check it. "No Sir" I said "I did so as you counted it out." He then said "sign here" and turned the ledger round and pointed to the space against the amount. This done, he told me to keep it safe. He must have seen the look of surprise on my face. "I will" I said as I placed the notes in my thigh pocket of the uniform and fastened the button. I had never seen so much money let alone own it. From the pay desk I then went to another office who gave me a travel pass that could be used for train or bus, my brown pay book together with my discharge paper. He then told me I was now discharged from military service. I was now placed on the 'Z' reserve which meant that if there was any conflict involving our country or empire I could be called up without notice. On stepping out into the warm August sunshine, I was met by the staff sergeant who asked me whether I was travelling by rail or road? I said rail. He then told me which truck, pointing to one of the two that were standing nearby but he said it won't be going for a while until everyone had passed through the centre. I could go and get a cup of tea in the Naffi. As everyone was going through in alphabetical order, one of my best pals who I had spent well over a year with, whose name was John Crockett – Davey to us – joined me and we picked up our gear and went for a welcoming cup of tea. In doing so it gave us the chance to put all our new clothes into the kit bag which made it much easier to handle. On reflection it must have looked a bit odd to see a pork pie hat sticking out from the top of our kit bags and not tin hats! We were eventually joined by another close pal of ours, Blondy Hall, (I believe his first name was Arthur) but he was always known as Blondy. Eventually we were given the call to get on the truck and off on our way to the station where we made enquiries for trains to Oxford. On being told the next one was in an hour and a half's time, it was time to find the buffet for the ever favourite cup of tea and a sandwich for it was dinner time. We duly arrived at Oxford in late afternoon. After spending so much time together, this was where we had to part company for Davey and Blondy came from the north. Blondy just outside Chesterfield in Derbyshire and Davey from Preston in Lancashire. They continued their journey together north to Birmingham, after making enquiries, they being on a major route where trains ran more frequently. They only had a short time to wait unlike me who having to travel on the lesser route, had a long and frustrating wait as my train didn't leave until just before nine o'clock. I had no option for bus travel was even worse and hitch hiking was out of the question at this time of day. So with Chipping Campden being our nearest station, I had no option but to wait. However, Oxford being quite a busy station, the cafe kept open until late and although the choice of food at that time of day was limited, the tea was welcome. At last I made my way to the platform which was almost deserted. I sat on the seat and waited. Eventually, I heard a train approaching then a porter appeared pulling a trolley loaded with what looked like mail bags. As the train came to a halt a voice came over the tanoy, "The train now standing at platform so and so is the eight forty-five to Evesham and calling at among other places, the welcoming sound of Chipping Campden. I opened the door of an empty compartment and sat down with a sigh of relief and thinking my comrades will be well on their way home by now. I well remember that final train journey seeming to take forever as we stopped everywhere and travelled not very fast between each station. At last, we arrived and on stepping out of the carriage I had no idea of the time. I asked the porter, just after 10.30 came his reply. As I placed my kit bag on my shoulder, I became resigned to the fact except for a huge slice of luck, I would be on foot the final four miles or so for the last part of my journey back to civy street. As I made my way, climbing steadily through the Gloucestershire countryside towards the highest point of Warwickshire on this fine summer night, the only sound to be heard were those of my footsteps as I made steady progress, past the Ebrington turn, then rising still higher, past Kytes Farm on the right, where Geoffrey Freeman and I used to help drive his grandfather's sheep to be dipped in the summer of our schooldays. Then, a little further on, the road on the left to the villages of Hidcote Boyce and Bartrum, home of the now famous gardens. Stopping every now and then, I changed my load from one shoulder to the other, the silence was quite eerie. No stars or Harvest Moon to light up the sky and I had given up any hope of someone coming along and a chance of a lift. Then, as I passed the turn to Larkstoke, it gave me a tremendous lift for I was now in Warwickshire and more than half way home. A little way ahead was what the locals called The Downes and the farm whose tenant was Mr John Bell, was part of the Foxcote Estate. A few yards more and the road leading to Foxcote House, known as The Avenue and the memories of the family walks on those summer Sunday evenings and then after another 300 yards I stopped. This time, it wasn't to admire the view as I had done so on countless days in years past but to stand by the road that lead to the farm called Wood Meadow, the former home of my grandparents, Joseph and Fanny Potter and where my mother and her brothers and sisters grew up. Then as I started to descend down Campden Hill, I pictured the scene that lay below me. The Church of St Marys, the Village Hall, The Grange, and the Old Rectory. As I made my way down through the village, all was quiet with no one around but then I didn't expect there would be for all the adult males would be at work the next day as there was no such thing as a five day week then, most people worked half days on Saturdays. As I came down Hobdays Bank and into our road, after leaving on that Thursday morning of the 15th August 1946, I had arrived home a few minutes past midnight on Saturday, 21st August 1948. The bacon sandwich and cup of tea that I was soon enjoying never tasted so good. The only downside to my homecoming, only one dog was there to welcome me. Nip, our oldest one who I had grown up with, had to be put down a few months before, having lost the use of her back legs.

CIVVY STREET

I spent the next few days adjusting to life as a civilian along with helping out on Dowlers Farm by helping with the harvesting. During the years of National Service whoever employed you at the time of your call-up were obliged to offer you employment when you were discharged. So after spending a week-end with army pal Blondy in Chesterfield, I cycled down to Armscote to see what the situation was regarding my job. Colonel Cardiff, who had recently been retired from the Army, was totally different from Mrs Cardiff. He had different ideas about the running of the place and seemed reluctant to change from military to civilian ways. He offered me a job of part-time groom, gardner, cowman for they now had two house cows, having first asked me if I could milk. I had done so when I was at Blackwell for Mr Hicks. He offered me £3 per week. I thought I would take it until I could find a better paid job elsewhere. I only stayed there a few weeks, being that work was taking place on the playing field, thanks to Mr Jewsbury, the force behind the scheme. Horace Terry and my father had been given the task of laying the water on. This is where I came in for I had the task of digging the trench for the pipeline. This had to be brought across two fields from a small reservoir in the field below The Grange that was fed by natural springs and it fed the surrounding field troughs. The trench across the playing field took priority for the reason that it was to be seeded down in order for it to germinate while the soil was still warm. The pipeline had to be connected and the trench filled in so this could be achieved. It was through this which led to my next job. Horace Terry was employed by the Shipston District Council, his job being the laying of sewage and water pipes. He said there was a vacancy in that department if I was interested and he would make me an appointment. I agreed and went and saw a Mr Cooper and was taken on a five and a half day week at one shilling and ten pence an hour which was very good money at that time. Now that I was cycling to Shipston to work I decided it was time for me to upgrade my transport for I was still riding the same bicycle that father bought me when I was still at school. So, after dinner on Saturday, I cycled into Stratford with twenty-five pounds of my gratuity money to see what I could find. There was, at that time, a bicycle shop on the corner of Wood Street and the Fountain so this is where I headed. About half an hour or so later, I came out with a brand new Raleigh, four speed, hub dynamo lighting with cable brakes. It had an orange frame with white mudguards and pump. The cost was £21.7s.6d. I rode it home and pushed my old one with the idea of getting Dickie Summers to repair it for it needed new brake cables and tyres and then selling it. This I did. Incidentally, I rode that bicycle up until I had my first car in the early 60s. Eventually I gave it to a neighbour.

In mid 1948, the lease on Middle Meadow smallholding, which was held by my grandmother and her son, Harry, my uncle, ran out so they had to move out. Gran was 89 and Uncle 68. There was little chance that the lease would be extended. Middle Meadow, was a substantial house and my father's brother Sid and his wife Clara lived in part of it with their children Sheila and Peter. So like my Gran they had to move. Sheila, however, had married and moved out by this time. They moved up the village close to the Church to a brick built house called Meadow View in Back Street, while my Gran moved to a house on Flea Bank owned by Jim Handy. He now moved to Middle Meadow -from what I understood was done under trying and controversial circumstances! Gran was now feeling the strain of a far from easy life having had eight children which she had brought up almost on her own. I could, on my visits, see a marked difference in her since I went into the Army and now I would frequently walk up with my parents on a Sunday evening to see her and Uncle. It was on one such occasion just before Christmas of 1948 that Gran was not well and confined to bed. The doctor had been but there was very little that he could do. She was just worn out. She passed away early in January leaving a large gap in our lives but I had and still have the memories of this wonderful person. She always dressed in long black clothes with lace top that came up to her throat and often fastened at the top with a broach and her snow-white hair that was swept to the back in a bun and held in place by combs. She was an imposing figure but then, as now, you have to carry on with life and things gradually returned to normal.

I continued working for the Shipston Council until early spring. On arrival at the yard one Monday morning, the Foreman Plumber whose name was Dick Gee, approached and said we have a problem. There is a man short on the dustcart, would I fill the vacancy on a temporary basis. I agreed with the understanding that I would return to my normal job as soon as the dustman returned and so for the next few days I went round emptying dustbins which I didn't enjoy it at all and when I was told that the person wasn't coming back and they wanted me to take it on, as a permanent role, I refused and said that I would leave if I wasn't restored to my former job. And so, with neither side giving way, I left.

ANOTHER JOB – SOMETHING CONCRETE

Aubrey Edwards, from two doors away, had worked as an apprentice mechanic at Taylor's Garage in Shipston from leaving school at fourteen, working with motorbikes and cars. He wanted a fresh challenge and, with vacancies for car and motor cycle mechanics being practically nil in the local area, had turned to lorry driving and for a time had driven a stone lorry, mostly for the laying of roads to outlying farms. This proved to be insecure for once the road was complete it could mean you would, in all probability, not be required for some time if at all. So, he made another change, this time to a firm in Shipston that made pre-cast reinforced concrete agricultural buildings in the form of dutch barns and smaller hay barns and even cow pens. The firm was known as Beecham Building and had been set up some time after the war by a son of Sir Thomas Beecham, the famous conductor. The son's name was also Thomas who lived at Tidmington. Another son, Adrian, had a working farm at Compton Scorpion, the access to this being from Shipston to Campden Road. Aubrey had a job there which involved a little driving while helping on site. When I was in company with him I told him that I was looking for employment. He said that the gang he was with needed someone and if I was interested to go and see Mr Hicks at the office. So, on the following Monday morning I made my way into Shipston. Up Station Road and up the lane opposite the Black Horse Public House that used to lead to the back entrance of the Workhouse, which was still in use then, as well as the home of Beecham's buildings. I made my way to the offices and asked if I could see Mr Hicks with regards to employment. After a while I was shown into a small office where a middle aged man was seated behind a desk. After introducing myself, he asked me if I had any experience in the construction industry. I said no but had previously worked for the local Council on underground services and had left there due to the fact that they wanted me to go on the dustcarts. After further talk he said they were an expanding company and were looking for recruits for different departments, among which was on-site erecting. He then asked me if I was single which I thought was a strange question. After answering yes with a smile, he then explained that the reason for asking was because persons that were employed on site work were mainly single, and new buildings being erected were not only local but could be further afield meaning travel on a daily basis would be impossible and staff would have to stay on site in caravans. After giving me the details of the job in the yard he asked me if I had a preference. I told him, yes, depending on pay I would prefer to go on site at Compton Scorpion where I believed there was a vacancy. "Very well," he said.

"The pay is one shilling and ten pence an hour plus if you stay on site we pay three and sixpence a night subsistence." It was then common practice to work a week in hand thus enabling time sheets to be handed in on Mondays for office staff to work out your wages for the previous week and paid on Saturdays or in some cases, Fridays, depending on where in the country you were. Mr Hicks then said "Alright, you have the job, report to Mr Bradley on Monday morning at eight o'clock. Your hours will be from eight until five, Monday to Friday and eight until twelve on Saturdays and let the site manager have your cards and P45," (ie cards meaning National Insurance).

So on Monday morning I cycled the two miles to Compton Scorpion along the gate road from home. Aubrey, had to go into the yard to pick up the lorry which he did often when we were working local to get materials and to pick up the foreman, Bert Bradley and Joe Minogue, a really nice Irish man who made up our gang. The job we were doing was replacing the roof of a building that was part of a field stockyard belonging to Adrian Beecham. The building was open-fronted whereas the ends and rear wall were of stone. The roof structure was, of course, reinforced concrete, replacing the previous wooden beams and rafters. The concrete sections were assembled on the ground and then lifted into place by a crane which had arrived on a trailer from another site and stayed on site until the frame of the roof was in place and then moved on. We then had to put the roofing sheets on. These were asbestos, a material widely used then well before it became a banned substance for health reasons. The sheets were held in place by special galvanised bolts, some five to six inches long, threaded one end and the other being a hook. Roofing was a three-man job. One passing the sheets up to the one on the roof and one underneath. The person passing the sheets up had the hardest job. On this building, because it was quite low, he could stand on the ground and pass them up but on Dutch and hay barns or taller buildings they had to be taken up a ladder on your shoulder. The person on the roof had to place the sheets in the correct position which were marked out by lines, one at the eaves, one at the gable end and the ridge. Once the end ones were in place and secured then it was quite straight forward. The person on the roof, in this case it was Joe had to drill the holes for the bolts which had to be the top side of the purlin. The holes were drilled with a hand drill, having first marked the positions using a straight edge held against the bolts on the previous sheets, then two pencil marks on the sheet to be fixed, one on the overlap and one on the centre. Once the holes were drilled the person underneath, in this case, Aubrey, would push the bolt through with the hook in the lip, to Joe on top who then placed a lead washer, followed by a hard rubberised one and then a galvernised nut and tightened with a spanner. I was passing the sheets up. They came in various sizes from about seven feet down to three. The width being a standard three foot and the lengths used depended on the span of the roof. When we had finished, we moved a little farther afield to Barton-on-the-Heath, a small village about seven miles from Shipston. This was where we stayed in the caravan for the first time. It was also at Barton where Bert Bradley, who was married, took a job in the yard and was replaced by a local from the village of Wolford whose name escapes me, while Joe took over as foreman. Aubrey was our cook which was done on a cooker fuelled by paraffin which was held in a glass bottle that held about a gallon. This had to be removed to fill and then turned upside-down and replaced in its holder. The paraffin was fed to the burners and oven by means of a valve – quite clever really and worked really well. For the lighting, we had a Tilly lamp that worked in a similar way to a primus stove except instead of a burner with a round spreader, the lamp had a small stem burner that had what was called a mantle, a cylindrical, flexible, fireproof, closely woven object that slid over the stem and like the primus stove, worked by pressure. The more you pumped, the brighter the light. They gave as good a light as electric. The caravans, like all the transport, were ex-military. There was among them an American truck with left-hand drive and with the company expanding, it now employed some five drivers so Aubrey had no need to drive anymore. He just carried on as one of the gang and, of course, our cook. This, however, changed, for when the Barton job was completed, Joe and the Wolford lad left us and went to form another gang while Aubrey and myself moved to Pebworth, a village north-west of Stratford and roughly around eight miles from Shipston. Our fellow workers there were Les Smith, a bricklayer by trade, married and foreman of the job and a man whose name was Philips, known by all as "Jagger". Aubrey and I were there for the sole purpose of putting the roof on the already erected building. We stayed in the van while the other two and a third man, travelled to and from Shipston each day. They were there building outer walls and partitions inside the building, using concrete blocks made at the yard. Whilst staying in the van during the week, we looked forward to our week-ends at home. Not only for a change of clothes but also more importantly to have a bath for this was impossible while in the van. You could have a strip wash but no laundry facilities so it was essential to come home. I also wanted to see my girlfriend who I had met some weeks earlier through my brother-in-law who worked at the liquor vaults where she worked in the offices as a book-keeper.

We were now into summer of 1949 and what a summer we had – very hot and very little rain. We continued to work locally then one Saturday morning the site manager, whose name was Webster, a north country person, on bringing our wages, asked Aubrey and me if we would consider a move as part of another gang who was

A Cole's crane, like the one used for erecting concrete buildings

employed mainly as erectors. He went on to explain with high demand for the company's buildings it was decided that they needed specialised gangs to do specific jobs, hence the reason for asking us. He said to think about it over the week-end and give him our answer on Monday when he collected the timesheets. After discussing it with Aubrey, we decided we would give it a go providing it was on erecting. So a week later we went into the yard to join up with the other two members of our gang. They were Jack Pine, our new foreman, a quietly spoken Irish man and Michael Sullivan, a Welsh man – our crane-driver and, of course, us, with Aubrey being the cook. This, then was the start of a very interesting part of my life for it involved travelling to a wide area of the country. Most of the buildings being agricultural involved meeting a whole range of farmers, farm workers and often gentry. Our job was to erect as the footings had all been done before we arrived. Mr Webster, the site manager/surveyor liaised with the clients so they dug out the yard square footings and put the concrete in once he had marked it all out. This made our job much easier for otherwise we would have had to spend an extra two or three weeks on each job which meant the crane standing idle for that length of time, whereas this system enabled us to start erecting at once. During the summer months there were Gymkhanas and agricultural shows around the country such as the Bath & West, Malvern, and Stoneleigh among others and these were where companies advertised their wares. Beechams were amongst them and this is where we had the task of erecting their samples. The first one that I remember was the Oxford Show. This was held on part of what is now Kidlington Airport. The erection buildings were on temporary foundations for when we dismantled them the site had to be restored to its original state. As a rule these buildings consisted of just three bays with a one bay lean-to and the roof was only partially covered. However, to give the visitors and potential customers a close up view, there were scale models of all the buildings in production at that time. There were cut away parts to all joins and types of plinths and bases for each one and used by the sales personnel to demonstrate. The majority of shows were held on Saturdays while others such as the Bath & West could be three days. The local ones gave us a chance to come home for the week-end and then on Monday morning we would go to the yard in order to return to the site to dismantle them and move on to the next job. During the long hot summer of 1949 we moved every week for six or seven weeks. Among the places visited was Charlbury in Oxfordshire, Great Rollright and a farm about five miles south east of Stratford where they had a large herd of Jersey dairy cows, Daventry in Northamptonshire and Leominster in Herefordshire, Pewsy in Wiltshire where they had a white horse carved out of the chalk hillside.

Another place of great interest where we erected a five bay dutch barn was on the outskirts of the village of Ironbridge where the famous cast iron bridge of that name spans the River Severn. Ironbridge is not the only reason for it staying fresh in my memory but an incident that occurred on the farm where they had a herd of dairy cows of mixed pedigree and in those days, where there were dairy cows there was at least one bull. This particular farm had a Hereford, nothing unusual about that, you might think, but most days we saw this one being led around the farm by a young girl of about sixteen or seventeen. Again, one would think, they are led around by the ring that all bulls have in their noses, either by a pole that is normally used by one person or by rope which is used by two, one on each side but this young lady was leading it around with a rope. From the first time we witnessed it, we remarked on the risks she was taking for no matter how quiet and docile they may seem they can never be trusted and this proved to be the case on this particular morning. We had finished our mid morning break, Aubrey had gone to the local shop for provisions. Jack and Mike were about to continue with fixing the crown boss that joined the span columns at the apex. I was up a ladder fixing the rods that secured the eave purlins to the columns, when suddenly on that warm summer morning, the relative quietness was broken by screaming coming from the buildings that were about 75 yards away. We all acted instantly, I don't think I have ever come down a ladder so fast. I just slid down, while Michael jumped down from the crane and Jack dropped his tools by the boson chair and we all ran to the building where the screams were coming from. As we looked over the bottom half of the stable type door, the sight that met us was of this young girl, lying on her back with the bull standing over her, its head in her abdomen and chest, moving it from side to side in a goring motion. We started shouting at the same time sliding the bolt to open the door. Michael had grabbed a wooden stake and Jack and I went in shouting and waving our arms while Michael started to prod it. With that, the bull moved away and while Mike stood posed with his stake, Jack and I picked up the girl, who was now crying and clearly frightened by what had happened, carried her out, sat her down and calmed her down. Mike disappeared while Jack and I asked her if she was in pain or did she have any problems breathing. She said she felt all right and no she had no pain. With that, Mike appeared with a hot sweet cup of tea. After a while, she got to her feet. We asked her if she would like us to contact anyone. "Oh no," she replied, "I'm alright". She dusted herself off and rather sheepishly said thank you. I think her pride had been hurt more than her body. I suppose from the time we first heard her scream to the point where she thanked us couldn't have been more than 20-25 minutes but I have often wondered what would have happened if we hadn't been there at that precise moment, for we never saw anyone around on that day. In fact, of all the places we had been to before or after, this farm in Shropshire was the one we had the least contact with the farmer or workers than anywhere. I don't think she told anyone for reasons only known to her. Could it be that she was working with the bull against the wishes of a person or persons? This is hard to believe for she had been doing it quite openly up to that point, unless she wanted to show off in front of us. Questions that we never knew the answers to but what we do know is that we never told anyone in the area what had happened even though we visited the local pub and chatted to the locals. One final mystery to this story is that we never knew who this girl was, whether she was the farmer's daughter or even a farmworker's, or even a local girl, employed. but for the rest of the time we never saw her with that three-quarters of a ton bull again.

Every six months or so, the crane was checked over and given a service. This was done in the yard. This always took place on a week-end so if we finished a job on Thursday or Friday, all the gear was loaded and secured on the crane, such as column braces, pudlocks, tools and acroprops and the items in the caravan were made secure and safe, then hitched to the crane we made our way back to the yard with Aubrey and me travelling in the van while Jack rode in the cab. Once back in the yard it gave us a chance to catch up with friends not only the ones that worked there but other friends from the town and our village. The yard was a hive of activity. We noticed the difference on this visit for there were more employees as the company expanded. There were, in fact, a lot of displaced persons, DPs for short, ie Polish, Latvians and Lithuanians. The majority were ex-Polish servicemen with many of them ex-service Army Officers. There was a Captain and a Major, both middle aged who worked on the casting slab. They were just ordinary workers whose jobs were cleaning and oiling the moulds then setting them up with the reinforcing frames and cores, ie the cores being the steel rods that formed lifting and fixing holes. Others worked in the frame shop. The foreman was Cyril McDonald whose brother Charlie, a carpenter was in charge of the Carpenters Shop where the moulds were maintained. Another gang was the Casting whose job was of course filling the moulds. This was done by a two wheeled barrow which brought the concrete from the mixer operated by one man and then by shovel into the moulds. Then, a Kango vibrating machine which was like a large drill but instead of a drill bit, it had a foot-plate. This was placed against the mould and by vibrating the mould ensured the concrete filled the moulds with no air pockets. The moulds were then finished by a person whose job was to trowel the tops to a smooth and level finish. A vital task that had to be done to finish the mould casting was removal of the cores and for this the concrete had to be at the right point of set for if it was done too soon, the core holes would collapse or if left for too long they would be difficult to remove. The responsibility of this operation was given to a person by the name of Peter Mumford who lived locally, with good reason for often he would have to return in late evening to remove them from the larger castings such as plinths and large columns. Although the general practice was to cast the larger components as early as possible, when the company was first started, it was not unusual to hear the sound of hammers being used to extract cores that had been left too long and often at the expense of the castings being damaged, some beyond repair but, with time, came experience that avoided such catastrophes. In those days before the development of quick drying concrete, the weather played a huge part in casting operations, winter being a really tricky time for long spells of freezing conditions, production fell dramatically when nothing could be cast so it was vital that during the rest of the year, casting was at a maximum level. To help with this a very large factory building was designed, cast and built alongside the boundary. This had huge columns with equally strong connecting beams that ran from one end of the building to the other – a distance of at least fifty yards with the height of some twelve to fifteen feet to the top of these. On these were two gantries which, like the one over the outside slab, were electric and with the roof on, ends closed and part of the sides, it gave a lot of shelter. The centre bays were open, the rear one for the large mixer that was fed by a hopper and then discharged down a shute into a bucket slung from one of the gantries. The gantry operator controlled this from his cab and moved it over the mould which was then discharged by trap door, operated by a hand lever. Quite labour-saving but still required the people on the floor to operate the bucket, Kango and the trowel. The front bay was used for loading onto the lorries and often trailers.

Another important part of the yard was the garage. The transport manager was my brother-in-law, Charles Steven Furniss, known by everyone as Dick, while the mechanic was a great friend of his, Roger Cawkell, a really nice person and a very good footballer. It was their responsibility to keep the fleet of lorries serviced and maintained in order to deliver the parts to the sites besides the sand and gravel from the quarries. The Blue Circle cement was delivered by lorry in one hundred weight bags. When drivers were not out on the road, they were moving the finished castings to the storage area where they were stacked on wooden spaces to allow air circulation for they were what was called in the green state where, although they were set enough to enable them to be lifted from the moulds, they were far from ready to be used. The saying goes that it takes 50 years to set and mature and more than 50 years to deteriorate. They were removed from the moulds by a large electrical gantry that could operate the length of the casting slab and part of the storage area. It was used to load the lorries and trailers. The person in charge of this and the casting was Harry Dunsby while the Yard Manager was a Mr Morgan. An amusing incident regarding Harry was on this particular occasion he was over-seeing the moving of a batch of intermediate purlins that were cast in sixes. With the gantry starting to move, a Polish man called Tom was busy working on another mould and was in danger of being hit by the load if he straightened up. So Harry called "Look out Tom" and with that a voice came from behind with the words "Oh, I'm sorry, am I in the way." It was only the boss, Tommy Beecham, crossing the slab. Poor Harry he was the most embarrassed I think but it was the cause of great amusement among the men. He too saw the funny side of it later. I mentioned earlier with the expansion of the company and the change to specialised gangs, now seemed to be the time with the Polish workers in mind to mention the gang of roofers that followed us around. This gang was all Polish. The foreman was a man by the name of Willy Karpe and his brother who was known to us as Billy plus another two, whose names I don't know. While Willy was an outgoing character and spoke very good English, Billy on the other hand was just the opposite, a very quiet and reserved man who only spoke very few words of English. Then, once we learnt what he had gone through we could understand why. While I have no details of all the facts of how all these DPs came to be over here, I do know that a lot of them had escaped from not only the Germans but the Russians also for they had made a pact where they would take over the Eastern Countries of Lithuania, Poland and Czechoslovakia to reclaim what they said was rightfully theirs. In the 1960s I worked with a Polish man whose first name was Walter who lived in the small village of Aston Magna which lies about a mile off the Fosse Way, north of Moreton-in-Marsh. He told me that in 1939 he had to run for his life for the Russians entered their farmhouse through the backdoor while he escaped through the front, with nothing except the clothes he stood in. He hid in nearby woods until it was safe to move on. He never saw his parents or home again. Home for the majority of these foreign personnel that were employed by Beecham Buildings were ex-Army Barracks such as the US Barracks at Northwick Park, Blockley, Gloucestershire and the ex POW Camp by the Ettington Park Hotel that lies some six hundred yards off the A3400 at Talton Bridge which spans the River Stour, mid way between the village of Newbold on Stour and Alderminster. This road that runs from Birmingham through Stratford to Oxford, Newbury and beyond, was at that time the A34. But to get back to Billy Karpe who, as mentioned earlier, was not only a very quiet and reserved man but also very slim with a pale complexion but once his story unfolded as told by his brother Willy, we understood the reasons why. As the British, American and Russian Forces advanced across Europe from the east and west into Germany, when they discovered the dreadful atrocities that man committed against his fellow-man. These places were the concentration camps where Jews, gypsies along with mentally and physically handicapped from all the occupied countries even Germany were taken by train in crowded cattle trucks, hundreds of miles with no food, water and no sanitation in all weathers. Upon arrival they were sectioned off, the elderly, pregnant women and young children, along with the disabled were sent straight to the gas chambers. They were told to take their clothes off and tie their shoes together for they were going to have a shower but instead they went to the gas chambers. The physically fit, men and girls were destined to work. Most of the men would work removing the bodies and removing any gold teeth, then putting them in the huge incinerators while the women and girls sorted through the belongings, clothes, spectacles, shoes and even false teeth. They were in fact, recycling. This they did from dawn to dusk, day in and day out with may be a bowl of what was supposed to be soup but more like coloured water, and if you were lucky, a small piece of bread or perhaps a small piece of potato. They were literally worked and starved to death if not from work, from disease. It was when the news broke that shocked the world. It was from one of these camps, (Belsen), that Billy was liberated in 1945 along with hundreds of others who were literally just walking skeletons of skin and bone. One can only imagine what it must have been like for the British and Allied Troops when they first came upon these places for the reports of the sweet sickly smell of burning flesh must have carried for miles. In fact, the Officers were so appalled by what they had came across that they forced the local people to come and see for themselves what their fellow countrymen had inflicted on those poor unfortunate people. Billy, like hundreds more spent months in hospital and rehabilitation centres under intense medical care, and specially prepared diets before they were well enough to rejoin the civilised world. Even in 1949, four years after the war had finished, Billy was far from the person he would have been under normal circumstances. I never knew how he was captured and for how long he was in that terrible place while his brother escaped. What I can say, in all honesty, having worked alongside them, they have repaid the Government and countries that brought them here and gave them employment by their loyalty and hard work. For those like Billy whose physical condition at that time would not allow them to do real manual work, they contributed by doing lighter tasks for Billy was the cook for his gang.

1949 CHRISTMAS AND NEW YEAR

Then, as now, Christmas was a time to spend with family and friends for with Christmas this year all the gangs came to Shipston for that purpose. For not only that but also to enjoy the Christmas party laid on by the company and held in Shipston's Townsend Hall which they said was to thank all the staff for all their hard work of that year. It also gave us the opportunity to get together with the members of other gangs that you rarely saw. On this particular occasion I met again a tall, handsome Latvian whom I knew as Arnold. He was a real nice person who I would say was in his early to mid twenties and very much like the British film star Stewart Granger. In fact, you could take them for brothers. He too, had escaped from the Russians and had made his way to Britain some years before and had mastered the English language really well. This was the last time I saw Arnold.

We were now into the New Year and the erecting was dependent on the weather and the state of the ground, not only on site but for transport as well as for snow and ice meant blocked country lanes could often delay or even halt deliveries. The situation for us, however, came with the move to erect a large building at a factory in Tewkesbury. This made a welcome change from the underfoot conditions we encountered on farms and with the site being on the edge of town, we enjoyed far better access. At this time, Aubrey owned a Triumph twin motorcycle – a powerful machine which he had with us. He used it not only to fetch provisions from the town but to come home at week-ends. We would leave after lunch on Saturday and return on Monday mornings. This enabled us to spend time with our girlfriends. After enjoying one such week-end we were returning at about 7.30 on the Monday morning. The weather was dull and grey and had rained overnight. We had passed the Teddington Cross Hands roundabout and heading towards Ashchurch, a nice stretch of road, at around 45-50 miles an hour. As we negotiated a gentle left hand bend, the next thing I remember was a burning sensation on my right thigh as I was sliding head-first along the road. As I slid to a halt, I turned round and saw Aubrey some two or three yards away and a little further head, slowly raising his head and shoulders up from the gutter and his bike some yards behind. He said "Are you alright?" to which I replied "I think so, are you?" He said "Likewise". As luck would have it the engine had cut out but there was a slight smell of petrol. We got to our feet and picked the bike up, put the stand down and looked for any damage. Luckily, apart from a few scratches, all seemed well. We then looked at ourselves. Aubrey, apart from a few sore spots was relatively unhurt for he had partially landed on the grass verge while I had finished near the centre of the road, consequently, having a harder landing. I suffered a little more as apart from having a very sore thigh and a bruised elbow, I had grazed the little finger of my left hand and my mackintosh which was part of my demob clothing was absolutely in tatters. My trousers were also badly torn plus my jacket sleeve was ripped but I think we had come out of it pretty well. With that, Aubrey said "Let's see if it will start". He put the kick start down. After two or three attempts the engine burst into life and we continued our journey, arriving only about twenty minutes after eight. We inspected the damage to my thigh which was really sore. I suppose the wound was about two inches across but luckily had no gravel in it. Aubrey said that at nine o'clock he would go into town and get some dressings for it. We didn't have first aid kits then. This he did and dressed it daily over the course of the week. At least that got better while my mackintosh was beyond repair. My trousers and jacket were repaired and we still came home each week-end we were on this site which was over a month for we also had to put the roof on as Willie, who normally followed us, had been diverted to other jobs.

It was now near the end of February and almost the end of the Tewkesbury job, So far, as our gang was concerned. The last week-end would be the only opportunity we would have to spend at home for a while as our new destination would be rather too far to travel. This was, as it turned out, the last time I would ride on the pillion of Aubrey's bike, as he was leaving it at home. We had arranged a lift on the Monday with a lorry taking material for the follow-up gang to us to block up the sides and ends of the building. Monday morning came and with it our lift back. We were picked up on what you might call our doorstep for the journey from Shipston passed along the road at the bottom of our garden. Two days later we were on the road to our next job. This was another big one - this time for the Power Station at Portishead, a small town on the outskirts of Bristol. Our journey was one of great interest for it gave us the chance to see for the first time the famous Clifton Suspension Bridge built by the famous engineer Isambard Kingdom Brunell for we travelled along the road that runs parallel to the gorge and under the famous landmark. On our arrival we met up with Willy and his gang. For them to be here was part of the reason why we had been given the job of putting the roof on the building we had just finished. An urgent job for Willy's gang of re-roofing a building at the power station. After they completed their job a few days later, they had to move on for it would be a while before they returned to roof the building we had just started to erect, which I am sure was the largest we had done by far. Being as our free time was spent on site, we welcomed the fact that the Power Station allowed us to use the showers and toilets. Saturday afternoons we took full advantage of this offer before visiting the local pub on Saturday evening. After we had been there for two weeks or so Aubrey said he intended to return home on Friday by taking a lift on the lorry that was bringing out purlins and returning on the Monday. So Friday evening Jack, Michael and myself had a fish and chip supper while on Saturday we decided to go into Bristol. This was not only as a social visit but also for Jack to visit a dentist for a few days he had been suffering from tooth ache and with tablets having little or no effect to relieve the pain he needed a dentist. Aubrey had made enquiries at the local shop and had been told that there was an emergency dentist in Bristol and so with instructions on how to find it we took a bus into town. Having found it, we entered and saw the receptionist who said the dentist would see Jack after the patient now being treated. After taking details she said take a seat. Michael and I said we would wait in the cafe we had passed on the way here. We ordered two teas from the lady and asked whether we could wait for our friend as he was at the dentist. "That's alright she said, I often have others on the same mission. After another two teas and three quarters of an hour later, Jack appeared, not as we thought minus a tooth and a frozen face but with a smile and the words that the dentist wouldn't take it out. The tooth was alright except for a small hole in the centre that was exposing the nerve. He would fill it and as far as a frozen face, No! - only if the tooth required a lot of drilling would they give you injections to deaden the pain. So Jack got away with a light drilling and filling and a couple of pain killers to take until it settled down. Jack said it was still a little uncomfortable but there was no way he was coming here to Bristol and not being able to have a few beers and with that we ordered sausage, egg and chips, bread and butter and more tea. After all, doesn't the old saying tell you not to drink on an empty stomach. We enjoyed those few beers in a pub named after the ship "Mauritania". On the Monday, Aubrey arrived back with another load of purlins and with the news that he had been summoned back for an interview with the Transport Manager (Dick Furniss) and Mr Hicks This was about a move from erecting to the garage to assist in the maintenance and repairs to the company's transport fleet, as the workload had increased to the point that existing staff of one mechanic (Roger Cawkell) was struggling to cope and often working until late in the evening. So it came as no surprise as he was never happier than working around engines, whether it was motor cycles, cars or lorries of any kind. He had been offered the job which he had accepted and would leave us on completion of the job at Portishead. So towards the end of March and the largest building we had erected so far completed, we returned to the yard with Aubrey for the last time.

With Aubrey leaving we needed replacements to our gang and with Jack saying that with one member of the gang doing the cooking, this was putting a larger work-load on us. On larger jobs, Michael often had to get off the crane to assist Jack and I with certain tasks, while Aubrey was attending to the domestic duties, leaving us short-handed. So after discussions in the office regarding the safety side of Michael having to leave the crane, they agreed to increase our gang to five. Our new members were John Bland, a local chap around my age whose parents owned and ran a fish and chip shop in Shipston. He wasn't to be our cook for that was to be the job of a short, well proportioned Irishman who was in his 30s by the name of Michael Duffey. He was a pleasant likeable character who turned out to be an excellent cook.

My girlfriend, Jean, who was now living with my sister Myra and her husband Bert in Shipston because the cottage where her parents lived with her two brothers in the village of Halford, only had two bedrooms and a landing large enough for a single bed, privacy was practically non-existent. Now not only did she have her own bedroom but she was only 50 yards from her work, saving her an eight mile round trip cycle ride. So on the week-ends I was at home, she would cycle over on Saturday evening, where we would meet up with friends in the Red Lion, have a couple of drinks and then made our way to the dance in the Village Hall, where the music was provided, as usual, by Laurie Hughes and his radiogram. It was then common practice in the majority of households to lay the table for breakfast before retiring which mother always did. So on Saturday nights we were there, she would leave supper out for us, usually with a note telling us to put the bread back in the breadbin and the rest in the pantry. It was on these week-ends that Jean would stay the night. After dinner on Sunday, weather permitting, we would go for walks, sometimes round the village but in the summer up Foxcote Hill to sit for a while half way up, to admire the views which on a clear day are a sight to behold and views that hold the same magic today as they did then. This particular week-end in early April, we could admire the early spring flowers along the hedgerows of celandines, violets and primroses and, of course, the song of the birds - simple things that cost nothing but gave us immense pleasure. After tea, we would ride back to Shipston and spend an hour with my sister, Myra, before meeting up with my sister Vera and her husband Dick for a drink in the White Horse. Then, after saying goodbye to them, we would make our way back to pick up my bicycle, say farewell to Jean with the words to ring her at the Liquor Vaults if I was anywhere near a phone-box on the following Saturday morning and then I cycled back to Ilmington.

Monday morning I made my way into the yard for half past seven for our reinforced gang had to stow two means of transport consisting of Michael's (our new Cook's) bicycle and Jack's motorbike which was one of America's famous makes – a Harley Davidson. These were secured to the rack at the back of the van and with the rest of the gear stowed securely we were on our way to our next job. This was a farm a few miles from the town of Ross-on-Wye to erect a five bay Dutch barn with a lean-to. After stopping on route for Michael to purchase provisions, we eventually arrived after asking directions on several occasions. It now became clear why we needed independent transport for it was, as far as I remember, the most isolated site we had been to with the nearest shop and pub about two miles away. Jack's motorbike proved a real god-send on Saturday evenings for strange as it seems, we all managed to get on board that big Harley Davidson with Jack perched on the front of that big saddle, Michael D on the fuel tank and three behind. We made it the two or three times we visited the pub without mishap. Our next job was on an estate farm near the Cotswold town of Stroud. It was just a routine job of a Dutch barn but as it turned out, one that brought home to us just how dangerous our job could be. It was here where we received the shocking news of an accident that had happened on another site while erecting columns of a Dutch Barn with tragic consequences. Without knowing the precise details, apparently it had happened at the stage where the arches were joined at the apex by a crown boss which is in the shape of a cross and bolted to the underneath. This operation is carried out by the foreman who is hoisted up on a bosun's chair a simple device made up of a plank of wood some 3-4 feet long, two inches thick and about a foot wide. A steel rod of about two and a half feet, threaded one end and a ring at the other which is passed through the centre of the board and fixed underneath with a steel plate, washers and a nut and locked in place by washers and a nut at the top. The operators sit astride one side, and the crown boss, the other and is hoisted up by the crane. This operation only takes about 15-20 minutes but it requires precise skill between the crane driver and the person on the chair. I don't remember hearing the cause of the accident but it could be a number of things. What I do know is it happened to the person that only a few months before had, like us and the rest of the company, enjoyed the Christmas Party. We had held a long conversation where he told me of his background and the way he had escaped from the Russians as they swept through his country of Latvia. He was a tall, good looking person who I knew as Arnold. It's hard to believe that someone had gone through his short life, fleeing to his adopted country only to lose his life crushed by over a ton of reinforced concrete in an unfortunate accident. At the inquest the Coroner, after hearing all the evidence, returned a verdict of accidental death. To us and everyone we had contact with, within the firm, were shocked and saddened by what had happened but one can only imagine what it must have been like for his fellow gang members.

JOURNEYS END

On completion of the job at Stroud we moved closer to home, this time it was to a farm at St Dennis owned by a Mr Wills and about two miles from Shipston which, for me, was like working at home as it allowed me to cycle into Shipston to see my girlfriend and sister on week day evenings and perhaps a visit to the Plaza Cinema – Shipston had a cinema then which was always well supported, especially weekends.   On Saturdays, for instance there was a matinee for the children in the afternoons and two shows in the evening, first house starting at six and the second at eight thirty.   These were often followed by a visit to one of the two fish and chip shops that Shipston had.   One in Market Place owned as I have mentioned earlier by the parents of John Bland, a member of our gang, the other, was in New Street owned and run by Mr & Mrs Hawkins.   The price of the fish supper then was one shilling and three pence – in today's currency about seven and a half pence.   If you only had three pennyworth of chips, the cost would be one shilling or five pence with salt and vinegar and wrapped up in greaseproof paper and newspaper and eaten out of it – absolutely delicious and a wonderful way to round off an evening.

When I first received the encouraging vibes from my family and friends to put into words my memories and stories of growing up in those early years of my life, it was my intention to end on reaching the age of twenty but, as I progressed and giving it some thought, I realised to do so would be like stopping before the journey was complete. How I became aware of this was simple and so I decided to complete that journey. In those days you were not considered to be an adult until you reached the age of twenty-one and mature enough to make decisions for yourself, hence the old song, "Twenty-one today, Twenty-one today, I've got the key of the door, never been twenty-one before. Father says I can do as I like, hip, hip, hip hip hooray, I won't be home till morning cos I'm twenty one today".

Despite this, it didn't stop the powers that be from calling up young people of 18 who then were not eligible to vote but old enough to be called up into the Armed Forces to serve King and Country, to fight and die in the course of duty. Laws are difficult to understand!

For some weeks my girlfriend, Jean and I had discussed where we were heading with our lives and the circumstances and situation we were in, especially for her as no matter how well she get on, as she did, with my sister Myra and Bert and their two young children, John and Gillian, It couldn't be the same as being in your own family home which for her was impossible due to circumstances described earlier.

Everyone, no matter who they are, needs time to themselves and when you are living in someone else's house it can be really difficult for both parties. With me being away often for weeks, it was really difficult for her especially during the week for there were only limited times you could visit family and friends in order to give both parties time on their own.

For me it was entirely different for being in the caravan with the rest of the gang, it was to some extent the same as being in the Armed Forces, only on a smaller scale and of course all being of the same gender.

So after talking things over, we decided that we cared enough for each other to get married. Nothing elaborate, just a quiet Church wedding in Shipston for families, the exception being my best friend Jackie Gaydon as my Best Man The reception was to be at my sister Myra & Bert's with all three of my sisters doing the food and of course, Bert and the Liquor Vaults taking care of the drinks. A major issue was where we were going to live. This was solved almost immediately by the parents of my sister, Rita's husband, Bill - Mr & Mrs Randall - who lived almost opposite to Myra's house. They lived in a large, red brick house just a few yards from the Council Offices where Mr Randall worked as the Clerk of the Council. He and his wife agreed to let us rent rooms in their house. This was ideal for us being that Jean would still be on the doorstep of her job. We decided after lengthy deliberation that I, for the time being, would continue with my job which I loved, despite the fact that Jean would be on her own even at week-ends on the occasions I couldn't get home if it was too far to travel. She assured me she would be OK and could spend evenings with my sister or Bert Bradley and his wife, the foreman on my first job with Beechams.

Now with most of our plans made, I returned to the job at St Dennis on the Monday morning with a certain spring in my step, and it was spring, We would be finishing the job in a few days and moving on. A day or so after, I realised that with all the goings on over the week-end, I had forgotten to bring my clean laundry and other things I needed, so I decided to travel to Ilmington the next evening. We would finish the job next day and with having to return to the yard anyway for a little maintenance on the crane, it would be a chance to go home for we would be moving on the following day. So after having our evening meal, parked in the yard, I made my way down to my sister's in New Street to see if Jean wanted to come to Ilmington with me, being a nice evening. On opening the back door and stepping into the utility room, I knew the answer to that question as Jean was bending over the sink, washing her hair. When she finally straightened up, having had my sister rinse all the lather off, she said she was about to have a home perm. This was about the time that this procedure was becoming popular for I remember the adverts in the papers and glossy magazines with the words, "Which twin has the Toni?" It was a procedure that really took off for to have it done at a hair salon was not only time consuming but rather expensive. What stands out in my mind was the smell of the solution that was put on the hair – it was far from pleasant. With the promise that I would see her later when I returned, for I would be leaving my bicycle there and walking back up to the yard and van in order to move on the following day.

As I cycled to Ilmington all seemed well with the world. The only sounds that could be heard came from the birds – a blackbird perched in a sapling singing out his message to others, claiming his territory, for he probably had a nest nearby. As I passed the Church in Darlingscote, the rooks that had nested and fledged their young, were holding a noisy meeting in the elms and oaks that lined the hedgerows and, as I neared home, perched on the top of a telegraph pole, a songthrush doing the same as the blackbird. I spent an hour or so with mother, father being down at the allotments as usual, for he still carried on the same even though they were the only two at home now, apart from me on the occasional week-ends – old habits die hard. Around nine o'clock, I picked up my things and said goodbye to mother and added that I expect father had gone up to have some refreshment at the Howard Arms. It wasn't really dark but more like twilight on that early May evening. As I made my way, I crossed the Fosse Way and then started the steady climb to the level crossing of the single track Moreton to Shipston Railway line which carried just one goods train a day. From there the hill gradually became steeper and this was where my four speed bicycle came into its own, allowing me to negotiate it easily whereas on my old single gear one, it would have meant either walking up or standing on the pedals to get more purchase and therefore putting more strain on the chain. Near the top, I passed the house on the right where some seven years before it was our first delivery stop on the Shipston milk round. As I reached the top and rode round the right hand bend onto the straight, I heard a sound coming from the direction of the railway line that ran some four hundred yards away across the field to my left. I listened on that quiet May evening and it became clear that what I was hearing was the sound I had heard often as a child when walking home across the fields and up the lane with my two younger sisters from Berryfields Farm. It was sadly, the last time I heard that unforgettable song, live. I have heard recordings but you don't get the same thrill that I experienced that night. I just had to stop and listen to hear a nightingale.